# THE CITY AND MAN

# LEO STRAUSS

# THE CITY AND MAN

The University of Chicago Press
*Chicago and London*

The University of Chicago Press, Chicago 60637
The University of Chicago Press, Ltd., London

© 1964 by The University Press of Virginia
All rights reserved. Published 1964 by Rand McNally & Company
Midway Reprint 1977
Printed in the United States of America

ISBN: 0-226-77699-9

# *Preface*

*This study is an enlarged version of the Page-Barbour Lectures* which I delivered at the University of Virginia in the Spring of 1962. I am grateful to the Committee on the Page-Barbour Lectures at the University of Virginia for having given me the opportunity to develop my views on a rather neglected aspect of classical political thought more fully than I otherwise might have done.

An earlier and shorter version of the lecture on Plato's *Republic* was published as a part of the chapter on Plato which I contributed to the *History of Political Philosophy*, edited by Joseph Cropsey and myself (Rand McNally, 1963).

L.S.

*July, 1963*

# Table of Contents

# INTRODUCTION

*It is not self-forgetting and pain-loving antiquarianism nor self-*forgetting and intoxicating romanticism which induces us to turn with passionate interest, with unqualified willingness to learn, toward the political thought of classical antiquity. We are impelled to do so by the crisis of our time, the crisis of the West.

It is not sufficient for everyone to obey and to listen to the Divine message of the City of Righteousness, the Faithful City. In order to propagate that message among the heathen, nay, in order to understand it as clearly and as fully as is humanly possible, one must also consider to what extent man could discern the outlines of that City if left to himself, to the proper exercise of his own powers. But in our age it is much less urgent to show that political philosophy is the indispensable handmaid of theology than to show that political philosophy is the rightful queen of the social sciences, the sciences of man and of human affairs: even the highest lawcourt in the land is more likely to defer to the contentions of social science than to the Ten Commandments as the words of the living God.

The theme of political philosophy is the City and Man. The City and Man is explicitly the theme of classical political philosophy. Modern political philosophy, while building on classical political philosophy, transforms it and thus no longer deals with that theme in its original terms. But one cannot understand the transformation, however legitimate, if one has not understood the original form.

Modern political philosophy presupposes Nature as understood by modern natural science and History as understood by the modern historical awareness. Eventually these presuppositions prove to be incompatible with modern political philosophy. Thus one seems to be confronted with the choice between abandoning political philosophy altogether and returning to classical political philosophy. Yet such a return seems to be impossible. For what has brought about the collapse of modern political philosophy seems to have buried classical political philosophy which did not even dream of

*1*

the difficulties caused by what we believe to know of nature and history. Certain it is that a simple continuation of the tradition of classical political philosophy—of a tradition which was hitherto never entirely interrupted—is no longer possible. As regards modern political philosophy, it has been replaced by ideology: what originally was a political philosophy has turned into an ideology. This fact may be said to form the core of the contemporary crisis of the West.

That crisis was diagnosed at the time of World War I by Spengler as the going down (or decline) of the West. Spengler understood by the West one culture among a small number of high cultures. But the West was for him more than one high culture among a number of them. It was for him the comprehensive culture. It is the only culture which has conquered the earth. Above all, it is the only culture which is open to all cultures and which does not reject the other cultures as forms of barbarism or which tolerates them condescendingly as "underdeveloped"; it is the only culture which has acquired full consciousness of culture as such. Whereas "culture" originally and naively meant *the* culture of *the* mind, the derivative and reflective notion of "culture" necessarily implies that there is a variety of equally high cultures. But precisely since the West is the culture in which culture reaches full self-consciousness, it is the final culture: the owl of Minerva begins its flight in the dusk; the decline of the West is identical with the exhaustion of the very possibility of high culture; the highest possibilities of man are exhausted. But man's highest possibilities cannot be exhausted as long as there are still high human tasks—as long as the fundamental riddles which confront man, have not been solved to the extent to which they can be solved. We may therefore say that Spengler's analysis and prediction is wrong: our highest authority, natural science, considers itself susceptible of infinite progress, and this claim does not make sense, it seems, if the fundamental riddles are solved. If science is susceptible of infinite progress, there cannot be a meaningful end or completion of history; there can only be a brutal stopping of man's onward march through natural forces acting by themselves or directed by human brains and hands.

However this may be, in one sense Spengler has proved to be right; some decline of the West has taken place before our eyes. In 1913 the West—in fact this country together with Great Britain and Germany—could have laid down the law for the rest of the earth without firing a shot. Surely for at least a century the West controlled the whole globe with ease. Today, so far from ruling the globe, the West's very survival is endangered by the East as it has not been since its beginning. From the Communist Manifesto it would appear that the victory of Communism would be the complete victory of the West—of the synthesis, transcending the national boundaries, of British industry, the French Revolution and German philosophy—over the East. We see that the victory of Communism would mean indeed the victory of originally Western natural science but surely at the same time the victory of the most extreme form of Eastern despotism.

However much the power of the West may have declined, however great the dangers to the West may be, that decline, that danger, nay, the defeat, even the destruction of the West would not necessarily prove that the West is in a crisis: the West could go down in honor, certain of its purpose. The crisis of the West consists in the West's having become uncertain of its purpose. The West was once certain of its purpose—of a purpose in which all men could be united, and hence it had a clear vision of its future as the future of mankind. We do no longer have that certainty and that clarity. Some among us even despair of the future, and this despair explains many forms of contemporary Western degradation. The foregoing statements are not meant to imply that no society can be healthy unless it is dedicated to a universal purpose, to a purpose in which all men can be united: a society can be tribal and yet healthy. But a society which was accustomed to understand itself in terms of a universal purpose, cannot lose faith in that purpose without becoming completely bewildered. We find such a universal purpose expressly stated in our immediate past, for instance in famous official declarations made during the two World Wars. These declarations merely restate the purpose stated originally by the most successful form of modern political philosophy—a kind of that political philosophy which aspired to build on the foundation laid by classical political philosophy but in opposition to the structure erected by classical political philosophy, a society superior in truth and justice to the society toward which the classics aspired. According to the modern project, philosophy or science was no longer to be understood as essentially contemplative and proud but as active and charitable; it was to be in the service of the relief of man's estate; it was to be cultivated for the sake of human power; it was to

*3*

enable man to become the master and owner of nature through the intellectual conquest of nature. Philosophy or science should make possible progress toward ever greater prosperity; it thus should enable everyone to share in all the advantages of society or life and therewith give full effect to everyone's natural right to comfortable self-preservation and all that that right entails or to everyone's natural right to develop all his faculties fully in concert with everyone else's doing the same. The progress toward ever greater prosperity would thus become, or render possible, the progress toward ever greater freedom and justice. This progress would necessarily be the progress toward a society embracing equally all human beings: a universal league of free and equal nations, each nation consisting of free and equal men and women. For it had come to be believed that the prosperous, free, and just society in a single country or in only a few countries is not possible in the long run: to make the world safe for the Western democracies, one must make the whole globe democratic, each country in itself as well as the society of nations. Good order in one country presupposes good order in all countries and among all countries. The movement toward the universal society or the universal state was thought to be guaranteed not only by the rationality, the universal validity, of the goal but also because the movement towards the goal seemed to be the movement of the large majority of men on behalf of the large majority of men: only small groups of men who, however, hold in thrall many millions of their fellow human beings and who defend their own antiquated interests, resist that movement.

This view of the human situation in general and of the situation in our century in particular retained a certain plausibility, not in spite of Fascism but because of it, until Communism revealed itself even to the meanest capacities as Stalinism and post-Stalinism, for Trotskyism, being a flag without an army and even without a general, is condemned or refuted by its own principle. For some time it appeared to many teachable Westerners—to say nothing of the unteachable ones—that Communism was only a parallel movement to the Western movement—as it were its somewhat impatient, wild, wayward twin who was bound to become mature, patient, and gentle. But except when in mortal danger, Communism responded to the fraternal greetings only with contempt or at most with manifestly dissembled signs of friendship; and when in mortal danger, it was as eager to receive Western help as it was determined to give

4

not even sincere words of thanks in return. It was impossible for the Western movement to understand Communism as merely a new version of that eternal reactionism against which it had been fighting for centuries. It had to admit that the Western project which had provided in its way against all earlier forms of evil could not provide against the new form in speech or in deed. For some time it seemed sufficient to say that while the Western movement agrees with Communism regarding the goal—the universal prosperous society of free and equal men and women—it disagrees with it regarding the means: for Communism, the end, the common good of the whole human race, being the most sacred thing, justifies any means; whatever contributes to the achievement of the most sacred end partakes of its sacredness and is therefore itself sacred; whatever hinders the achievement of that end is devilish. The murder of Lumumba was described by a Communist as a reprehensible murder by which he implied that there can be irreprehensible murders, like the murder of Nagy. It came to be seen then that there is not only a difference of degree but of kind between the Western movement and Communism, and this difference was seen to concern morality, the choice of means. In other words, it became clearer than it had been for some time that no bloody or unbloody change of society can eradicate the evil in man: as long as there will be men, there will be malice, envy and hatred, and hence there cannot be a society which does not have to employ coercive restraint. For the same reason it could no longer be denied that Communism will remain, as long as it lasts in fact and not merely in name, the iron rule of a tyrant which is mitigated or aggravated by his fear of palace revolutions. The only restraint in which the West can put some confidence is the tyrant's fear of the West's immense military power.

The experience of Communism has provided the Western movement with a twofold lesson: a political lesson, a lesson regarding what to expect and what to do in the foreseeable future, and a lesson regarding the principles of politics. For the foreseeable future there cannot be a universal state, unitary or federative. Apart from the fact that there does not exist now a universal federation of nations but only of those nations which are called peace-loving, the federation that exists masks the fundamental cleavage. If that federation is taken too seriously, as a milestone on man's onward march toward the perfect and hence universal society, one is bound to take great risks supported by nothing but an inherited and perhaps antiquated hope, and thus to endanger the very progress one endeavors to bring about. It is imaginable that in the face of the danger of thermonuclear destruction, a federation, however incomplete, of nations outlaws wars, *i.e.* wars of aggression; but this means that it acts on the assumption that all present boundaries are just, *i.e.* in accordance with the self-determination of nations; but this assumption is a pious fraud of which the fraudulence is more evident than the piety. In fact, the only changes of present boundaries for which there is any provision are those not disagreeable to the Communists. One must also not forget the glaring disproportion between the legal equality and the factual inequality of the confederates. The factual inequality is recognized in the expression "underdeveloped nations." The expression implies the resolve to develop them fully, *i.e.* to make them either Communist or Western, and this despite the fact that the West claims to stand for cultural pluralism. Even if one would still contend that the Western purpose is as universal as the Communist, one must rest satisfied for the foreseeable future with a practical particularism. The situation resembles the one which existed during the centuries in which Christianity and Islam each raised its universal claim but had to be satisfied with uneasily coexisting with its antagonist. All this amounts to saying that for the foreseeable future, political society remains what it always has been: a partial or particular society whose most urgent and primary task is its self-preservation and whose highest task is its self-improvement. As for the meaning of self-improvement, we may observe that the same experience which has made the West doubtful of the viability of a world-society has made it doubtful of the belief that affluence is the sufficient and even necessary condition of happiness and justice: affluence does not cure the deepest evils.

The doubt of the modern project is more than merely a strong but vague feeling. It has acquired the status of scientific exactitude. One may wonder whether there is a single social scientist left who would assert that the universal and prosperous society constitutes the rational solution of the human problem. For present-day social science admits and even proclaims its inability to validate any value-judgments proper. The teaching originated by modern political philosophy in favor of the universal and prosperous society has admittedly become an ideology—a teaching not superior in truth

6

and justice to any other among the innumerable ideologies. Social science which studies all ideologies is itself free from all ideological biases. Through this Olympian freedom it overcomes the crisis of our time. That crisis may destroy the conditions of social science: it cannot affect the validity of its findings.

Social science has not always been as skeptical or restrained as it has become during the last two generations. The change in the character of social science is not unconnected with the change in the status of the modern project. The modern project was originated as required by nature (natural right), *i.e.* it was originated by philosophers; the project was meant to satisfy in the most perfect manner the most powerful natural needs of men: nature was to be conquered for the sake of man who himself was supposed to possess a nature, an unchangeable nature; the originators of the project took it for granted that philosophy and science are identical. After some time it appeared that the conquest of nature requires the conquest of human nature and hence in the first place the questioning of the unchangeability of human nature: an unchangeable human nature might set absolute limits to progress. Accordingly, the natural needs of men could no longer direct the conquest of nature; the direction had to come from reason as distinguished from nature, from the rational Ought as distinguished from the neutral Is. Thus philosophy (logic, ethics, esthetics) as the study of the Ought or the norms became separated from science as the study of the Is. The ensuing depreciation of reason brought it about that while the study of the Is or science succeeded ever more in increasing men's power, one could no longer distinguish between the wise or right and the foolish or wrong use of power. Science cannot teach wisdom. There are still some people who believe that this predicament will disappear when social science and psychology catch up with physics and chemistry. This belief is wholly unreasonable, for social science and psychology, however perfected, being sciences, can only bring about a still further increase of man's power; they will enable men to manipulate man still better than ever before; they will as little teach man how to use his power over man or non-man as physics and chemistry do. The people who indulge this hope have not grasped the bearing of the distinction between facts and values.

The decay of political philosophy into ideology reveals itself most obviously in the fact that in both research and teaching, political philosophy has been replaced by the history of political philosophy. This substitution can be excused as a well-meaning attempt to prevent, or at least to delay, the burial of a great tradition. In fact it is not merely a half measure but an absurdity: to replace political philosophy by the history of political philosophy means to replace a doctrine which claims to be true by a survey of more or less brilliant errors. The discipline which takes the place of political philosophy is the one which shows the impossibility of political philosophy. That discipline is logic. What for the time being is still tolerated under the name of history of political philosophy will find its place within a rational scheme of research and teaching in footnotes to the chapters in logic textbooks which deal with the distinction between factual judgments and value-judgments; those footnotes will supply slow learners with examples of the faulty transition, by which political philosophy stands or falls, from factual judgments to value-judgments.

It would be wrong to believe that in the new dispensation the place once occupied by political philosophy is filled entirely by logic however enlarged. A considerable part of the matter formerly treated by political philosophy is now treated by a non-philosophic political science which forms part of social science. This new political science is concerned with discovering laws of political behavior and ultimately universal laws of political behavior. Lest it mistake the peculiarities of the politics of the time and the places in which social science is at home for the character of all politics, it must study also the politics of other climes and other ages. The new political science thus becomes dependent on a kind of study which belongs to the comprehensive enterprise called universal history. It is controversial whether history can be modelled on the natural science on which the new political science aspires to be modelled. At any rate, the historical studies in which the new political science must engage must become concerned not only with the working of institutions but with the ideologies informing those institutions as well. Within the context of these studies, the meaning of an ideology is primarily the meaning in which its adherents understand it. In some cases the ideologies are known to have been originated by outstanding men. In such cases it becomes necessary to consider whether and how the ideology as conceived by the originator was modified by the adherents. For precisely if only the crude understanding of ideologies can be politically effective, it is necessary to grasp the characteristics of crudity: if the routinization of charisma is a permitted theme, the vulgarization of thought ought to be a permitted theme. One kind of ideology consists of the teachings of the political philosophers. These teachings may have played only a minor political role, but one cannot know this before one knows them solidly. This solid knowledge consists primarily in understanding the teachings of the political philosophers as they themselves meant them. Each of them was undoubtedly mistaken in believing that his teaching is the true and final teaching regarding political things: we know through a reliable tradition that this belief forms part of a rationalization; but the process of rationalization is not so thoroughly understood that it would not be worthwhile to study it in the case of the greatest minds; for all we know there may be various kinds of rationalization. It is then necessary to study the political philosophies as they were understood by their originators in contradistinction to the way in which they were understood by their adherents, and various kinds of their adherents, but also by their adversaries and even by detached or indifferent bystanders or historians. For indifference does not offer a sufficient protection against the danger that one identifies the view of the originator with a compromise between the views of his adherents and those of his adversaries. The genuine understanding of the political philosophies which is then necessary may be said to have been rendered possible by the shaking of all traditions; the crisis of our time may have the accidental advantage of enabling us to understand in an untraditional or fresh manner what was hitherto understood only in a traditional or derivative manner. This may apply especially to classical political philosophy which has been seen for a considerable time only through the lenses of modern political philosophy and its various successors.

Social science will then not live up to its claim if it does not concern itself with a genuine understanding of the political philosophies proper and therewith primarily of classical political philosophy. As has been indicated, such an understanding cannot be presumed to be available. It is frequently asserted today that such an understanding is not possible: all historical understanding is relative to the point of view of the historian, in particular to his country and his time; the historian cannot understand a teaching as it was meant by its originator but he necessarily understands it differently than its originator understood it; ordinarily the historian's understanding is inferior to the originator's understanding; in the best case the understanding will be a creative transformation of the original understanding. Yet it is hard to see how one can speak of a creative transformation of the original teaching if it is not possible to grasp the original teaching as such. Besides, one may grant that the initial point of view of the historian who studies a teaching expounded in the past necessarily differs from that of the originator of the teaching or, in other words, that the question which the historian addresses to his author necessarily differs from the question which his author attempted to answer; yet surely the primary duty of the historian consists in suspending his initial question in favor of the question with which his author is concerned or in learning to look at the subject matter in question from his author's point of view. To the extent to which the social scientist succeeds in this kind of study which is imposed on him by the requirements of social science, he not only enlarges the horizon of present-day social science, he even transcends the limitations of social science, for he learns to look at things in a manner which is as it were forbidden to the social scientist. He will have learned from his logic that his science rests on certain hypotheses, certainties or assumptions. He learns now to suspend these assumptions. He is thus compelled to make these assumptions his theme. Far from being merely one of the innumerable themes of social science, history of political philosophy, and not logic, proves to be the pursuit concerned with the presuppositions of social science.

Those presuppositions prove to be modifications of the principles of modern political philosophy, and these principles in turn prove to be modifications of the principles of classical political philosophy. One cannot understand the presuppositions of present-day social science without a return to classical political philosophy. Social science claims to be decisively superior to classical political philosophy which surely lacked the alleged insight into the radical difference between facts and values. When attempting to understand classical political philosophy on its own terms, the social scientist is compelled to wonder whether the distinction is as necessary or as evident as it seems today. He is compelled to wonder whether not present-day social science but classical political philosophy is the true science of political things. This suggestion is dismissed out of hand because a return to an earlier position is believed to be impossible. But one must realize that this belief is a dogmatic assumption whose hidden basis is the belief in progress or in the rationality of the historical process.

The return to classical political philosophy is both necessary and tentative or experimental. Not in spite but because of its tentative character, it must be carried out seriously, *i.e.* without squinting at our present predicament. There is no danger that we can ever become oblivious of this predicament since it is the incentive to our whole concern with the classics. We cannot reasonably expect that a fresh understanding of classical political philosophy will supply us with recipes for today's use. For the relative success of modern political philosophy has brought into being a kind of society wholly unknown to the classics, a kind of society to which the classical principles as stated and elaborated by the classics are not immediately applicable. Only we living today can possibly find a solution to the problems of today. But an adequate understanding of the principles as elaborated by the classics may be the indispensable starting point for an adequate analysis, to be achieved by us, of present-day society in its peculiar character, and for the wise application, to be achieved by us, of these principles to our tasks.

One can come to doubt the fundamental premise of present-day social science—the distinction between values and facts—by merely considering the reasons advanced in its support as well as the consequences following from it. These considerations lead one to see that the issue concerning that distinction is part of a larger issue. The distinction is alien to that understanding of political things which belongs to political life but it becomes necessary, it seems, when the citizens' understanding of political things is replaced by the scientific understanding. The scientific understanding implies then a break with the pre-scientific understanding, yet at the same time it remains dependent on the pre-scientific understanding. Regardless of whether the superiority of the scientific understanding to the pre-scientific understanding can be demonstrated or not, the scientific understanding is secondary or derivative. Hence, social science cannot reach clarity about its doings if it does not possess a coherent and comprehensive understanding of what is frequently called the common sense view of political things, *i.e.* if it does not primarily understand the political things as they are experienced by the citizen or statesman; only if it possesses such a coherent and comprehensive understanding of its basis or matrix can it possibly show the legitimacy, and make intelligible the character, of that peculiar modification of the primary understanding of political things which is their scientific understanding. We contend that that coherent and comprehensive understanding of political things is available to us in Aristotle's *Politics* precisely because the *Politics* contains the original form of political science: that form in which political science is nothing other than the fully conscious form of the common sense understanding of political things. Classical political philosophy is the primary form of political science because the common sense understanding of political things is primary.

Our description of the character of the *Politics* is manifestly provisional. "Common sense" as used in this description is understood in contradistinction to "science," *i.e.* primarily modern natural science, and therewith presupposes "science" whereas the *Politics* itself does not presuppose "science." We shall first attempt to reach a more adequate understanding of the *Politics* by considering the objections to which our contention is exposed.

# Chapter I

# ON ARISTOTLE'S POLITICS

*According to the traditional view, it was not Aristotle but Socrates* who originated political philosophy or political science. More precisely, according to Cicero, Socrates was the first to call philosophy down from heaven, to establish it in the cities, to introduce it also into the households, and to compel it to inquire about men's life and manners as well as about the good and bad things. In other words, Socrates was the first philosopher who concerned himself chiefly or exclusively, not with the heavenly or divine things, but with the human things. The heavenly or divine things are the things to which man looks up or which are higher than the human things; they are super-human. The human things are the things good or bad for man as good or bad for man and particularly the just and noble things and their opposites. Cicero does not say that Socrates called philosophy down from heaven to earth, for the earth, the mother surely of all earthly things and perhaps the oldest and therefore the highest goddess, is itself super-human. The divine things are higher in rank than the human things. Man manifestly needs the divine things but the divine things do not manifestly need man. In a parallel passage Cicero speaks not of "heaven" but of "nature": the higher than human things from whose study Socrates turned to the study of the human things, is "the whole nature," "the *kosmos*," "the nature of all things." This implies that "the human things" are not "the nature of man"; the study of the nature of man is part of the study of nature.[1] Cicero draws our attention to the special effort which was required to turn philosophy toward the

---

[1] Cicero, *Tusc. disput.* V 10, and *Brutus* 31. Cf. Xenophon, *Memorabilia* I 1.11–12 and 1.15–16, *Hiero* 7.9, *Oeconomicus* 7.16 and 7.29–30, as well as Aristotle, *Metaphysics* 987b1–2 and *Eth. Nic.* 1094b7, 14–17; 1141a20–22, b7–8; 1143b21–23; 1177b31–33.

human things: philosophy turns primarily away from the human things toward the divine or natural things; no compulsion is needed or possible to establish philosophy in the cities or to introduce it into the households; but philosophy must be compelled to turn back toward the human things from which it originally departed.

The traditional view regarding the beginnings of political philosophy or political science is no longer accepted. Prior to Socrates, we are told, the Greek sophists turned to the study of the human things. As far as we know, Socrates himself did not speak about his predecessors as such. Let us then see what the man who takes Socrates' place in Plato's *Laws,* the Athenian stranger, says about his predecessors, about all or almost all men who prior to him concerned themselves with inquiries about nature. According to him, these men assert that all things which are have come into being ultimately out of and through certain "first things" which are not strictly speaking "things" but which are responsible for the coming into being and perishing of everything that comes into being and perishes; it is the first things and the coming into being attending on the first things which these men mean by "nature"; both the first things and whatever arises through them, as distinguished from human action, are "by nature." The things which are by nature stand at the opposite pole from the things which are by *nomos* (ordinarily rendered as "law" or "convention"), *i.e.* things which are not only not by themselves, nor by human making proper, but only by men holding them to be or positing that they are or agreeing as to their being. The men whom the Athenian stranger opposes assert above all that the gods are only by law or convention. For our present purpose it is more immediately important to note that according to these men the political art or science has little to do with nature and is therefore not something serious. The reason which they advance is that the just things are radically conventional and the things which are by nature noble differ profoundly from the things which are noble by convention: the way of life which is straight or correct according to nature consists in being superior to others or in lording it over the others whereas the way of life which is straight or correct according to convention consists in serving others. The Athenian stranger disagrees entirely with his predecessors. He asserts that there are things which are just by nature. He can also be said to show by deed—by the fact that he teaches legislators—that he regards the political art or science as a most serious pursuit.[2]

In order to be able to act and to speak as he does, the Athenian stranger need not abandon the fundamental distinction from which the men whom he opposes start. Despite the most important difference between him and them, the distinction between nature and convention, between the natural and the positive, remains as fundamental for him, and for classical political philosophy in general, as it was for his predecessors.[3] Our failure to recognize this is partly due to modern philosophy. We cannot do more than to remind readers of the most obvious points. The distinction mentioned became questionable primarily through the reasoning which was meant also to dispose of chance. The "explanation" of a chance event is the realization that it is a chance event: the fortuitous meeting of two men does not cease to be fortuitous when we know the whole prehistory of the two men prior to their meeting. There are then events which cannot meaningfully be traced to preceding events. The tracing of something to convention is analogous to the tracing of something to chance. However plausible a convention may appear in the light of the conditions in which it arose, it nevertheless owes its being, its "validity," to the fact that it became "held" or "accepted."[4] Against this view the following reasoning was advanced: the conventions originate in human acts, and these acts are as necessary, as fully determined by preceding causes, as natural as any natural event in the narrow sense of the term; hence the distinction between nature and convention can only be provisional or superficial.[5] Yet this "universal consideration regarding the concatenation of the causes" is not helpful as long as one does not show the kind of preceding causes which are relevant for the explanation of conventions. Natural conditions like climate, character of a territory, race, fauna, flora appear to be especially relevant. This means, however, that in each case the "legislator" has prescribed what was best for his people or that all customs are sensible or that all legislators

---

[2] *Laws* 631d1–2; 690b7–c3; 870e1–2; 888e4–6; 889b1–2, 4, c4, d–890a; 891c2–3, 7–9, e5–6; 892a2–3, c2–3; 967a7–d2.

[3] Consider especially *Laws* 757c–e.

[4] *Eth. Nic.* 1134b19–21.

[5] Spinoza, *Tr. theol.-pol.* IV (sect. 1–4 Bruder).

are wise. Since this sanguine assumption cannot be maintained, one is compelled to have recourse also to the errors, superstitions, or follies of the legislators. But one can do this only as long as one possesses a natural theology of one kind or another as well as knowledge of what constitutes the well-being, the common good, of any people. The difficulties which were encountered along this way of explaining conventions led people to question the very notion of convention as some sort of making; customs and languages, it was asserted, cannot be traced to any positing or other conscious acts but only to growth, to a kind of growth essentially different from the growth of plants and animals but analogous to it; that growth is more important and of higher rank than any making, even the rational making according to nature. We shall not insist on the kinship between the classical notion of "nature" and this modern notion of "growth." It is more urgent to point out that partly as a consequence of the modern notion of "growth," the classical distinction between nature and convention, according to which nature is of higher dignity than convention, has been overlaid by the modern distinction between nature and history according to which history (the realm of freedom and of values) is of higher dignity than nature (which lacks purposes or values), not to say, as has been said, that history comprehends nature which is essentially relative to the essentially historical mind.

The Athenian stranger, to return, unlike his predecessors, takes the political art or science seriously because he acknowledges that there are things which are by nature just. He traces his divergence from his predecessors to the fact that the latter admitted as first things only bodies whereas, according to him, the soul is not derivative from the body or inferior in rank to it but by nature the ruler over the body. In other words, his predecessors did not recognize sufficiently the fundamental difference between body and soul.[6] The status of the just things depends on the status of the soul. Justice is the common good *par excellence;* if there are to be things which are by nature just there must be things which are by nature common; but the body appears to be by nature each one's own or private.[7] Aristotle goes to the end of this road by asserting that the political association is by nature and that man is by nature political

---

[6] *Laws* 891c1–4, e5–892b1; 896b10–c3.
[7] *Laws* 739c6–d1 (cf. *Republic* 464d8–9 and 416d5–6).

because he is the being characterized by speech or reason and thus capable of the most perfect, the most intimate union with his fellows which is possible: the union in pure thought.[8]

The assertion of the Athenian stranger is confirmed by what Aristotle says about the sophists' manner of dealing with the political things. He says that the sophists either identify political science with rhetoric or subordinate it to rhetoric. If there are no things which are by nature just or if there is not by nature a common good, if therefore the only natural good is each man's own good, it follows that the wise man will not dedicate himself to the community but only use it for his own ends or prevent his being used by the community for its end; but the most important instrument for this purpose is the art of persuasion and in the first place forensic rhetoric. Someone might say that the most complete form in which one could use or exploit the political community would be the exercise of political power and especially of tyrannical power and that such exercise requires, as Machiavelli showed later on, deep knowledge of political things. According to Aristotle, the sophists denied this conclusion; they believed that it is "easy" to discharge well the non-rhetorical functions of government and to acquire the knowledge needed for this purpose: the only political art to be taken seriously is rhetoric.[9]

Aristotle does not deny however that there was a kind of political philosophy prior to Socrates. For Aristotle, political philosophy is primarily and ultimately the quest for that political order which is best according to nature everywhere and, we may add, always.[10] This quest will not come into its own as long as men are entirely immersed in political life, be it even in the founding of a political community, for even the founder is necessarily limited in his vision by what can or must be done "here and now." The first political philosopher will then be the first man not engaged in political life who attempted to speak about the best political order. That man, Aristotle tells us, was a certain Hippodamus. Before presenting the political order proposed by Hippodamus, Aristotle speaks at some length of Hippodamus' way of life. Apart from being the first polit-

---

[8] *Politics* 1253a1–18, 1281a2–4.
[9] *Eth. Nic.* 1181a12–17. Cf. Isocrates, *Antidosis* 80–83; Plato, *Gorgias* 460a3–4 (and context), *Protagoras* 318e6–319a2 and *Theaetetus* 167c2–7.
[10] Cf. *Eth. Nic.* 1135a4–5.

ical philosopher, Hippodamus was also a famous town planner, he lived, from ambition, in a somewhat overdone manner in other respects also (for instance he paid too much attention to his clothing), and he wished to be learned also regarding the whole nature. It is not Aristotle's habit to engage in what could even appear to be slightly malicious gossip. The summarized remark is the only one of its kind in his entire work. Shortly before speaking of Hippodamus, when discussing Plato's political writings, Aristotle describes "Socrates' speeches" (i.e. particularly the speeches occurring in the Republic and the Laws) by setting forth their high qualities; but he does this in order to legitimate his disagreement with those speeches: since the Socratic speeches, especially those about the simply best political order, exert an unrivaled charm, one must face that charm as such. When speaking of Eudoxus' hedonistic teaching, Aristotle remarks that Eudoxus was reputed to be unusually temperate; he makes this remark in order to explain why Eudoxus' speeches were regarded as more trustworthy than those of other hedonists.[11] We may therefore assume that Aristotle did not make his remark about Hippodamus' way of life without a good reason. Whereas the first philosopher became ridiculous on a certain occasion in the eyes of a barbarian slave woman,[12] the first political philosopher was rather ridiculous altogether in the eyes of sensible freemen. This fact indicates that political philosophy is more questionable than philosophy as such. Aristotle thus expresses in a manner somewhat mortifying to political scientists the same thought which Cicero expresses by saying that philosophy had to be compelled to become concerned with political things. Aristotle's suggestion was taken up in modern times by Pascal who said that Plato and Aristotle, being not pedants but gentlemen, wrote their political works playfully: "this was the least philosophic and the least serious part of their life . . . they wrote of politics as if they had to bring order into a madhouse." Pascal goes much beyond Aristotle, for, while admitting that there are things which are by nature just, he denies that they can be known to unassisted man owing to original sin.[13]

---

[11] Politics 1267b22–30; cf.1265a10–13 and 1263b15–22 as well as Eth. Nic. 1172b15–18.

[12] Plato, Theaetetus 173e1–174b7; Aristotle, Politics 1259a6–18.

[13] Pensées (ed. Brunschvicg) frs. 331 and 294. Cf. Plato, Laws 804b3–c1.

The best political order proposed by Hippodamus is distinguished by unusual simplicity: the citizen body is to consist of 10,000 men and of 3 parts; the land is to be divided into 3 parts; there are only 3 kinds of laws, for there are only 3 things about which lawsuits take place; regarding verdicts in lawcourts provision must be made for the 3 alternatives. After having considered this scheme which seems to be so clear, Aristotle is forced to note that it involves great confusion: the confusion is caused by the desire for a kind of clarity and simplicity which is alien to the subject matter.[14] It looks as if some account of "the whole nature"—an account which used the number 3 as the key to all things—enabled or compelled Hippodamus to go on toward his plan of the best political order as that political order which is entirely according to nature. But he merely arrived at great confusion because he did not pay attention to the peculiar character of political things: he did not see that the political things are in a class by themselves. In spite or because of his ambition, Hippodamus did not succeed in founding political philosophy or political science because he did not begin by raising the question "what is political?" or rather "what is the *polis*?" This question, and all questions of this kind, were raised by Socrates who for this reason became the founder of political philosophy.

The "what is" questions point to "essences," to "essential" differences—to the fact that the whole consists of parts which are heterogeneous, not merely sensibly (like fire, air, water, and earth) but noetically: to understand the whole means to understand the "What" of each of these parts, of these classes of beings, and how they are linked with one another. Such understanding cannot be the reduction of one heterogeneous class to others or to any cause or causes other than the class itself; the class, or the class character, is the cause *par excellence*. Socrates conceived of his turn to the "what is" questions as a turn, or a return, to sanity, to "common sense": while the roots of the whole are hidden, the whole manifestly consists of heterogeneous parts. One may say that according to Socrates the things which are "first in themselves" are somehow "first for us"; the things which are "first in themselves" are in a manner, but necessarily, revealed in men's opinions. Those opinions have as opinions a certain order. The highest opinions, the authoritative opinions, are

---

[14] *Politics* 1267b30–1268a6; 1268b3–4, 11; *Eth. Nic.* 1094b11–27.

the pronouncements of the law. The law makes manifest the just and noble things and it speaks authoritatively about the highest beings, the gods who dwell in heaven. The law is the law of the city; the city looks up to, holds in reverence, "holds" the gods of the city. The gods do not approve of man's trying to seek out what they did not wish to reveal, the things in heaven and beneath the earth. A pious man will therefore not investigate the divine things but only the human things, the things left to man's investigation. It is the greatest proof of Socrates' piety that he limited himself to the study of the human things. His wisdom is knowledge of ignorance because it is pious and it is pious because it is knowledge of ignorance.[15] Yet the opinions however authoritative contradict one another. Even if it should happen that a given city orders a matter of importance without contradicting itself, one can be certain that the verdict of that city will be contradicted by the verdicts of other cities.[16] It becomes then necessary to transcend the authoritative opinions as such in the direction of what is no longer opinion but knowledge. Even Socrates is compelled to go the way from law to nature, to ascend from law to nature. But he must go that way with a new awakeness, caution, and emphasis. He must show the necessity of the ascent by a lucid, comprehensive, and sound argument which starts from the "common sense" embodied in the accepted opinions and transcends them; his "method" is "dialectics." This obviously implies that, however much the considerations referred to may have modified Socrates' position, he still remains chiefly, if not exclusively, concerned with the human things: with what is by nature right and noble or with the nature of justice and nobility.[17] In its original form political philosophy broadly understood is the core of philosophy or rather "the first philosophy." It also remains true that human wisdom is knowledge of ignorance: there is no knowledge of the whole but only knowledge of parts, hence only partial knowledge of parts, hence no unqualified transcending, even by the wisest man as such, of the sphere of opinion. This Socratic or Platonic conclusion differs radically from a typically modern conclusion according to which the unavailability of knowledge of the

---

[15] Xenophon, *Mem.* I 1.11–16; IV 3.16, 6.1–4 and 7.6. Plato, *Apol. Soc.* 19b4–c8, 20d7–e3, 23a5–b4; *Phaedo* 99d4ff.; *Phaedrus* 249e4–5.

[16] Consider Plato, *Laches* 190e4–191c6.

[17] *Republic* 501b2; cf. *ibid.* 597b–e and *Phaedrus* 254b5–6.

whole demands that the question regarding the whole be abandoned and replaced by questions of another kind, for instance by the questions characteristic of modern natural and social science. The elusiveness of the whole necessarily affects the knowledge of every part. Because of the elusiveness of the whole, the beginning or the questions retain a greater evidence than the end or the answers; return to the beginning remains a constant necessity. The fact that each part of the whole, and hence in particular the political sphere, is in a sense open to the whole, obstructs the establishment of political philosophy or political science as an independent discipline. Not Socrates or Plato but Aristotle is truly the founder of political science: as one discipline, and by no means the most fundamental or the highest discipline, among a number of disciplines. This difference between Plato and Aristotle can be illustrated by the contrast between the relation of the *Republic* to the *Timaeus* on the one hand, and of the *Politics* to the *Physics* or *On the Heaven* on the other. Aristotle's cosmology, as distinguished from Plato's, is unqualifiedly separable from the quest for the best political order. Aristotelian philosophizing has no longer to the same degree and in the same way as Socratic philosophizing the character of ascent. Whereas the Platonic teaching presents itself necessarily in dialogues, the Aristotelian teaching presents itself necessarily in treatises. As regards the political things, Aristotle acts directly as the teacher of indefinitely many legislators or statesmen whom he addresses collectively and simultaneously, whereas Plato presents his political philosopher as guiding, in a conversation, one or two men who seek the best political order or are about to legislate for a definite community. Nevertheless it is no accident that the most fundamental discussion of the *Politics* includes what is almost a dialogue between the oligarch and the democrat.[18] It is equally characteristic however that that dialogue does not occur at the beginning of the *Politics*.

Aristotle is especially concerned with the proposal of Hippodamus that those who invent something useful to the city should receive honors; his examination of this proposal takes up about a half of his examination of Hippodamus' whole scheme. He is much less sure than Hippodamus of the virtues of innovation. It seems that Hippodamus had not given thought to the difference between

---

[18] See especially 1281a16 and b18.

innovation in the arts and innovation in law, or to the possible tension between the need for political stability and what one might call technological change. On the basis of some observations made nearer home, one might suspect a connection between Hippodamus' unbridled concern with clarity and simplicity and his unbridled concern with technological progress. His scheme as a whole seems to lead, not only to confusion, but to permanent confusion or revolution. At any rate Aristotle cannot elucidate innovation without bringing out a most important difference between the arts and law. The arts are susceptible of infinite refinement and hence progress and they do not as such in any way suffer from progress. The case of law is different, for law owes its strength, *i.e.* its power of being obeyed, as Aristotle says here, entirely to custom and custom comes into being only through a long time. Law, in contradistinction to the arts, does not owe its efficacy to reason at all or only to a small degree.[19] However evidently reasonable a law may be, its reasonableness becomes obscured through the passions which it restrains. Those passions support maxims or opinions incompatible with the law. Those passion-bred opinions in their turn must be counteracted by passion-bred and passion-breeding opposite opinions which are not necessarily identical with the reasons of the law. The law, the most important instrument for the moral education of "the many," must then be supported by ancestral opinions, by myths—for instance, by myths which speak of the gods as if they were human beings—or by a "civil theology." The gods as meant in these myths have no being in and by themselves but only "by law." Yet given the necessity of law one may say that the principle of the whole both wishes and does not wish to be called Zeus.[20] Because the city as a whole is characterized by a specific recalcitrance to reason, it requires for its well-being a rhetoric different from forensic and deliberative rhetoric as a servant to the political art.

"The very nature of public affairs often defeats reason." One illustration taken from Aristotle's *Politics* must suffice. In the first book, Aristotle sets forth the dictate of reason regarding slavery: it is just to enslave men who are by nature slaves; men who are slaves

---

[19] *Politics* 1268b22–1269a24, 1257b25–27. Cf. Isocrates, *Antidosis* 82 and Thomas Aquinas, S. *th.* 1 2 q. 97. a. 2. ad 1.

[20] Aristotle, *Metaphysics* 1074b1–14 (cf. Thomas Aquinas *ad loc.*). Cf. Heraclitus (Diels, *Vorsokratiker*, 7th ed.) fr. 32.

not by nature but only by law and compulsion are unjustly enslaved; a man is a slave by nature if he is too stupid to guide himself or can do only a kind of work little superior to the work done by beasts of burden; such a man is better off as a slave than free. But when discussing the best polity, Aristotle takes it for granted that the slave population of that polity consists of men each of whom can safely be rewarded with freedom for his service, *i.e.* is not a natural slave. After all, a man may have by nature a slavish character, a lack of pride or manliness which disposes him to obey a stronger man, while being intelligent and thus much more useful to his master than a fellow who is as strong and as stupid as an ox.[21] Plato who also allows, to Aristotle's displeasure, that the defenders of the city be savage toward strangers, expresses the same thought more directly by admitting, with Pindar, that superiority in strength ✓is a natural title to rule. From this we understand why the nature of political things defeats to some extent not only reason but persuasion in any form and one grasps another reason why the sophistic reduction of the political art to rhetoric is absurd. Xenophon's companion Proxenus had been a pupil of Gorgias, the famous rhetorician. Thanks to Gorgias' instruction he was capable of ruling gentlemen by means of praise or abstention from praise. Yet he was utterly incapable of instilling his soldiers with respect and fear of himself: he was unable to discipline them. Xenophon on the other hand, the pupil of Socrates, possessed the full political art. The very same thought—the insufficiency of persuasion for the guidance of "the many" and the necessity of laws with teeth in them—constitutes the transition from Aristotle's *Ethics* to his *Politics*. It is within this context that he denounces the sophists' reduction of politics to rhetoric.[22] So far from being "Machiavellians," the sophists—believing in the omnipotence of speech—were blind to the sternness of politics.

Hitherto we have spoken of the apparent superiority of the arts to laws. But precisely Aristotle's critique of Hippodamus implies that the arts must be regulated by law and hence are subordinate to law. Law owes this dignity to the facts that it is meant to be a

---

[21] Aristotle, *Politics* 1254b22–1255a3, 1255b4–15, 1285a19–22, 1327b27–29, 1330a25–33. Cicero, *Republic* II 57.

[22] *Eth. Nic.* 1179b4ff.; Plato, *Laws* 690b; Xenophon, *Anabasis* II 16–20; Cicero, *Republic* I 2–3.

dictate of reason and that the reason effective in the arts is lower than the reason effective in law as law should be.[23] Laws are the work of the legislative art, but the legislative art is the highest form of practical wisdom or prudence, the prudence concerned with the common good of a political society, as distinguished from prudence in the primary sense which is concerned with a man's own good. The difference between arts and law is then founded on the difference between arts and prudence. Prudence is of higher dignity than the arts because every art is concerned with a partial good whereas prudence is concerned with the whole human good, the good life. Prudence alone enables one to distinguish between genuine arts (like medicine) and sham arts (like cosmetics) and to decide which use of an art (for instance, of strategy) is good. The arts point to Right or Law which makes them arts by being their limit and norm.[24] The artisan as artisan is concerned with producing the work peculiar to his art (the cobbler with making shoes, the physician with restoring health) but not with his own good; he is concerned with his own good in so far as he is concerned with receiving pay for his work or with practicing the art which accompanies all arts, the art of money-making; thus the art of money-making could appear to be the universal art, the art of arts; the art of money-making knows no limits: it enables a man to make greater and ever greater gains; yet the view that money-making is an art presupposes that unlimited acquisitiveness is good for a man and this presupposition can well be questioned; it appears that acquisition is for the sake of use, of the good use of wealth, i.e. of an activity regulated by prudence.[25] The distinction between prudence and the arts implies that there is no art that tells me which partial good supplied by an art I ought to choose here and now in preference to other goods. There is no expert who can decide the prudent man's vital questions for him as well as he can. To be prudent means to lead a good life, and to lead a good life means that one deserves to be one's own master or that one makes one's own decisions well. Prudence is that kind of knowledge which is inseparable from "moral virtue," i.e. goodness of character or of the habit of choosing, just as moral virtue is inseparable from prudence. The arts as arts do not have this close

---

[23] *Eth. Nic.* 1094a27–b6, 1180a18–22; cf. 1134a34 with *Politics* 1287a28–30.
[24] *Eth. Nic.* 1094b7–10, 1140a26–30, 1141b23–29, 1181a23; cf. Sophocles, *Antigone* 332–372.
[25] *Politics* 1257b4ff.; Plato, *Republic* 341c4–7 and 346.

connection with moral virtue. Aristotle goes so far as to suggest that the virtue required of artisans as artisans is less than that required of slaves.[26] Prudence and moral virtue united and as it were fused enable a man to lead a good life or the noble life which seems to be the natural end of man. The best life is the life devoted to understanding or contemplation as distinguished from the practical or political life. Therefore practical wisdom is lower in rank than theoretical wisdom which is concerned with the divine things or the *kosmos,* and subservient to it—but in such a way that within its sphere, the sphere of all human things as such, prudence is supreme.[27] The sphere ruled by prudence is closed since the principles of prudence—the ends in the light of which prudence guides man—are known independently of theoretical science. Because Aristotle held that art is inferior to law or to prudence, that prudence is inferior to theoretical wisdom, and that theoretical wisdom (knowledge of the whole, *i.e.* of that by virtue of which "all things" are a whole) is available, he could found political science as an independent discipline among a number of disciplines in such a way that political science preserves the perspective of the citizen or statesman or that it is the fully conscious form of the "common sense" understanding of political things.

The Athenian stranger may be said to assert that the men who preceded him conceived of nature as superior to art and of art as superior to law. Aristotle conceives of nature as superior to law—for the good law is the law which is according to nature—and of law as superior to the arts. Aristotle's view must also be distinguished from another extreme view by virtue of which nature and law become fused and oppose themselves to the arts which thus appear to defile a sacred order.

According to Aristotle it is moral virtue that supplies the sound principles of action, the just and noble ends, as actually desired; these ends come to sight only to the morally good man; prudence seeks the means to these ends. The morally good man is the properly bred man, the well-bred man. Aristotle's political science is addressed only to such men.[28] The sphere of prudence is then closed by principles which are fully evident only to gentlemen. In seeking

---

[26] *Politics* 1260a33–41.

[27] *Eth. Nic.* 1141a28–b9, 1145a6–11.

[28] *Eth. Nic.* 1095a30–b8, 1103a24–26, 1144a7–9, 1144a20–1145a6, 1178a-16–19.

for higher principles, one would raise the question "why should one be decent?" but in doing so one would already have ceased to be a gentleman, for decency is meant to be choiceworthy for its own sake. The gentleman is recognized as gentleman not only by other gentlemen but also by people of deficient breeding. Yet among the latter there may be men of great power of persuasion who question the goodness of moral virtue. It is therefore not sufficient to know what justice, magnanimity and the other virtues are and to be moved by their beauty; one must show that they are good.[29] One must then transcend the sphere of prudence or of what one may call the moral consciousness. One must show that the practice of the moral virtues is the end of man by nature, *i.e.* that man is inclined toward such practice by nature. This does not require that man by nature know his natural end without any effort on his part. The natural end of man as well as of any other natural being becomes genuinely known through theoretical science, through the science of the natures.[30] More precisely, knowledge of the virtues derives from knowledge of the human soul: each part of the soul has its specific perfection. Plato sketches such a purely theoretical account of the virtues in the *Republic*. But it is characteristic of Aristotle that he does not even attempt to give such an account. He describes all the moral virtues as they are known to morally virtuous man without trying to deduce them from a higher principle; generally speaking, he leaves it at the fact that a given habit is regarded as praiseworthy without investigating why this is so. One may say that he remains within the limits of an unwritten *nomos* which is recognized by well-bred people everywhere. This *nomos* may be in agreement with reason but is not as such dictated by reason. It constitutes the sphere of human or political things by being its limit or its ceiling. By proceeding differently, Aristotle would make political or practical science dependent on theoretical science.

In order to grasp the ground of Aristotle's procedure, one must start from the facts that according to him the highest end of man by nature is theoretical understanding or philosophy and this per-

---

[29] Cf. Plato, *Republic* I end and Aristotle, *Eth. Nic.* 1101b25–27 (cf. 1132b31–1133a2).

[30] Aristotle, *On the Soul* 434a16–21 (cf. 432b27–30). Cf. Averroës, *Commentary on Plato's Republic* (ed. E.I.J. Rosenthal) I 23.5 and II 8.1; Thomas Aquinas, *Commentary on the Nicomachean Ethics* VI lectio 2. (nr. 1131), *S. th.* 2 2 q. 47. a. 6. ad 3.

fection does not require moral virtue as moral virtue, *i.e.* just and noble deeds as choiceworthy for their own sake.[31] It goes without saying that man's highest end cannot be achieved without actions resembling moral actions proper, but the actions in question are intended by the philosopher as mere means toward his end. That end also calls for prudence, for the philosopher must deliberate about how he can secure the conditions for his philosophizing here and now. The moral virtues are more directly related to man's second natural end, his social life; one could therefore think that the moral virtues are intelligible as being essentially in the service of the city. For instance, magnanimity is praiseworthy because the city needs men who are born to command and who know that they are born to command. But it suffices to read Aristotle's description of magnanimity in order to see that the full phenomenon of magnanimity cannot be understood in that way. The moral virtues cannot be understood as being for the sake of the city since the city must be understood as being for the sake of the practice of moral virtue.[32] Moral virtue is then not intelligible as a means for the only two natural ends which could be thought to be its end. Therefore, it seems, it must be regarded as an "absolute." Yet one cannot disregard its relations to those two natural ends. Moral virtue shows that the city points beyond itself but it does not reveal clearly that toward which it points, namely, the life devoted to philosophy. The man of moral virtue, the gentleman, may very well know that his political activity is in the service of noble leisure but his leisurable activity hardly goes beyond the enjoyment of poetry and the other imitative arts.[33] Aristotle is the founder of political science because he is the discoverer of moral virtue. For Plato, what Aristotle calls moral virtue is a kind of halfway house between political or vulgar virtue which is in the service of bodily well-being (of self-preservation or peace) and genuine virtue which, to say the least, animates only the philosophers as philosophers.[34] As for the Stoics, who went so far as to assert that only the noble is good, they identified the man of nobility with the wise man who as such possesses the

---

[31] *Eth. Nic.* 1177b1–8, 1178a28ff.; cf. *E.E.* 1248b9ff. Cf. Averroës, *loc. cit.* III 12 and 16.10; Thomas, *S. th.* 1 2 q. 58. a. 4.–5. and 2 2 q. 45. a. 4.

[32] *Eth. Nic.* 1095b30–31, 1099b29–32, 1178b5; *Politics* 1278b21–24. Cf. Averroës, *loc. cit.* I 4.7.

[33] *Politics* 1337b33–1338b4.

[34] *Phaedo* 68b2–69c3, 82a11ff., *Republic* 518d9–e3.

"virtues" called logic and physics.[35] We must beware of mistaking Aristotle's man of moral virtue or "good man" who is the perfect gentleman for the "good man" who is just and temperate but lacks all other virtues, like the members of the lowest class in Plato's *Republic*.[36] The latter notion of "goodness" prepared Machiavelli's and Rousseau's distinction, or opposition, between "goodness" and "virtue."

When the philosopher Aristotle addresses his political science to more or less perfect gentlemen, he shows them as far as possible that the way of life of the perfect gentleman points toward the philosophic way of life; he removes a screen. He articulates for his addressees the unwritten *nomos* which was the limit of their vision while he himself stands above that limit. He is thus compelled or enabled to correct their opinions about things which fall within their purview. He must speak of virtues and vices which were "nameless" and hence hitherto unknown. He must deny explicitly or tacitly that habits as highly praised as sense of shame and piety are virtues. The gentleman is by nature able to be affected by philosophy; Aristotle's political science is an attempt to actualize this potentiality. The gentleman affected by philosophy is in the highest case the enlightened statesman, like Pericles who was affected by Anaxagoras.[37] The moral-political sphere is then not unqualifiedly closed to theoretical science. One reason why it seemed necessary to make a radical distinction between practical wisdom on the one hand and the sciences and the arts on the other was the fact that every art is concerned with a partial good, whereas prudence is concerned with the whole human good. Yet the highest form of prudence is the legislative art which is the architectonic art, the art of arts, because it deals with the whole human good in the most comprehensive manner. It is concerned with the whole human good by being concerned with the highest human good with reference to which all partial human goods are good. It deals with its subject in the most comprehensive manner because it establishes the framework within which political prudence proper, the right handling of situations, can take place. Moreover, "legislative art" is an ambiguous term; it may mean the art practiced "here and now" by a legis-

---

[35] Cicero, *De finibus* III 11, 17–18, 72–73. Consider, however, *ibid.* V 36.
[36] Cf. *Phaedo* 82a11–b2 with Cicero, *Offices* II 35.
[37] *Phaedrus* 269d–270a.

lator acting on behalf of this or that political community; but it may also mean the "practical science" of legislation taught by the teacher of legislators which is superior in dignity to the former since it supplies guidance for it. As a practical science it differs from prudence in all its forms because it is free from that involvement the dangers of which cannot be averted except by moral virtue.[38] Hence prudence appears to be ultimately subject to a science. Considerations like these induced Socrates and Plato to assert that virtue is knowledge and that quest for prudence is philosophy. Just as the partial human goods cannot be known to be goods except with reference to the highest or the whole human good, the whole human good cannot be known to be good except with reference to the good simply, the idea of the good, which comes to sight only beyond and above all other ideas: the idea of the good, and not the human good or in particular gentlemanship, is the principle of prudence. But since love of wisdom is not wisdom and philosophy as prudence is the never-to-be-completed concern with one's own good, it seems impossible to know that the philosophic life is the best life. Socrates could not know this if he did not know that the only serious alternative to the philosophic life is the political life and that the political life is subordinate to the philosophic life: political life is life in the cave which is partly closed off by a wall from life in the light of the sun; the city is the only whole within the whole or the only part of the whole whose essence can be wholly known. In spite of their disagreement Plato and Aristotle agree as to this, that the city is both closed to the whole and open to the whole, and they are agreed as to the character of the wall separating the city from the rest of the whole. Given the fact that the only political work proper of Plato is the *Laws* in which Socrates does not occur, one is tempted to draw this conclusion: the only reason why not Socrates but Aristotle became the founder of political science is that Socrates who spent his life in the unending ascent to the idea of the good and in awakening others to that ascent, lacked for this reason the leisure not only for political activity but even for founding political science.—

---

[38] *Eth. Nic.* 1094a15–b10, 1099b31, 1104a3–10, 1141b24–27, 1152b1–3, 1181a23; *Politics* 1287a32–b3, 1288b10ff., 1325b40ff. Cf. Thomas Aquinas, *S. th.* 1 q. 1. a. 6. ad 3. and q. 14. a. 16. c. as well as *Commentary on Ethics* VI lectio 7. (nr. 1200–1201).

Our provisional contention according to which Aristotle's political science is the fully conscious form of the common sense understanding of political things is open to the objection that the matrix of that science is not common sense simply but the common sense of the Greeks, not to say the common sense of the Greek upper class. This is said to show itself immediately in the theme of Aristotle's *Politics,* the Greek city-state. It is true that city-states were much more common among the Greeks than among the non-Greeks,[39] but the fact that Aristotle respects the Carthaginian city-state hardly less than the Spartan and much more than the Athenian suffices to dispose of the assertion that the city-state is essentially Greek. A more serious difficulty appears when we turn our attention to the expression "city-state." The city-state is meant to be a particular form of the state, and this thought cannot even be stated in Aristotle's language. Furthermore, when we speak today of "state," we understand "state" in contradistinction to "society," yet "city" comprises "state" and "society." More precisely, "city" antedates the distinction between state and society and cannot therefore be put together out of "state" and "society." The nearest English equivalent to "the city" is "the country": one can say "my country right or wrong," but one cannot say "my society right or wrong" or "my state right or wrong." "City" can be used synonymously with "fatherland."[40] Yet the difference between "city" and "country" must not be neglected. "City" is not the same as "town," for "city" comprises both "town" and "country," yet the city as Aristotle understands it is essentially an urban society[41]: the core of the city is not the tillers of the soil. The alternative to "city" is not another form of "state" but the "tribe" or "nation" as a lower, not to say barbarian, kind of society which in contradistinction to the city is unable to combine civilization with freedom.[42]

While for the citizen the modern equivalent of the city is the country, for the theoretical man that equivalent is the unity of state and society which transforms itself into "society" simply as well as into "civilization" or "culture." Through our understanding of "the

---

[39] Cf. Aristophanes, *Peace* 59 and 63.

[40] Cf. Xenophon, *Hiero* 4.3–5; Plato, *Crito* 51c1, *Laws* 856d5. Consider, above all, Aristotle's treatment of "the fatherland."

[41] *Politics* 1276a26–30; 1319a9–10, 29–38; 1321b19, 28. Cf. Plato, *Laws* 758d–e.

[42] *Politics* 1284a38–b3, b38–39; 1326b3–5.

country" we would have a direct access to "the city," but that access is blocked by the modern equivalents of the "city" which originate in theory. It is therefore necessary to understand the ground of the difference between "city" on the one hand and these modern equivalents on the other.

The city is a society which embraces various kinds of smaller and subordinate societies; among these the family or the household is the most important. The city is the most comprehensive and the highest society since it aims at the highest and most comprehensive good at which any society can aim. This highest good is happiness. The highest good of the city is the same as the highest good of the individual. The core of happiness is the practice of virtue and primarily of moral virtue. Since the theoretical life proves to be the most choiceworthy for the individual, it follows that at least some analogue of it is the aim also of the city. However this may be, the chief purpose of the city is the noble life and therefore the chief concern of the city must be the virtue of its members and hence liberal education.[43] There is a great variety of opinions as to what constitutes happiness but Aristotle is satisfied that there is no serious disagreement on this subject among sufficiently thoughtful people. In modern times it came to be believed that it is wiser to assume that happiness does not have a definite meaning since different men, and even the same man at different times, have entirely different views as to what constitutes happiness. Hence happiness or the highest good could no longer be the common good at which political society aims. Yet however different the notions of happiness may be, the fundamental conditions of happiness, it was believed, are in all cases the same: one cannot be happy without being alive, without being a free man, and without being able to pursue happiness however one understands happiness. Thus it became the purpose of political society to guarantee those conditions of happiness which came to be understood as the natural rights of each, and to refrain from imposing on its members happiness of any sort, for no notion of happiness can be intrinsically superior to any other notion. One may indeed call the security of all members of society in life, liberty, and the pursuit of happiness, public or political happiness, but one thus merely confirms the fact that true happiness is private. Some

---

[43] *Eth. Nic.* 1094a18–28, 1095a14–20, 1098a15–17; *Politics* 1252a1–7, 1278b21–24, 1324a5–8, 1325b14–32.

kind of virtue is indispensable even for political society thus understood—as a means for peaceably living together and ultimately for
each man's happiness whatever that happiness may be. Hence the
purpose of the individual and the purpose of political society are
essentially different. Each individual strives for happiness as he
understands happiness. This striving, which is partly competitive
with and partly cooperative with the strivings of everyone else, produces or constitutes a kind of web; that web is "society" as distinguished from the "state" which merely secures the conditions for the
striving of the individuals. It follows that in one respect the state is
superior to society, for the state is based on what all must equally
desire because they all equally need it, on the conditions of happiness, and that in another respect society is superior to the state, for
society is the outcome of each individual's concern with his end,
whereas the state is concerned only with certain means. In other
words, the public and the common is in the service of the merely
private whatever that private may be, or the highest or ultimate
purpose of the individual is merely private. This difficulty cannot be
overcome except by transcending the plane on which both society
and the state exist.

Aristotle knew and rejected a view of the city which seems to
foreshadow the modern view of political society and hence the
distinction between state and society. According to that view, the
purpose of the city is to enable its members to exchange goods and
services by protecting them against violence among themselves
and from foreigners, without its being concerned at all with the
moral character of its members.[44] Aristotle does not state the reasons
which were adduced for justifying this limitation of the purpose of
the city unless his reference in this context to a sophist is taken to
be a sufficient indication. The view reported by Aristotle reminds
us of the description given in Plato's *Republic* of the "city of pigs"[45]
—of a society which is sufficient for satisfying the natural wants of
the body, *i.e.* of the naturally private. We shall say that society
as distinguished from the state first comes to sight as the market in
which competitors buy and sell and which requires the state as its
protector or rather servant. On this basis the "political" comes to be

---

[44] *Politics* 1280a25–b35. Cf. the kindred criticism of this kind of society
by Augustine in *De Civitate Dei* II 20.

[45] *Republic* 372d4 and e6–7.

understood eventually as derivative from the "economic." The actions of the market are as such voluntary whereas the state coerces. Yet voluntariness is not a preserve of the market; it is above all of the essence of genuine, as distinguished from merely utilitarian, virtue. From this it was inferred in modern times that since virtue cannot be brought about by coercion, the promotion of virtue cannot be the purpose of the state; not because virtue is unimportant but because it is lofty and sublime, the state must be indifferent to virtue and vice as such, as distinguished from transgressions of the state's laws which have no other function than the protection of the life, liberty, and property of each citizen. We note in passing that this reasoning does not pay sufficient attention to the importance of habituation or education for the acquisition of virtue. This reasoning leads to the consequence that virtue, and religion, must become private, or else that society, as distinguished from the state, is the sphere less of the private than of the voluntary. Society embraces then not only the sub-political but the supra-political (morality, art, science) as well. Society thus understood is no longer properly called society, nor even civilization, but culture. On this basis the political must be understood as derivative from the cultural: culture is the matrix of the state. "Culture" as susceptible of being used in the plural is the highest modern equivalent of "city." In its original form "culture" in the sense indicated was thought to have its originating core in religion: "it is in religion that a nation [Volk] gives itself the definition of what it regards as the truth."⁴⁶ According to Aristotle too, the concern with the divine occupies somehow the first place among the concerns of the city but this is not true according to him in the last analysis. His reason is that that concern with the divine which occupies the place of honor among the concerns of the city is the activity of the priesthood,

---

⁴⁶ Hegel, *Die Vernunft in der Geschichte* (ed. Hoffmeister) 125. In his "Wissenschaftliche Behandlungsarten des Naturrechts" (*Schriften zur Politik und Rechtsphilosophie* [ed. Lasson] 383 and 393) Hegel renders Plato's and Aristotle's *polis* by "Volk." Hegel does not speak of cultures but of *Volksgeister* and *Weltanschauungen*. Cf. Burke, *Reflections on the Revolution in France* (*Works* [Bohn Standard Library] II 351 and 362) and *Letters on a Regicide Peace* I (*ed. cit.* V 214–215). The kinship between trade, "society," and "culture" as the spontaneous or non-coercive (in contradistinction to the state as well as to religion) appears in Jakob Burckhardt's *Weltgeschichtliche Betrachtungen* (Gesamtausgabe, VII [Basel, 1929] 20, 42–43 and 47–48).

whereas the true concern with the divine is the knowledge of the divine, *i.e.* transpolitical wisdom which is devoted to the cosmic gods as distinguished from the Olympian gods. In the words of Thomas Aquinas, reason informed by faith, not natural reason simply, to say nothing of corrupted reason, teaches that God is to be loved and worshipped.[47] Natural reason cannot decide which of the various forms of divine worship is the true one, although it is able to show the falsity of those which are plainly immoral; each of the various forms of divine worship appears to natural reason to owe its validity to political establishment and therefore to be subject to the city. Aristotle's view is less opposed to the Biblical view than it might seem: he too is concerned above all with the truth of religion. But to return to the relation between "city" and "culture," "culture" as commonly used now differs from the original notion decisively because it no longer implies the recognition of an order of rank among the various elements of culture. From this point of view Aristotle's assertion that the political element is the highest or most authoritative element in human society must appear to be arbitrary or at best the expression of one culture among many.

The view according to which all elements of culture are of equal rank, is meant to be adequate for the description or analysis of all human societies present or past. Yet it appears to be the product of one particular culture, modern Western culture, and it is not certain that its use for the understanding of other cultures does not do violence to them: these cultures must be understood as they are in themselves. It would seem that each culture must be understood in the light of what it looks up to; that to which it looks up may appear to it to become reflected in a particular kind of human being, and that kind of human being may rule the society in question in broad daylight; it is this special case of rule which Aristotle regarded as the normal case. But is it merely a special case? The view according to which all elements of a culture are of equal rank, which we may call the egalitarian view of culture, reflects an egalitarian society—a society which derives its character from its looking up to equality (and ultimately to a universe not consisting of essentially different parts) and which therefore looks up to such uncom-

---

[47] *Politics* 1328b11–13 and 1322b12–37. Thomas, *S. th.* 1 2 q. 104. a. 1. ad 3.; cf. 2 2 q. 85. a. 1. ad 1.

mon men as devote themselves to the service of the common man.
The present interest in the variety of cultures was foreshadowed by
the interest of certain Greek travellers in the variety of nations.
Herodotus may be said to have studied the various nations with a
view to the nature of the land and of its inhabitants, their arts or
crafts, their laws written or unwritten, and their stories or accounts;
in this scheme the political element was not manifestly the highest
or the most authoritative. In contradistinction to this descriptive
approach, Aristotle's approach is practical; he sees the various societies as they appear when one is guided by the question of the
good society or of the good life; those societies themselves come to
sight then as attempting to answer that question, given the conditions imposed on them; in this perspective the nature of the land and
of its inhabitants, to some extent even the arts and the accounts, appear as conditions and the political order alone as the intended.—

We must now say a few words about Aristotle's alleged anti-
democratic prejudice. The democracy with which he takes issue is
the democracy of the city, not modern democracy or the kind of
democracy which presupposes the distinction between state and
society. The democracy of the city is characterized by the presence
of slavery: citizenship was a privilege not a right. That democracy
did not allow the claim to freedom of man as man but of freeman
as freeman and in the last analysis of men who are by nature freemen, not to say of people descended on both sides from citizens.
The freeman is distinguished from the slave by the fact that he
lives as he likes; the claim to live as he likes is raised for every
freeman equally. He refuses to take orders from anyone or to be
subject to anyone. But since government is necessary, the freeman
demands that he not be subject to anyone who is not in turn subject
to him: everyone must have as much access to magistracies as
everyone else, merely because he is a freeman. The only way in
which this can be guaranteed is election by lot, as distinguished
from voting for candidates where considerations other than whether
the candidate is a free man—especially merit—inevitably enter;
voting for candidates is aristocratic rather than democratic. Hence
modern democracy would have to be described with a view to its
intention from Aristotle's point of view as a mixture of democracy
and aristocracy. Since freedom as claimed by the democracy of the
city means to live as one likes, that democracy permits only the

minimum of restraint on its members; it is "permissive" to the extreme.[48] One may find it strange that Aristotle does not allow for the possibility of an austere, stern, "Puritan" democracy; but this kind of regime would be theocratic rather than democratic. We must note, however, that Aristotle does not suggest a connection between the democracy of the city and the city which limits itself to enabling its members to exchange goods and services by protecting them against violence without its being concerned with the moral character of its members. Democracy as he understands it is no less passionately and comprehensively political than any other regime.

It could seem that democracy is not merely one form of the city among many but its normal form, or that the city tends to be democratic. The city is, or tends to be, a society of free and equal men. As city it is the people or belongs to the people and this would seem to require that it be ruled by the people. It is no accident that Aristotle introduces the fundamental reflections of the third book of the *Politics* by an argument of democratic origin and that the first definition of the citizen which suggests itself to him is that of the citizen in a democracy. In contradistinction to oligarchy and aristocracy, democracy is the rule of all and not the rule of a part; oligarchy and aristocracy exclude the common people from participation in government whereas democracy does not exclude the wealthy and the gentlemen.[49] Nevertheless, according to Aristotle, the apparent rule of all in democracy is in fact the rule of a part. Among equals, the fair, nay, the only possible way compatible with deliberation, of deciding issues where unanimity is lacking is to abide by the will of the majority, but it so happens that the majority of freemen in practically every city is the poor; hence democracy is the rule of the poor.[50] Democracy presents itself as the rule of all or it bases its claim on freedom and not on poverty, because titles to rule are more credible if based on an excellence rather than on a defect or a need. But if democracy is rule of the poor, of those who lack leisure, it is the rule of the uneducated and therefore undesirable. Since it is not safe to exclude the *demos* where it

---

[48] *Politics* 1273b40–41, 1275b22–25, 1317a40–b21, 1323a3–6. Cf. Plato, *Republic* 557a9ff. and 562b9–c2, *Statesman* 303a4–7.

[49] *Politics* 1255b20, 1259b4–6, 1274b32–36, 1275b5–7, 1280a5, 1281b34–38, 1282a16–17, 1295b25–26. Cf. Cicero, *Republic* I 39–43. Consider Plato, *Republic* 557d4–9.

[50] *Politics* 1294a9–14, 1317b5–10.

exists from participation in rule, Aristotle devised as his best polity a city without a *demos*, a city consisting only of gentlemen on the one hand and metics and slaves on the other.[51] This perfect solution is however possible only under the most favorable conditions. Aristotle considered therefore a variety of less extreme solutions—of regimes in which the common people participate without being predominant. He comes closest to accepting democracy—at least in the case when the common people is not too depraved—in the fundamental reflections of the third book. After having laid the broadest possible foundations, he states first the case for democracy and then for the absolute rule of one outstanding man.[52] He acts as if he agreed with the suggestion made in Plato's *Laws* according to which there are two "mothers" of all other regimes, namely, democracy and monarchy.[53] The argument in favor of a certain kind of democracy appears to be conclusive on the political level. Why then is Aristotle not wholly satisfied with it? What induces him to turn from democracy to a certain kind of absolute monarchy? Who is that Zeus-like man who has the highest natural title to rule, a much higher title than any multitude? He is the man of the highest self-sufficiency who therefore cannot be a part of the city: is he not, if not the philosopher, at least the highest political reflection of the philosopher? He is not likely to be the philosopher himself, for kingship in the highest sense belongs to the dawn of the city, whereas philosophy belongs to a later stage and the completion of philosophy—Aristotle's own philosophy—belongs rather to its dusk: the peak of the city and the peak of philosophy belong to entirely different times.[54] However this may be, we suggest that the ultimate reason why Aristotle has reservations against even the best kind of democracy is his certainty that the *demos* is by nature opposed to philosophy.[55] Only the gentlemen can be open to philosophy, *i.e.* listen to the philosopher. Modern democracy on the other hand presupposes a fundamental harmony between philosophy and the people, a harmony brought about by universal enlightenment, or by

---

[51] *Politics* 1274a17–18, 1281b28–30, 1328b24–1329a2, 1329a19–26.

[52] Compare the argument in favor of democracy from 1281a39 to 1283b35 with 1282b36; 1283b16–23; 1284a3–8, b13, 28–33. Cf. 1282a15–16.

[53] *Laws* 693d2–e8.

[54] *Politics* 1253a27–29, 1267a10–12, 1284b25–34, 1286b20–22, 1288a26–28, 1313a4–5; *Eth Nic.* 1160b3–6, 1177a27–b1.

[55] Cf. *Gorgias* 481d3–5 and *Republic* 494a4–7.

philosophy (science) relieving man's estate through inventions and discoveries recognizable as salutary by all, or by both means. On the basis of the break with Aristotle, one could come to believe in the possibility of the simply rational society, *i.e.* of a society each member of which would be of necessity perfectly rational so that all would be united by fraternal friendship, and government of men, as distinguished from administration of things, would wither away. It also became possible to integrate philosophy into the city or rather into its modern equivalent, "culture," and thus to achieve the replacement of the distinction between nature and convention by the distinction between nature and history.

For Aristotle political inequality is ultimately justified by the natural inequality among men. The fact that some men are by nature rulers and others by nature ruled points in its turn to the inequality which pervades nature as a whole: the whole as an ordered whole consists of beings of different rank. In man the soul is by nature the ruler of the body and the mind is the ruling part of the soul. It is on the basis of this that thoughtful men are said to be the natural rulers of the thoughtless ones.[56] It is obvious that an egalitarianism which appeals from the inequality regarding the mind to the equality regarding breathing and digestion does not meet the issue. Entirely different is the case of an egalitarianism which starts from morality and its implications. In passing moral judgments—in praising good men or good actions and in blaming bad men or bad actions—we presuppose that a man's actions, and hence also his being a good or a bad man, are in his power.[57] We presuppose therefore that prior to the exercise of their wills, or by nature, all men are equal with respect to the possibility of becoming good or bad men, *i.e.* in what seems to be the highest respect. Yet a man's upbringing or the conditions in which he lives would seem to affect greatly, if not decisively, his potentiality of becoming or being good or bad. To maintain a man's moral responsibility in the face of the unfavorable conditions which moulded him, one seems to be compelled to make him responsible for those conditions: he himself must have willed the conditions which as it were compel him to act badly. More generally, the apparent inequality among men in respect of the possibility of being good must be due to

---

[56] *Politics* 1254a28–b16.
[57] *Eth. Nic.* 1113b6ff.

human fault.[58] Moral judgment seems then to lead up to the postulate that a God concerned with justice has created all men equal as regards their possibility of becoming good or bad. Yet "matter" might counteract this intention of the just God. One must therefore postulate creation *ex nihilo* by an omnipotent God who as such must be omniscient, by the absolutely sovereign God of the Bible who will be what He will be, *i.e.* who will be gracious to whom He will be gracious; for, to say nothing of other considerations, the assumption that His grace is a function of human merit necessarily leads men into pride. In agreement with this, Thomas Aquinas teaches that even in the state of innocence, if it had lasted, men would have been unequal regarding justice and there would have been government by the superior man over men inferior to him. God is not unjust in creating beings of unequal rank and in particular men of unequal rank, since the equality of justice has its place in retribution, but not in creation which is an act, not of justice, but of liberality and is therefore perfectly compatible with the inequality of gifts; God does not owe anything to His creatures.[59] Considering the connection between intelligence and prudence on the one hand, and between prudence and moral virtue on the other, one must admit a natural inequality among men regarding morality; that inequality is perfectly compatible with the possibility that all men possess by nature equally the capability to comply with the prohibition against murder, for example, as distinguished from the capability of becoming morally virtuous in the complete sense or of becoming perfect gentlemen. One reaches the same conclusion even if one grants that the creatures have claims against God—claims which appeal to God's goodness or liberality, provided one understands by justice not a firm will to give everyone his due, but goodness tempered by wisdom; for given these assumptions, even such claims of some creatures as are justified on the ground of God's goodness might have to be denied on grounds of His wisdom, *i.e.* of His concern with the common good of the universe.[60] Equivalent considerations led Plato to trace vice to ignorance and to make

---

[58] Cf. Plato, *Timaeus* 41e3–4 and 90e6ff. Cf. *Gorgias* 526e1–4, *Republic* 379c5–7, 380a7–b8, 617e1–5.

[59] *S. th.* I. q. 21. a. l., q. 23. a. 5., q. 65. a. 2., q. 96. a. 3–4.; *S. c. G.* II 44.

[60] Leibniz, *Principes de la Nature et de la Grâce* sect. 7, *Monadologie* sect. 50–51, 54, *Théodicée* sect. 151, 215.

knowledge the preserve of men endowed with particularly good natures. As for Aristotle, it may suffice here to say that moral virtue as he understands it is not possible without "equipment" and that for this reason alone, to say nothing of natural inequality, moral virtue in the full sense is not within the reach of all men.

For a better understanding of the classical view, one does well to cast a glance at that kind of egalitarianism which is most characteristically modern. According to Rousseau, through the foundation of society, natural inequality is replaced by conventional equality; the social contract which creates society is the basis of morality, of moral freedom or autonomy; but the practice of moral virtue, the fulfillment of our duties to our fellow men is the one thing needful.[61] A closer analysis shows that the core of morality is the good will as distinguished from the fulfillment of all duties; the former is equally within the reach of all men, whereas as regards the latter natural inequality necessarily asserts itself. But it cannot be a duty to respect that natural inequality, for morality means autonomy, *i.e.* not to bow to any law which a man has not imposed upon himself. Accordingly, man's duty may be said to consist in subjugating the natural within him and outside of him to that in him to which alone he owes his dignity, to the moral law. The moral law demands from each virtuous activity, *i.e.* the full and uniform development of all his faculties and their exercise jointly with others. Such a development is not possible as long as everyone is crippled as a consequence of the division of labor or of social inequality. It is therefore a moral duty to contribute to the establishment of a society which is radically egalitarian and at the same time on the highest level of the development of man. In such a society, which is rational precisely because it is not natural, *i.e.* because it has won the decisive battle against nature, everyone is of necessity happy if happiness is indeed unobstructed virtuous activity; it is a society which therefore does no longer have any need for coercion.[62] There may be some relics of natural inequality which are transmitted by

---

[61] Cf. *Contrat Social* I 8–9 with the thesis of the *First Discourse*.

[62] Cf. Fichte, *Ueber die Bestimmung des Gelehrten* I–III on the one hand, Marx-Engels, *Die Deutsche Ideologie* (Berlin: Dietz Verlag, 1953) 27–30, 68–69, 74, 221, 414–415, 449, and Marx, *Die Fruehschriften* (ed. Landshut) 233 and 290–295 on the other. Cf. the treatment of natural inequality by Hegel in his *Rechtsphilosophie* sect. 200.

the natural process of procreation, but they will gradually disappear since, as one can hope, the acquired faculties can also become inherited, to say nothing of human measures which may have to be taken during the transition period in which coercion cannot yet be dispensed with.—

For Aristotle, natural inequality is a sufficient justification for the non-egalitarian character of the city and is as it were part of the proof that the city is the natural association *par excellence*. The city is by nature, *i.e.* the city is natural to man; in founding cities men only execute what their nature inclines them to do. Men are by nature inclined to the city because they are by nature inclined to happiness, to living together in a manner which satisfies the needs of their nature in proportion to the natural rank of these needs; the city, one is tempted to say, is the only association which is capable of being dedicated to the life of excellence. Man is the only earthly being inclined toward happiness and he is capable of happiness. This is due to the fact that he is the only animal which possesses reason or speech, or which strives for seeing or knowing for its own sake, or whose soul is somehow "all things": man is the microcosm. There is a natural harmony between the whole and the human mind. Man would not be capable of happiness if the whole of which he is a part were not friendly to him. Man could not live if nature did not supply him with food and his other wants: nature has made, if not all animals, at least most of them for the sake of man, although not necessarily exclusively for this purpose, so that man acts according to nature if he captures or kills the animals useful to him.[63] One may describe this view of the relation of man to the whole as "optimism" in the original sense of the term: the world is the best possible world; we have no right to assume that the evils with which it abounds, and especially the evils which do not originate in human folly, could have been absent without bringing about still greater evils; man has no right to complain and to rebel. This is not to deny but to assert that the nature of man is enslaved in many ways so that only very few, and even these not always, can achieve happiness or the highest freedom of which man is by nature capable, so that the city actually dedicated to human excellence is,

---

[63] *Politics* 1252b27–1253a2, 1253a9–10, 1256b7–24, 1280b33–1281a2; *Eth. Nic.* 1178b24–28; *On the Soul* 431b21–23.

to say the least, very rare, and so that chance rather than human reason seems to be responsible for the various laws laid down by men.[64]

Aristotle was compelled to defend his view of happiness or of the end of man against the poets' assertion that the divine is envious of man's happiness or bears malice to man.[65] He did not take seriously this assertion. It was taken up after his time in a considerably modified form: the whole as we know it is the work of an evil god or demon, as distinguished from the good or highest god; hence, the end toward which man is inclined as part of the visible whole or by nature, cannot be good. This view presupposes that man possesses knowledge of true goodness as distinguished from natural goodness; he cannot know true goodness by his natural powers, for otherwise the visible whole would not be simply bad; but for this reason the alleged knowledge of true goodness lacks cogency. Let us then turn to the modern criticism of Aristotle's principle. It does not suffice to say that the new, anti-Aristotelian science of the seventeenth century rejected final causes, for the classical "materialists" had done the same and yet not denied, as the modern anti-Aristotelians did, that the good life is the life according to nature and that "Nature has made the necessary things easy to supply." If one ponders over the facts which Aristotle summarizes by saying that our nature is enslaved in many ways, one easily arrives at the conclusion that nature is not a kind mother but a harsh stepmother to man, *i.e.* that the true mother of man is not nature. What is peculiar to modern thought is not this conclusion by itself but the consequent resolve to liberate man from that enslavement by his own sustained effort. This resolve finds its telling expression in the demand for the "conquest" of nature: nature is understood and treated as an enemy who must be subjugated. Accordingly, science ceases to be proud contemplation and becomes the humble and charitable handmaid devoted to the relief of man's estate. Science is for the sake of power, *i.e.* for putting at our disposal the means for achieving our natural ends. Those ends can no longer include knowledge for its own sake; they are reduced to comfortable self-preservation. Man as the potential conqueror of nature stands outside of nature. This

---

[64] *Metaphysics* 982b29 (cf. Plato, *Phaedo* 66d1–2 and context); *Eth. Nic.* 1154b7; *Politics* 1331b39–1332a3, 1332a29–31; Plato, *Laws* 709a–b.

[65] *Metaphysics* 982b32–983a4.

presupposes that there is no natural harmony between the human mind and the whole. The belief in such harmony appears now as a wishful or good-natured assumption. We must reckon with the possibility that the world is the work of an evil demon bent on deceiving us about himself, the world, and ourselves by means of the faculties with which he has supplied us or, which amounts to the same thing, that the world is the work of a blind necessity which is utterly indifferent as to whether it and its product ever becomes known. Surely we have no right to trust in our natural faculties; extreme skepticism is required. I can trust only in what is entirely within my control: the concepts which I consciously make and of which I do not claim more than that they are my constructs, and the naked data as they impress themselves upon me and of which I do not claim more than that I am conscious of them without having made them. The knowledge which we need for the conquest of nature must indeed be dogmatic, but its dogmatism must be based on extreme skepticism; the synthesis of dogmatism and skepticism eventually takes the form of an infinitely progressive science as a system or agglomeration of confirmed hypotheses which remain exposed to revision *in infinitum*. The break with the primary or natural understanding of the whole which is presupposed by the new dogmatism based on extreme skepticism leads to the transformation and eventually to the abandonment of the questions which on the basis of the primary understanding reveal themselves as the most important questions; the place of the primary issues is taken by derivative issues. This shift may be illustrated by the substitution of "culture" for "city."

From what has been said it follows that the modern posture both demands and cannot admit natural ends. The difficulty is indicated by the term "state of nature" which means no longer a completed or perfected but the initial state of man. This state is, because it is entirely natural, not only imperfect but bad: the war of everybody against everybody. Man is not by nature social, *i.e.* Nature dissociates men. This however means that nature compels man to make himself social; only because nature compels man to avoid death as the greatest evil can man compel himself to become and to be a citizen. The end is not something towards which man is by nature inclined but something towards which he is by nature compelled; more precisely, the end does not beckon man but it must be invented by man so that he can escape from his natural misery.

Nature supplies men with an end only negatively: because the state of nature is intolerable. This would seem to be the root of what Nietzsche discerned as the essentially ascetic character of modern morality. Man conquers nature (universal compulsion) because nature compels him to do so. The result is freedom. It looks as if freedom were the end towards which nature tends. But this is surely not what is meant. The end is not natural but only devised by man against nature and only in this sense devised on the basis of nature.

According to Aristotle, man is by nature meant for the life of human excellence; this end is universal in the sense that no man's life can be understood, or seen as what it is, except in the light of that end. That end however is very rarely achieved. Must there not then be a natural obstacle to the life of human excellence as Aristotle understood it? Can that life be the life according to nature? To discover a truly universal end of man as man, one must seek primarily not for the kind of natural laws for which a certain Aristotelian tradition sought, i.e. "normative" laws, laws which can be transgressed and which perhaps are more frequently transgressed than observed, but for natural laws as laws which no one can transgress because everyone is compelled to act according to them. Laws of the latter kind, it was hoped, would be the solid basis of a new kind of "normative" laws which as such can indeed be transgressed but are much less likely to be transgressed than the normative laws preached up by the tradition. The new kind of normative laws did no longer claim to be natural laws proper; they were rational laws in contradistinction to natural laws; they eventually become "ideals."[66] The ideal "exists" only by virtue of human reasoning or "figuring out"; it exists only "in speech." It has then an entirely different status from the end or perfection of man in classical political philosophy; it has however the same status as the best political order (the best regime) in classical political philosophy. One must keep this in mind if one wishes to understand the politicization of philosophic thought in modern times or in other words the obsolescence in modern thought of the distinction between nature and convention.

The fundamental change which we are trying to describe shows

---

[*] Hobbes, *De Cive* I 2, *Leviathan* ch. 13 and ch. 15 (see both versions); Spinoza, *Tr. theol.-pol.* IV sect. 1–5 (Bruder), *Ethics* IV praef.; Locke, *Essay* III 11.15.

itself in the substitution of "the rights of man" for "the natural law": "law" which prescribes duties has been replaced by "rights," and "nature" has been replaced by "man." The rights of man are the moral equivalent of the *Ego cogitans*. The *Ego cogitans* has emancipated itself entirely from "the tutelage of nature" and eventually refuses to obey any law which it has not originated in its entirety or to dedicate itself to any "value" of which it does not know that it is its own creation.—

It is not sufficient to say that the theme of the *Politics* is not the Greek city-state but the *polis* (the city): the theme of the *Politics* is the *politeia* (the regime), the "form" of a city. This appears immediately from the beginnings of each book of the *Politics* except the first.[67] At the beginning of the first book, Aristotle deals with the city without raising the question of the regime because his first task is to establish the dignity of the city as such: he must show that the city as city is by nature, *i.e.* that the city as essentially different from the household and other natural associations is by nature, for some men had denied that there is an essential difference between the city and the household, to say nothing of those who had denied that there are any natural associations. One may say that at the beginning of the *Politics*, Aristotle presents the city as consisting of certain associations as its parts. However this may be, at the beginning of the third book, he presents as parts of the city not other associations, not even human individuals, but the citizens.[68] It appears that "citizen" is relative to "regime," to the political order: a man who would be a citizen in a democracy would not necessarily be a citizen in an oligarchy, and so on. Whereas the consideration of those "parts" of the city which are the natural associations remains on the whole politically neutral, the consideration of those parts of the city which are the citizens necessarily becomes involved in a divisive, a political issue: by raising the question of what the citizen is, Aristotle approaches the core of the political question *par excellence*. What is true of the citizen is true of the good citizen, since the activity or the work of the citizen belongs to the same genus as that of the good citizen:[69] "good citizen," in contradistinction to "good man," too is relative to "regime"; obviously a good

---

[67] Cf. also *Eth. Nic.* 1181b12–23.
[68] *Politics* 1252a7–23, 1253a8–10, 1274b38–41.
[69] *Eth. Nic.* 1098a8–11.

Communist cannot but be a bad citizen in a liberal democracy and vice versa. The regime is the "form" of the city in contradistinction to its "matter," that matter consisting above all of the human beings who inhabit the city in so far as they are considered as not formed by any regime. The citizen as citizen does not belong to the matter, for who is or is not a citizen depends already on the form.[70] The form is higher in dignity than the matter because of its direct connection with the "end": the character of a given city becomes clear to us only if we know of what kind of men its preponderant part consists, i.e. to what end these men are dedicated.

Aristotle apparently draws the conclusion that a change of regime transforms a given city into another city. This conclusion seems to be paradoxical, not to say absurd: it seems to deny the obvious continuity of a city in spite of all changes of regime. For is it not obviously better to say that the same France which was first an absolute monarchy became thereafter a democracy than to say that democratic France is a different country from monarchic France? Or, generally stated, is it not better to say that the same "substance" takes on successively different "forms" which, compared with the "substance," are "mere" forms? It goes without saying that Aristotle was not blind to the continuity of the "matter" as distinguished from the discontinuity of the "forms"; he did not say that the sameness of a city depends exclusively on the sameness of the regime, for in that case there could not be, for instance, more than one democratic city; he says that the sameness of a city depends above all on the sameness of the regime.[71] Nevertheless what he said runs counter to our notions. It does not run counter to our experience. In order to see this, one must follow his presentation more closely than is usually done. He starts from an experience. Immediately after a city has become democratic, the democrats sometimes say of a certain action (say, of a certain contractual obligation) that it is the action not of the city but of the deposed oligarchs or tyrant. The democrat, the partisan of democracy, implies that when there is not democracy, there is no city. It is no accident that Aristotle refers to a statement made by democrats as distinguished from oligarchs; perhaps the oligarchs will only say, after the transformation of the oligarchy into a democracy, that the city is going to pieces, leaving us

[70] *Politics* 1274b38, 1275a7–8.
[71] *Politics* 1276b3–11.

wondering whether a city which is going to pieces can still be said simply to be. Let us say then that for the partisan of any regime the city "is" only if it is informed by the regime which he favors. There are other people, the moderate and sober people, who reject this extreme view and therefore say that the change of regime is a surface event which does not affect the being of the city at all. Those people will say that, however relative the citizen may be to the regime, the good citizen is a man who serves his city well under any regime. Let us call these men the patriots. The partisans will call them turncoats.[72] Aristotle disagrees with both the partisans and the patriots. He says that a change of regime is much more radical than the patriots admit but less radical than the partisans contend: through a change of regime, the city does not cease to be but becomes another city—in a certain respect, indeed in the most important respect; for through a change of regime the political community becomes dedicated to an end radically different from its earlier end. In making his apparently strange assertion, Aristotle thinks of the highest end to which a city can be dedicated, namely, human excellence: is any change which a city can undergo comparable in importance to its turning from nobility to baseness or vice versa? We may say that his point of view is not that of the patriot or the ordinary partisan, but that of the partisan of excellence. He does not say that through a change of regime a city becomes another city in every respect. For instance, it will remain the same city in regard to obligations which the preceding regime has undertaken. He fails to answer the question regarding such obligations, not because he cannot answer it, but because it is not a political question strictly speaking, but rather a legal question.[73] It is easy to discern the principle which he would have followed in answering this legal question because he was a sensible man: if the deposed tyrant undertook obligations which are beneficial to the city, the city ought to honor them; but if he undertook the obligations merely in order to feather his own nest, the city is not obliged to honor them.

In order to understand Aristotle's thesis asserting the supremacy of the regime, one has only to consider the phenomenon now known as loyalty. The loyalty demanded from every citizen is not mere loyalty to the bare country, to the country irrespective of the regime,

---

[72] Aristotle, *Resp. Ath.* 28.5; cf. Xenophon, *Hellenica* II 3.30–31.
[73] *Politics* 1276b10–15; cf. 1286a2–4.

but to the country informed by the regime, by the Constitution. A Facist or Communist might claim that he undermines the Constitution of the United States out of loyalty to the United States, for in his opinion the Constitution is bad for the people of the United States; but his claim to be a loyal citizen would not be recognized. Someone might say that the Constitution could be constitutionally changed so that the regime would cease to be a liberal democracy and become either Fascist or Communist and that every citizen of the United States would then be expected to be loyal to Fascism or Communism; but no one loyal to liberal democracy who knows what he is doing would teach this doctrine precisely because it is apt to undermine loyalty to liberal democracy. Only when a regime is in a state of decay can its transformation into another regime become publicly defensible.—We have come to distinguish between legality and legitimacy: whatever is legal in a given society derives its ultimate legitimation from something which is the source of all law ordinary or constitutional, from the legitimating principle, be it the sovereignty of the people, the divine right of kings, or whatever else. The legitimating principle is not simply justice, for there is a variety of principles of legitimacy. The legitimating principle is not natural law, for natural law is as such neutral as between democracy, aristocracy, and monarchy. The principle of legitimacy is in each case a specific notion of justice: justice democratically understood, justice oligarchically understood, justice aristocratically understood, and so on. This is to say, every political society derives its character from a specific public or political morality, from what it regards as publicly defensible, and this means from what the preponderant part of society (not necessarily the majority) regards as just. A given society may be characterized by extreme permissiveness, but this very permissiveness is in need of being established and defended, and it necessarily has its limits: a permissive society which permits to its members also every sort of non-permissiveness will soon cease to be permissive; it will vanish from the face of the earth. Not to see the city in the light of the variety of regimes means not to look at the city as a political man does, i.e. as a man concerned with a specific public morality does. The variety of specific public moralities or of regimes necessarily gives rise to the question of the best regime, for every kind of regime claims to be the best. Therefore the guiding question of

Aristotle's *Politics* is the question of the best regime. But this subject is better discussed on another occasion.

We conclude with a remark about a seeming self-contradiction of Aristotle's regarding the highest theme of his *Politics*. He bases his thematic discussion of the best regime on the principle that the highest end of man, happiness, is the same for the individual and the city. As he makes clear, this principle would be accepted as such by everyone. The difficulty arises from the fact that the highest end of the individual is contemplation. He seems to solve the difficulty by asserting that the city is as capable of the contemplative life as the individual. Yet it is obvious that the city is capable at best only of an analogue of the contemplative life. Aristotle reaches his apparent result only by an explicit abstraction, appropriate to a political inquiry strictly and narrowly conceived, from the full meaning of the best life of the individual;[74] in such an inquiry the trans-political, the supra-political—the life of the mind in contradistinction to political life—comes to sight only as the limit of the political. Man is more than the citizen or the city. Man transcends the city only by what is best in him. This is reflected in the fact that there are examples of men of the highest excellence whereas there are no examples of cities of the highest excellence, *i.e.* of the best regime—that men of the highest excellence (Plato and Aristotle) are known to have lived in deed, whereas of the best regime it is known only that it necessarily "lives" in speech. In asserting that man transcends the city, Aristotle agrees with the liberalism of the modern age. Yet he differs from that liberalism by limiting this transcendence only to the highest in man. Man transcends the city only by pursuing true happiness, not by pursuing happiness however understood.

---

[74] *Politics* 1323b40–1325b32; see particularly 1324a19–23. Consider, however, [Thomas'] *Commentary on Politics* VII, lectio 2.

*Chapter II*

# ON PLATO'S REPUBLIC

*Generally speaking, we can know the thought of a man only through* his speeches oral or written. We can know Aristotle's political philosophy through his *Politics*. Plato's *Republic* on the other hand, in contradistinction to the *Politics*, is not a treatise but a dialogue among people other than Plato. Whereas in reading the *Politics* we hear Aristotle all the time, in reading the *Republic* we hear Plato never. In none of his dialogues does Plato ever say anything. Hence we cannot know from them what Plato thought. If someone quotes a passage from the dialogues in order to prove that Plato held such and such a view, he acts about as reasonably as if he were to assert that according to Shakespeare life is a tale told by an idiot, full of sound and fury, signifying nothing. But this is a silly remark: everyone knows that Plato speaks through the mouth not indeed of his Protagoras, his Callicles, his Menon, his Hippias, and his Thrasymachus, but of his Socrates, his Eleatic stranger, his Timaeus and his Athenian stranger. Plato speaks through the mouths of his spokesmen. But why does he use a variety of spokesmen? Why does he make his Socrates a silent listener to his Timaeus' and his Eleatic stranger's speeches? He does not tell us; no one knows the reason; those who claim to know mistake guesses for knowledge. As long as we do not know that reason, we do not know what it means to be a spokesman for Plato; we do not even know whether there is such a thing as a spokesman for Plato. But this is still sillier: every child knows that the spokesman *par excellence* of Plato is his revered teacher or friend Socrates to whom he entrusted his own teaching fully or in part. We do not wish to appear more ignorant than every child and shall therefore repeat with childlike docility that the spokesman *par excellence* for Plato is Socrates. But it is one of Socrates' peculiarities that he was a master of irony. We are back where we started: to speak through the mouth of a man who is

notorious for his irony seems to be tantamount to not asserting anything. Could it be true that Plato, like his Socrates, the master of the
knowledge of ignorance, did not assert anything, *i.e.* did not have
a teaching?

Let us then assume that the Platonic dialogues do not convey a
teaching, but, being a monument to Socrates, present the Socratic
way of life as a model. Yet they cannot tell us: live as Socrates
lived. For Socrates' life was rendered possible by his possession of a
"demonic" gift and we do not possess such a gift. The dialogues
must then tell us: live as Socrates tells you to live; live as Socrates
teaches you to live. The assumption that the Platonic dialogues do
not convey a teaching is absurd.

Very much, not to say everything, seems to depend on what
Socratic irony is. Irony is a kind of dissimulation, or of untruthful-
ness. Aristotle therefore treats the habit of irony primarily as a vice.
Yet irony is the dissembling, not of evil actions or of vices, but
rather of good actions or of virtues; the ironic man, in opposition
to the boaster, understates his worth. If irony is a vice, it is a
graceful vice. Properly used, it is not a vice at all: the magnanimous
man—the man who regards himself as worthy of great things while
in fact being worthy of them—is truthful and frank because he is in
the habit of looking down and yet he is ironical in his intercourse
with the many.[1] Irony is then the noble dissimulation of one's worth,
of one's superiority. We may say, it is the humanity peculiar to the
superior man: he spares the feelings of his inferiors by not display-
ing his superiority. The highest form of superiority is the superiority
in wisdom. Irony in the highest sense will then be the dissimulation
of one's wisdom, *i.e.* the dissimulation of one's wise thoughts. This
can take two forms: either expressing on a "wise" subject such
thoughts (*e.g.* generally accepted thoughts) as are less wise than
one's own thoughts or refraining from expressing any thoughts
regarding a "wise" subject on the ground that one does not have
knowledge regarding it and therefore can only raise questions but
cannot give any answers. If irony is essentially related to the fact
that there is a natural order of rank among men, it follows that
irony consists in speaking differently to different kinds of people.[2]

While there can be no doubt that Socrates was notorious for his

---

[1] Aristotle, *Eth. Nic.* 1108a19–22; 1124b29–31; 1127a20–26, b22–31.
[2] Plato, *Rivals* 133d8–e1; cf. 134c1–6.

irony, it is not much of an exaggeration to say that irony and
kindred words "are only used of Socrates by his opponents and have
always an unfavorable meaning."[3] To this one could reply that
where there was so much smoke there must have been some fire or
rather that avowed irony would be absurd. But be this as it may,
we certainly must return to the beginning. One cannot understand
Plato's teaching as he meant it if one does not know what the
Platonic dialogue is. One cannot separate the understanding of
Plato's teaching from the understanding of the form in which it is
presented. One must pay as much attention to the How as to the
What. At any rate to begin with one must even pay greater attention to the "form" than to the "substance," since the meaning of the
"substance" depends on the "form." One must postpone one's concern
with the most serious questions (the philosophic questions) in order
to become engrossed in the study of a merely literary question. Still,
there is a connection between the literary question and the philosophic question. The literary question, the question of presentation,
is concerned with a kind of communication. Communication may
be a means for living together; in its highest form, communication *is*
living together. The study of the literary question is therefore an
important part of the study of society. Furthermore, the quest for
truth is necessarily, if not in every respect, a common quest, a quest
taking place through communication. The study of the literary question is therefore an important part of the study of what philosophy
is. The literary question properly understood is the question of the
relation between society and philosophy.

Plato's Socrates discusses the literary question—the question
concerning writings—in the *Phaedrus*. He says that writing is an
invention of doubtful value. He thus makes us understand why he
abstained from writing speeches or books. But Plato wrote dialogues. We may assume that the Platonic dialogue is a kind of
writing which is free from the essential defect of writings. Writings
are essentially defective because they are equally accessible to all
who can read or because they do not know to whom to talk and
to whom to be silent or because they say the same things to everyone. We may conclude that the Platonic dialogue says different
things to different people—not accidentally, as every writing does,

---

[3] Burnet on Plato, *Apology of Socrates* 38a1. Cf. *Symposion* 218d6–7 and
Aristotle, *Eth. Nic.* 1127b25–26.

but that it is so contrived as to say different things to different people, or that it is radically ironical. The Platonic dialogue, if properly read, reveals itself to possess the flexibility or adaptability of oral communication. What it means to read a good writing properly is intimated by Socrates in the *Phaedrus* when he describes the character of a good writing. A writing is good if it complies with "logographic necessity," with the necessity which ought to govern the writing of speeches: every part of the written speech must be necessary for the whole; the place where each part occurs is the place where it is necessary that it should occur; in a word, the good writing must resemble the healthy animal which can do its proper work well.[4] The proper work of a writing is to talk to some readers and to be silent to others. But does not every writing admittedly talk to all readers?

Since Plato's Socrates does not solve this difficulty for us, let us have recourse to Xenophon's Socrates. According to Xenophon, Socrates' art of conversation was twofold. When someone contradicted him on any point, he went back to the assumption underlying the whole dispute by raising the question "what is . . ." regarding the subject matter of the dispute and by answering it step by step; in this way the truth became manifest to the very contradictors. But when he discussed a subject on his own initiative, *i.e.* when he talked to people who merely listened, he proceeded through generally accepted opinions and thus produced agreement to an extraordinary degree. This latter kind of the art of conversation which leads to agreement, as distinguished from evident truth, is the art which Homer ascribed to the wily Odysseus by calling him "a safe speaker." It may seem strange that Socrates treated the contradictors better than the docile people. The strangeness is removed by another report of Xenophon. Socrates, we are told, did not approach all men in the same manner. He approached differently the men possessing good natures by whom he was naturally attracted on the one hand, and the various types of men lacking good natures on the other. The men possessing good natures are the gifted ones: those who are quick to learn, have a good memory and are desirous for all worthwhile subjects of learning. It would not be strange if Socrates had tried to lead those who are able to think toward the truth and to lead the others toward agreement in salutary opinions or to

---

[4] *Phaedrus* 275d4–276a7 and 264b7–c5.

confirm them in such opinions. Xenophon's Socrates engaged in his most blissful work only with his friends or rather his "good friends." For, as Plato's Socrates says, it is safe to say the truth among sensible friends.[5] If we connect this information with the information derived from the *Phaedrus*, we reach this conclusion: the proper work of a writing is truly to talk, or to reveal the truth, to some while leading others to salutary opinions; the proper work of a writing is to arouse to thinking those who are by nature fit for it; the good writing achieves its end if the reader considers carefully the "logographic necessity" of every part, however small or seemingly insignificant, of the writing.

But "good writing" is only the genus of which the Platonic dialogue is a species. The model for the good writing is the good conversation. But there is this essential difference between any book and any conversation: in a book the author addresses many men wholly unknown to him, whereas in a conversation the speaker addresses one or more men whom he knows more or less well. If the good writing must imitate the good conversation, it would seem that it must be addressed primarily to one or more men known to the author; the primary addressee would then act as a representative of that type of reader whom the author wishes to reach above all. It is not necessary that that type should consist of the men possessing the best natures. The Platonic dialogue presents a conversation in which a man converses with one or more men more or less well known to him and in which he can therefore adapt what he says to the abilities, the characters, and even the moods of his interlocutors. But the Platonic dialogue is distinguished from the conversation which it presents by the fact that it makes accessible that conversation to a multitude wholly unknown to Plato and never addressed by Plato himself. On the other hand the Platonic dialogue shows us much more clearly than an Epistle Dedicatory could, in what manner the teaching conveyed through the work is adapted by the main speaker to his particular audience and therewith how that teaching would have to be restated in order to be valid beyond the particular situation of the conversation in question. For in no Platonic dialogue do the men who converse with the main speaker possess the perfection of the best nature. This is one reason why Plato employs a

---

[5] *Memorabilia* I 6.14, IV 1.2–2.1; cf. IV 6.13–15 with *Symposion* 4.56–60; Plato, *Republic* 450d10–e1.

variety of spokesmen: by failing to present a conversation between Socrates and the Eleatic stranger or Timaeus, he indicates that there is no Platonic dialogue among men who are, or could be thought to be, equals.

One could reject the preceding observations on the ground that they too are based chiefly and at best on what Platonic characters say and not on what Plato himself says. Let us then return once more to the surface. Let us abandon every pretense to know. Let us admit that the Platonic dialogue is an enigma—something perplexing and to be wondered at. The Platonic dialogue is one big question mark. A question mark in white chalk on a blackboard is wholly unrevealing. Two such question marks would tell us something; they would draw our attention to the number 2. The number of dialogues which has come down to us as Platonic is 35. Some of them are at present generally regarded as spurious; but the atheteses ultimately rest on the belief that we know what Plato taught or thought or what he could possibly have written or that we have exhausted his possibilities. At any rate, we are confronted with many individuals of the same kind: we can compare; we can note similarities and dissimilarities; we can divide the genus "Platonic dialogue" into species; we can reason. Let us regard the 35 dialogues as individuals of one species of strange things, of strange animals. Let us proceed like zoologists. Let us start by classifying those individuals and see whether we do not hear Plato himself, as distinguished from his characters, speak through the surface of the surface of his work. Even if we make the most unintelligent assumption which, as it happens, is the most cautious assumption, that for all we know the Platonic dialogues might be verbatim reports of conversations, the selection of these particular 35 conversations would still be the work of Plato; for Socrates must have had more conversations known to Plato than there are Platonic dialogues presenting Socratic conversations: Socrates must have had some conversations with Plato himself, and there is no Platonic dialogue in which Socrates converses with Plato.[6]

While everything said in the Platonic dialogues is said by Plato's characters, Plato himself takes full responsibility for the titles of the dialogues. There are only four dialogues whose titles designate the subject matter: the *Republic*, the *Laws*, the *Sophist*, and the *States-*

---

[6] Consider *Republic* 505a2–3.

*man*. There is no Platonic *Nature* or *Truth*. The subject matter of
the dialogues as it is revealed by the titles is preponderantly political. This suggestion is strengthened by the observation that according to Plato's Socrates the greatest sophist is the political multitude.[7]
There are 25 dialogues whose titles designate the name of a human
being who in one way or another participates in the conversation
recorded in the dialogue in question; that human being is invariably
a male contemporary of Socrates; in these cases the titles are as unrevealing or almost as unrevealing as regards the subject matter of
the dialogues in question as the titles of *Anna Karenina* or *Madame
Bovary*. Only in three cases (*Timaeus, Critias, Parmenides*) does
the title clearly designate the chief character of the dialogue concerned. In two cases (*Hipparchus* and *Minos*) the title consists of
the name, not of a participant, but of a man of the past who is only
spoken about in the dialogue; these titles remind of the titles of
tragedies. The name of Socrates occurs only in the title *Apology of
Socrates*. One may say that seven titles indicate the theme of the
dialogues concerned: *Republic, Laws, Sophist, Statesman, Hipparchus, Minos,* and *Apology of Socrates;* the theme of the dialogues,
in so far as it is revealed by the titles, is preponderantly political.

The fact that the name of Socrates occurs in no title except that
of the *Apology of Socrates* is hardly an accident. Xenophon devoted
four writings to Socrates; he too mentions the name of Socrates in
no title except that of his *Apology of Socrates;* his most extensive
writing devoted to Socrates is called *Recollections* and not, as one
would expect from its content, *Recollections of Socrates;* Xenophon,
just as Plato, deliberately refrained from mentioning Socrates in a
title except when conjoined with "apology." Plato's *Apology of Socrates* presents Socrates' official and solemn account of his way of life,
the account which he gave to the city of Athens when he was compelled to defend himself against the accusation of having committed
a capital crime. Socrates calls this account a conversation.[8] It is his
only conversation with the city of Athens, and it is not more than
an incipient conversation: it is rather one-sided. In this official account Socrates speaks at some length of the kind of people with
whom he was in the habit of having conversations. It appears that
he conversed with many Athenian citizens in public, in the market

---

[7] *Republic* 492a8–494a6.
[8] 37a6–7; cf. 39e1–5 and *Gorgias* 455a2–6.

at the tables of the money-changers. His peculiar "business" which made him suspect to his fellow citizens consisted in examining them with regard to their claim to be wise. He examined all who were supposed to possess some knowledge. But he mentions in his detailed statement only three kinds of such men: the politicians, the poets, and the craftsmen. It is true that in a brief repetition he adds the orators to the three classes mentioned before and shortly before the repetition he says that he examined whichever Athenian or stranger he believed to be wise.[9] But it cannot be denied that according to the suggestions of the *Apology of Socrates* one would expect to find more Platonic dialogues presenting Socratic conversations with Athenian common men and in particular with Athenian politicians, craftsmen, and poets than Platonic dialogues presenting Socratic conversations with foreign sophists, rhetoricians, and the like. The Platonic Socrates is famous or ridiculed for speaking about shoemakers and the like; but we never see or hear him speak to shoemakers or the like. He converses in deed (as distinguished from his self-presentation in his sole public speech) only with people who are not common people—who belong in one way or the other to an elite, although never, or almost never, to the elite in the highest sense. Xenophon devotes a whole chapter of the *Memorabilia*, although only one chapter, to showing how useful Socrates was to craftsmen when he happened to converse with such people. In the chapter following, Xenophon records a conversation between Socrates and a beautiful woman of easy manners who was visiting Athens.[10] In the Platonic dialogues we find two Socratic reports about conversations which he had with famous women (Diotima and Aspasia) but on the stage we see and hear only one woman, and her only once: his wife Xanthippe. Above all, Plato presents no Socratic conversation between Socrates and men of the *demos*, and in particular craftsmen; he presents only one Socratic conversation with poets and very few with Athenian citizens who were actual or retired politicians at the time of the conversation, as distinguished from young men of promise. It is above all through this selection of conversations, apart from the titles, that we hear Plato himself as distinguished from his characters.

---

[9] Cf. 17c8–9, 19d2–3, 21e6–22a1 (and context) with 23b5–6 and 23e3–24a1.

[10] III 10–11.

The division of the Platonic dialogues which comes next in obviousness is that between performed dialogues of which there are 26, and narrated dialogues of which there are 9. The narrated dialogues are narrated either by Socrates (6) or by someone else mentioned by name (3) and they are narrated either to a named man (2) or to a nameless companion (2) or to an indeterminate audience (5). Plato is mentioned as present in the *Apology of Socrates* which is a performed dialogue and as absent in the *Phaedo* which is a narrated dialogue. One cannot infer from this that Plato must be thought to have been present at all performed dialogues and absent from all narrated dialogues. One must rather say that Plato speaks to us directly, without the intermediacy of his characters, also by the fact that he presented most of the dialogues as performed and the others as narrated. Each of these two forms has its peculiar advantages. The performed dialogue is not encumbered by the innumerable repetitions of "he said" and "I said." In the narrated dialogue on the other hand a participant in the conversation gives an account directly or indirectly to nonparticipants and hence also to us, while in the performed dialogue there is no bridge between the characters of the dialogue and the reader; in a narrated dialogue Socrates may tell us things which he could not tell with propriety to his interlocutors, for instance why he made a certain move in the conversation or what he thought of his interlocutors; he thus can reveal to us some of his secrets. Plato himself does not tell us what he means by his division of his dialogues into performed and narrated ones and why any particular dialogue is either narrated or performed. But he permits us a glimpse into his workshop by making us the witnesses of the transformation of a narrated dialogue into a performed one. Socrates had narrated his conversation with Theaetetus to the Megarian Euclides; Euclides, who apparently did not have as good a memory as some other Platonic characters, had written down what he had heard from Socrates, not indeed verbatim as Socrates had narrated it, but "omitting . . . the narratives between the speeches" like Socrates' saying "I said" and "Theaetetus agreed";[11] Euclides had transformed a narrated dialogue into a performed dialogue. The expressions used by Euclides are used by Socrates in the *Republic*. As he makes clear there at great length, if a writer speaks only as if he were one or the other of his characters, *i.e.* if he "omits"

---

[11] *Theaetetus* 142c8–143c5.

"what is between the speeches" of the characters (the "*a* said"'s and "*b* replied"'s), the writer conceals himself completely, and his writings are dramas.[12] It is clear that the writer conceals himself completely also when he does not "omit what is between the speeches" but entrusts the narrative to one of his characters. According to Plato's Socrates, we would then have to say that Plato conceals himself completely in his dialogues. This does not mean that Plato conceals his name; it was always known that Plato was the author of the Platonic dialogues. It means that Plato conceals his opinions. We may draw the further conclusion that the Platonic dialogues are dramas, if dramas in prose. They must then be read like dramas. We cannot ascribe to Plato any utterance of any of his characters without having taken great precautions. To illustrate this by our example, in order to know what Shakespeare, in contradistinction to his Macbeth, thinks about life, one must consider Macbeth's utterance in the light of the play as a whole; we might thus find that according to the play as a whole, life is not senseless simply, but becomes senseless for him who violates the sacred law of life, or the sacred order restores itself, or the violation of the law of life is self-destructive; but since that self-destruction is exhibited in the case of Macbeth, a human being of a particular kind, one would have to wonder whether the apparent lesson of the play is true of all men or universally; one would have to consider whether what appears to be a natural law is in fact a natural law, given the fact that Macbeth's violation of the law of life is at least partly originated by preternatural beings. In the same way we must understand the "speeches" of all Platonic characters in the light of the "deeds." The "deeds" are in the first place the setting and the action of the individual dialogue: on what kind of men does Socrates act with his speeches? what is the age, the character, the abilities, the position in society, and the appearance of each? when and where does the action take place? does Socrates achieve what he intends? is his action voluntary or imposed on him? Perhaps Socrates does not primarily intend to teach a doctrine but rather to educate human beings—to make them better, more just or gentle, more aware of their limitations. For before men can genuinely listen to a teaching, they must be willing to do so; they must have become aware of their need to listen; they must be liberated from the charms

---

[12] *Republic* 392c1–394c6.

which make them obtuse; this liberation is achieved less by speech than by silence and deed—by the silent action of Socrates which is not identical with his speech. But the "deeds" also include the relevant "facts" which are not mentioned in the "speeches" and yet were known to Socrates or to Plato; a given Socratic speech which persuades his audience entirely may not be in accordance with the "facts" known to Socrates. We are guided to those "facts" partly by the unthematic details and partly by seemingly casual remarks. It is relatively easy to understand the speeches of the characters: everyone who listens or reads perceives them. But to perceive what in a sense is not said, to perceive how what is said is said, is more difficult. The speeches deal with something general or universal (*e.g.* with justice), but they are made in a particular or individual setting: these and those human beings converse there and then about the universal subject; to understand the speeches in the light of the deeds means to see how the philosophic treatment of the philosophic theme is modified by the particular or individual or transformed into a rhetorical or poetic treatment or to recover the implicit philosophic treatment from the explicit rhetorical or poetic treatment. Differently stated, by understanding the speeches in the light of the deeds, one transforms the two-dimensional into something three-dimensional or rather one restores the original three-dimensionality. In a word, one cannot take seriously enough the law of logographic necessity. Nothing is accidental in a Platonic dialogue; everything is necessary at the place where it occurs. Everything which would be accidental outside of the dialogue becomes meaningful within the dialogue. In all actual conversations chance plays a considerable role: all Platonic dialogues are radically fictitious. The Platonic dialogue is based on a fundamental falsehood, a beautiful or beautifying falsehood, *viz.* on the denial of chance.

When Socrates explains in the *Republic* what a drama in contradistinction to other poetry is, the austere Adeimantus thinks only of tragedy. In the same way the austere reader of the Platonic dialogues—and the first thing which Plato does to his readers is to make them austere—understands the Platonic dialogue as a new kind of tragedy, perhaps as the finest and best kind. Yet Socrates adds to Adeimantus' mention of tragedy the words "and comedy."[13] At this point we are compelled to have recourse, not only to an author other

---

[13] *Republic* 394b6–c2.

than Plato but to an author whom Plato could not have known since he lived many centuries after Plato's death. The reason is this. We have access to Plato primarily only through the Platonic tradition, for it is that tradition to which we owe the interpretations, translations, and editions. The Platonic tradition has been for many centuries a tradition of Christian Platonism. The blessings which we owe to that tradition must not blind us however to the fact that there is a difference between Christian and primitive Platonism. It is not surprising that perhaps the greatest helper in the effort to see that difference should be a Christian saint. I have in mind Sir Thomas More. His *Utopia* is a free imitation of Plato's *Republic*. More's perfect commonwealth is much less austere than Plato's. Since More understood very well the relation between speeches and deeds, he expressed the difference between his perfect commonwealth and Plato's by having his perfect commonwealth expounded after dinner, whereas the exposition of Plato's commonwealth takes the place of a dinner. In the thirteenth chapter of his *Dialogue of Comfort against Tribulation* More says: "And for to prove that this life is no laughing time, but rather the time of weeping, we find that our saviour himself wept twice or thrice, but never find we that he laughed so much as once. I will not swear that he never did, but at the least wise he left us no example of it. But, on the other side, he left us example of weeping." More must have known that exactly the opposite is true of Plato's—or Xenophon's—Socrates: Socrates left us no example of weeping, but, on the other side, he left us example of laughing.[14] The relation of weeping and laughing is similar to that of tragedy and comedy. We may therefore say that the Socratic conversation and hence the Platonic dialogue is slightly more akin to comedy than to tragedy. This kinship is noticeable also in Plato's *Republic* which is manifestly akin to Aristophanes' *Assembly of Women*.[15]

Plato's work consists of many dialogues because it imitates the manyness, the variety, the heterogeneity of being. The many dia-

---

[14] *Phaedo* 115c5; Xenophon, *Apology of Socrates* 28.

[15] Cf. *Assembly of Women* 558–567, 590–591, 594–598, 606, 611–614, 635–643, 655–661, 673–674, and 1029 with *Republic* 442d10–443a7, 416d3–5, 417a6–7, 464b8–c3, 372b–c, 420a4–5, 457c10–d3, 461c8–d2, 465b1–4, 464d7–e7, 416d6–7, 493d6. Cf. *Republic* 451c2 with *Thesmophoriazusae* 151, 452b6–c2 with *Lysistrata* 676–678, and 473d5 with *Lysistrata* 772. Consider also 420e1–421b3.

logues form a *kosmos* which mysteriously imitates the mysterious
*kosmos*. The Platonic *kosmos* imitates or reproduces its model in
order to awaken us to the mystery of the model and to assist us in
articulating that mystery. There are many dialogues because the
whole consists of many parts. But the individual dialogue is not a
chapter from an encyclopaedia of the philosophic sciences or from
a system of philosophy, and still less a relic of a stage of Plato's
development. Each dialogue deals with one part; it reveals the
truth about that part. But the truth about a part is a partial truth,
a half truth. Each dialogue, we venture to say, abstracts from something that is most important to the subject matter of the dialogue.
If this is so, the subject matter as presented in the dialogue is
strictly speaking impossible. But the impossible—or a certain kind
of the impossible—if treated as possible is in the highest sense ridiculous or, as we are in the habit of saying, comical. The core of
every Aristophanean comedy is something impossible of the kind
indicated. The Platonic dialogue brings to its completion what could
be thought to have been completed by Aristophanes.—

The *Republic*, the most famous political work of Plato, the most
famous political work of all times, is a narrated dialogue whose
theme is justice. While the place of the conversation is made quite
clear to us, the time, *i.e.* the year, is not. We lack therefore certain
knowledge of the political circumstances in which the conversation
about the political principle took place. Yet we are not left entirely
in the dark on this point. In the *Republic* Socrates tells the story of
a descent. The day before, he had gone down from Athens in the
company of Glaucon to the Piraeus, the seat of Athenian naval and
commercial power, the stronghold of the democracy. He had not
gone down to the Piraeus in order to have a conversation there
about justice but in order to pray to the goddess—perhaps a goddess new and strange to Athens—and at the same time because he
was desirous to look at a novel festival which included not only
an indigenous but also a foreign procession. When hurrying back
to town he and his companion are detained by some acquaintances
who induce them to go with them to the house of one of them, a
wealthy metic, from which they are supposed to go, after dining,
to look at a novel torchrace in honor of the goddess as well as
at a night festival. In that house they meet some other men. The
*synontes* (those who are together with Socrates on the occasion
and are mentioned by name) are altogether ten, only five of

whom are Athenians whereas four are metics and one a famous foreign teacher of rhetoric. (Only six of the ten participate in the conversation.) We are clearly at the opposite pole from Old Athens, from the ancestral polity, the Athens of the Marathon-fighters. We breathe the air of the new and the strange—of decay. At any rate Socrates and his chief interlocutors, Glaucon and Adeimantus, prove to be greatly concerned with that decay and to think of the restoration of political health. The harshest possible indictment of the reigning democracy, the novel polity favoring novelty, which was ever uttered is uttered in the *Republic* without a voice being raised in its defense. Besides, Socrates makes very radical proposals of reform without encountering serious resistance. Some years after the conversation, men linked to Socrates and Plato by kinship or friendship attempted a political restoration, putting down the democracy and restoring an aristocratic regime dedicated to virtue and justice. Among other things they established an authority called the Ten in the Piraeus. Yet the characters of the *Republic* are different from these statesmen. Some of the characters of the *Republic* (Polemarchus, Lysias, and Niceratus) were mere victims of the latter, of the so-called Thirty Tyrants. The situation resembles that in the *Laches* where Socrates discusses courage with generals defeated or about to be defeated and in the *Charmides* where he discusses moderation with future tyrants; in the *Republic* he discusses justice in the presence of victims of an abortive attempt made by most unjust men to restore justice.[16] We are thus prepared for the possibility that the restoration attempted in the *Republic* will not take place on the political plane.

The character of the Socratic restoration begins to reveal itself by the action preceding the conversation. The conversation about justice is not altogether voluntary. When Socrates and Glaucon hasten homeward, Polemarchus (the War Lord), seeing them from afar, orders his slave to run after them and to order them to wait for him. Not Socrates but Glaucon answers the slave that they will wait. A little later Polemarchus appears in the company of Adeiman-

---

[16] Lysias, *Against Eratosthenes* 4–23; Xenophon, *Hellenica* II 3.39, 4.19, 38; Plato, *Seventh Letter* 324c5; Aristotle, *Politics* 1303b10–12 and *Constitution of the Athenians* 35.1. The Archon Polemarchus was the Athenian magistrate in charge of lawsuits in which metics were involved (Aristotle, *Constitution of the Athenians* 68).

tus, Niceratus and some others not mentioned by name; the name of Adeimantus, the most important man in this group, is put in the center as is meet. Polemarchus, pointing to the numerical and hence brachial superiority of his group, demands of Socrates and Glaucon that they stay in the Piraeus. Socrates replies that they might prevent the coercion by persuasion. Yet, Polemarchus replies, he and his group could make themselves immune to persuasion by refusing to listen. Thereupon Glaucon, and not Socrates, cedes to force. Fortunately, before Socrates too might be compelled to cede to force, Adeimantus begins to use persuasion; he promises Socrates and Glaucon a novel spectacle if they stay: a torchrace on horseback in honor of the goddess which is so exciting not because of the goddess but because of the horses. Polemarchus following Adeimantus promises yet another sight for the time after dinner and still another attraction. Thereupon Glaucon, and not Socrates, makes the decision, his third decision: "it seems as if we should have to stay." The vote is now almost unanimous in favor of Socrates' and Glaucon's staying in the Piraeus: Socrates has no choice but to abide by the decision of the overwhelming majority. Ballots have taken the place of bullets: ballots are convincing only as long as bullets are remembered. We owe then the conversation on justice to a mixture of compulsion and persuasion. To cede to such a mixture, or to a kind of such a mixture, is an act of justice. Justice itself, duty, obligation, is a kind of mixture of compulsion and persuasion, of coercion and reason.

Yet the initiative soon passes to Socrates. Owing to his initiative, all sight-seeing and even the dinner are completely forgotten in favor of the conversation about justice, which must have lasted from the afternoon until the next morning. Especially the central part of the conversation must have taken place without the benefit of the natural light of the sun and perhaps in artificial light (cf. the beginning of the fifth book). The action of the *Republic* thus proves to be an act of moderation, of self-control regarding the pleasures, and even the needs, of the body and regarding the pleasures of seeing sights or of gratifying curiosity. This action too reveals the character of the Socratic restoration: the feeding of the body and of the senses is replaced by the feeding of the mind. Yet was it not the desire to see sights which had induced Socrates to go down to the Piraeus and hence, as it happened, to expose himself to the compulsion to stay in the Piraeus and thus to engage in the conversation about justice? Is Socrates punished by others or by himself for an act of self-indulgence? Just as his staying in the Piraeus is due to a combination of compulsion and persuasion, his going down to the Piraeus was due to a combination of piety and curiosity. His descending to the Piraeus would seem to remain a mystery unless we assume that he was prompted by his piety as distinguished from any desire. Yet we must not forget that he descended together with Glaucon. We cannot exclude the possibility that he descended to the Piraeus for the sake of Glaucon and at the request of Glaucon. After all, all decisions made prior to the conversation in so far as we could observe them were made by Glaucon. Xenophon[17] tells us that Socrates, being well-disposed toward Glaucon for the sake of Charmides and of Plato, cured him of his extreme political ambition. In order to achieve this cure he had first to make him willing to listen to him by gratifying him. Plato's Socrates may have descended to the Piraeus together with Glaucon who was eager to descend, in order to find an unobtrusive opportunity for curing him of his extreme political ambition. Certain it is that the *Republic* supplies the most magnificent cure ever devised for every form of political ambition.

At the beginning of the conversation, Cephalus, the aged father of Polemarchus and two other characters, occupies the center. He is the father in the full sense, one reason being that he is a man of wealth; wealth strengthens paternity. He stands for what seems to be the most natural authority. He possesses the dignity peculiar to old age and thus presents the order which is based on reverence for the old, the old order as opposed to the present decay. We can easily believe that the old order is superior even to any restoration. Although he is a lover of speeches, Cephalus leaves the conversation about justice when it has barely begun in order to perform an act of piety, and he never returns: his justice is not in need of speeches or reasons. After he has left, Socrates occupies the center. However lofty Cephalus' justice may be, it is animated by the traditional notion of justice, and that notion is radically deficient (366d–e). The old order is deficient, for it is the origin of the present disorder: Cephalus is the father of Polemarchus. And assuredly, the metic Cephalus is not the proper representative of the old order, of the old Athenian order. The good is not identical with the paternal or ancestral. Piety is replaced by philosophy.

Since the conversation about justice was not planned, one must

---

[17] *Memorabilia* III 6.

see how it came about. The conversation opens with Socrates' addressing a question to Cephalus. The question is a model of propriety. It gives Cephalus an opportunity to speak of everything good which he possesses, to display his happiness as it were, and it concerns the only subject of a general character about which Socrates could conceivably learn something from him: how it feels to be very old. Socrates surely meets very rarely men of Cephalus' age (cf. *Apology of Socrates* 23c2) and when he does, they do not give him as good an opportunity to ask them this question as Cephalus does. Cephalus on the other hand converses ordinarily only with men of his own age and they ordinarily talk about old age. Disagreeing with most of his contemporaries, but agreeing with the aged poet Sophocles, he praises old age with special regard to the fact that old men are free from sexual desire, a raging and savage master. Obviously Cephalus, as distinguished from Socrates, had suffered greatly under that master when he was not yet very old; and, as distinguished from Sophocles, who had spoken so harshly about sexual desire when he was indelicately asked about his condition in this respect, he brings up this subject spontaneously when asked about old age in general (cf. already 328d2–4). The first point made by Socrates' first interlocutor in the *Republic* concerns the evils of *eros*. Old age is then worthy of praise since it brings freedom from sensual desires or since it brings moderation. But Cephalus corrects himself immediately: what is relevant for a man's well-being is not age but character; for men of good character, even old age is only moderately burdensome—which implies that old age is of course more burdensome than youth. One might think of the weakening of memory and of the sense of sight but Cephalus does not say a word about these infirmities. How his final judgment on old age can be true if sexual desire, that scourge of youth, is such a very great hardship, is not easy to see. No wonder that Socrates wonders at Cephalus' statement. Desiring that Cephalus should reveal himself more fully, Socrates mentions the possibility that Cephalus' bearing old age lightly is due, not to his good character, but to his great wealth. Cephalus does not deny that wealth is the necessary condition for bearing old age lightly (he thus unwittingly advises poor Socrates against becoming very old) but he denies that it is the sufficient condition: the most important condition is good character. Socrates gives Cephalus an occasion to speak of another facet of his moderation—a facet which did not have to wait for old age to be brought out—his moderation regarding the acquisition of wealth; it becomes clear beyond the shadow of a doubt that Cephalus' moderation in this respect is genuine. Socrates has only one further question (his third and last question prior to the question regarding justice) to address to Cephalus: What in your opinion is the greatest good which you have enjoyed through your wealth? Cephalus himself does not regard his answer as very convincing. To appreciate it, one needs the experience of old age which apart from him no one else present has, or at least an equivalent experience (cf. *Phaedo* 64a4–6): one must be close to believing that one is going to die. Once one is in that state, one begins to fear that the stories told about the things in Hades might be true: that he who has acted unjustly here may have to undergo punishment there, and one begins to ask oneself whether one has not done injustice to anyone in anything. In this scrupulous search one may find that one has involuntarily cheated someone or lied to him or that one owes some sacrifices to a god or money to a human being. Only if one possesses wealth can one pay those debts while there is still time. This then is the greatest good which Cephalus enjoys from his wealth since he has begun to believe that he is going to die. We note that the last point, just as the first, deals with Cephalus' present state only: only the central point (his moderation regarding the acquisition of wealth) deals with the whole course of his life.

Cephalus' reply could have given occasion to more than one question: what was the greatest good which Cephalus enjoyed from his wealth when he was of middle age and when he was young? how trustworthy are the stories regarding punishment after death? is involuntary deception an unjust action? is a man as moderate as Cephalus in regard to wealth likely ever to have acted unjustly? Socrates raises none of these questions for they ultimately lead back to the question which he does raise: is the view of justice implied in Cephalus' reply correct? is justice simply identical with truthfulness and restoring what one has taken or received from someone? Socrates seems to narrow unduly the view of the pious merchant Cephalus who had spoken of paying what one owes to gods or men; Socrates seems to disregard entirely Cephalus' reference to sacrifices to the gods. Could he have thought that bringing sacrifices means to restore to the gods what one has received from them, since everything good we have we owe to the gods (379cff.)? One cannot say that the restoration takes place naturally, by our dying, for in that case Cephalus would have no reason to worry about his debt to the gods, to say nothing of the fact that Cephalus leaves everything he owns to his children; but this fact shows also that bringing sacrifices is not a special case of restoring what one has received or taken. Let us then assume that Socrates regards the bringing of sacrifices as an act of piety as distinguished from justice (cf. 331a4 with *Gorgias* 507b1–3) or that he limits the conversation to justice as distinguished from piety.

Socrates shows with ease that Cephalus' view of justice is untenable: a man who has taken or received a weapon from a sane man would act unjustly if he returned it to him when he asked for it after having become insane; in the same way one would act unjustly by being resolved to say nothing but the truth to a madman. Cephalus seems to be about to concede his defeat when his son and heir Polemarchus, acting as a dutiful son, rising in defense of his father, takes the place of his father in the conversation. But the opinion which he defends is not exactly the same as his father's; if we may make use of a joke of Socrates, Polemarchus inherits only a half, perhaps even less than a half, of his father's intellectual property. Polemarchus no longer maintains that saying the truth is unqualifiedly required by justice. Without knowing it, he thus lays down one of the principles of the teaching of the *Republic*. As appears later in the work, in a well-ordered society it is required that one tell untruths of a certain kind to children and even to the grown-up subjects. This example reveals the character of the discussions which occur in the first book of the *Republic*. There Socrates refutes a number of false opinions about justice. Yet this negative or destructive work contains within itself the positive or edifying assertions of the bulk of the work. Let us consider from this point of view the three opinions on justice discussed in the first book.

Cephalus' opinion, as taken up by Polemarchus after his father had left both piously and laughingly, is to the effect that justice consists in paying one's debts. Only Cephalus' particular preoccupation can justify this very particular view of justice. The complete view after which he gropes is none other than the one stated in the traditional definition of justice: justice consists in returning, leaving or giving to everyone what he is entitled to, what belongs to him.[18] It is this view of justice with which Socrates takes issue in his dis-

---

[18] Thomas Aquinas, S. *th.* 2 2 q. 58. a. 1. Cf. Cicero, *Laws* I 19 and 45.

cussion with Cephalus. In his refutation he tacitly appeals to another view of justice tacitly held by Cephalus, *viz.* that justice is good, not only for the giver (who is rewarded for his justice) but also for the receiver. The two views of justice are not simply compatible. In some cases giving to a man what belongs to him is harmful to him. Not all men make a good or wise use of what belongs to them, of their property. If we judge very strictly, we might be driven to say that very few people make a wise use of their property. If justice is to be good or salutary, one might be compelled to demand that everyone own only what is "fitting" for him,[19] what is good for him and for as long as it is good for him. We might be compelled to demand the abolition of private property or the introduction of communism. To the extent to which there is a connection between private property and the family, one would even be compelled to demand in addition the abolition of the family or the introduction of absolute communism, *i.e.* of communism regarding property, women, and children. Above all, very few people will be able to determine exactly what things and what amount of things are good for each individual, or at any rate for each individual who counts, to use; only men of exceptional wisdom are able to do this. We shall then be compelled to demand that society be ruled by simply wise men, by philosophers in the strict sense wielding absolute power. Socrates' refutation of Cephalus' view of justice contains then the proof of the necessity of absolute communism as well as of the absolute rule of philosophers. This proof, as is hardly necessary to say, is based on the disregard of, or the abstraction from, a number of most relevant things; it is "abstract" in the extreme. If one wishes to understand the *Republic,* one must try to find out what these disregarded things are and why they are disregarded. The *Republic* itself, properly read, supplies the answers to these questions.

Whereas the first opinion was only implied by Cephalus but stated by Socrates (and even by him only partly), the second opinion is stated by Polemarchus, although not without Socrates' assistance. To begin with, Polemarchus' thesis presents itself as identical with Cephalus' thesis: undeterred by Socrates' refutation, he appropriates his father's thesis while his father is still present, bolstering it by an additional authority, that of the poet Simonides. Only after

---

[19] Cf. 332c2 and Xenophon, *Cyropaedia* I 3.17.

Cephalus has left and Socrates has repeated the refutation of Cephalus' thesis does Polemarchus admit that the first opinion about justice is wrong and that Simonides' opinion differs from Cephalus' opinion: Simonides' opinion is not exposed to Socrates' powerful objection. Simonides' thesis as Polemarchus understands it is to the effect that justice consists, not in giving to everyone what belongs to him, but in giving to everyone what is good for him. More precisely, remembering that Socrates in refuting Cephalus' view had spoken of what belongs to a friend (331c6), Polemarchus says in the name of Simonides that justice consists in doing good to one's friends. Only when Socrates asks him about what justice requires in regard to enemies does he say that justice also requires that one harm one's enemies. The view according to which justice consists in helping one's friends and harming one's enemies is the only one of the three views discussed in the first book of the *Republic* of which the discussion may be said to begin and to end with a Socratic praise of the poets as wise men. It is also according to the Clitophon (410a6–b1)—the dialogue preceding the *Republic* in the traditional order of Plato's works—the only view of justice which is Socrates' own. Justice thus understood is obviously good, not only to those receivers who are good to the giver but for this very reason to the giver as well; it does not need to be supported by divine rewards and punishments, as does justice as understood by Cephalus; divine retribution is therefore dropped by Polemarchus who is followed therein by Thrasymachus. Yet Polemarchus' view is exposed to difficulties of its own. The difficulty is not that justice understood in Polemarchus' sense, as giving tit for tat, is merely reactive or does not cover the actions by which one originally acquires friends or enemies, for justice however understood presupposes things which in themselves are neither just nor unjust. One might say for instance that every human being has friends from the moment of his birth, namely his parents (330c4–6), and therewith enemies, namely the enemies of his family: to be a human being means to have friends and enemies. The difficulty is rather this. If justice is taken to be giving to others what belongs to them, the only thing which the just man must know is what belongs to anyone with whom he has any dealings or perhaps only what does and what does not belong to himself. This knowledge is supplied by law, which in principle can be known easily by everybody through mere listening. But if justice is giving to one's friends what is good for them, the just man himself must judge; he himself must know what is good for each of his friends; he himself must be able to distinguish correctly his friends from his enemies. Justice must include knowledge of a high order. To say the least, justice must be an art comparable to medicine, the art by virtue of which one knows and produces what is good for human bodies and therefore also knows and produces what is bad for them. This means however that the man who is best at healing his sick friends and poisoning his enemies is not the just man but the physician; yet the physician is also best at poisoning his friends. Confronted with these difficulties Polemarchus is unable to identify the knowledge or art which goes with justice or which is justice. His refutation takes place in three stages. In the central stage Socrates points out to him the difficulty of knowing one's friends and one's enemies. One may erroneously believe that some-one is one's friend or that one has been benefited by him; by bene-fiting him one might in fact help an enemy. One might also harm a man who does not hurt anyone, a just or good man. It seems then better to say that justice consists in helping the just and in harming the unjust, or, since there is no reason to help a man who is not likely ever to help oneself and to harm a man who may have harmed others but is not likely to harm oneself, that justice consists in helping good men if they are one's friends[20] and in harming bad men if they are one's enemies. It is obvious that justice understood as helping men who help oneself is advantageous to both parties. But is it advantageous to harm those who have harmed one? This question is taken up by Socrates in the third stage of his conversa-tion with Polemarchus. Harming human beings, just as harming dogs and horses, makes them worse. A sensible or just man will then not harm any human being, as little as a horse or a dog (cf. *Apology of Socrates* 25c3–e3 and *Euthyphro* 13a12–c3). In this stage Socra-tes makes use of the premise that justice is an art, a premise which is discussed in the first stage but absent from the second stage.

Polemarchus, we recall, was supposed to say which art justice is. Since justice is concerned with friends and enemies, it must be something like the art of war (332e4–6): justice is the art which enables men to become a fighting team each member of which helps every other so that they can jointly defeat their enemies and inflict on them any harm they deem good. Yet Socrates induces Pole-

---

[20] Cf. 450d10–e1 with *Gorgias* 487a.

marchus to grant that justice is useful also in peace, in peaceful exchange, in matters of money, but not indeed regarding the use of money but regarding the safekeeping of money or of other things; justice will then be the art of safekeeping; but that art proves to be identical with the art of stealing: the knowledge required for safe-keeping is identical with the knowledge required for stealing; the just man thus proves to be identical with the thief, *i.e.* with a manifestly unjust man. The argument refutes, not Polemarchus' thesis but the assumption that justice is an art; the identity of the honest guard and the thief follows necessarily if one considers only the knowledge, the intellectual part, of their work, and not their opposite moral intentions. Yet Polemarchus' thesis was altogether amoral —this was also the reason why he had not provided for the difference between the genuine friends and the merely seeming friends; therefore he gets what he deserves. The difficulty did not exist for his father in whose view justice was linked to the gods who know everything. This explanation is however not sufficient, for Socrates does not know of moral virtue as such: virtue is knowledge. In other words, one must raise the question: what is the intention or the will as distinguished from knowledge? is not a good intention based on a knowledge absent from the bad intention? is it not possible that the good intention is identical with knowledge of a certain kind? The good intention is based on an opinion absent from the bad intention. But every opinion on a subject seems to point toward knowledge of that subject. Prior to investigation we cannot even know whether justice is not an art comparable to the art of medicine, namely, the medicine of the soul or philosophy. Polemarchus' first mistake in the conversation was his failure to stick to the identification of justice with the art of war: justice in "peace" is the allied individuals' conduct toward neutrals; there is never simply peace. Secondly, Socrates' refutation of Polemarchus is valid only on the premise that justice and stealing are incompatible, but at least the compatibility of justice with lying had been established in the conversation with his father, and the Greek word for stealing can also mean cheating and to do anything stealthily. But by far the most important point is the fact that the complete refutation of Polemarchus' thesis culminates in the thesis that justice consists in helping the good men who are one's friends and in not harming anybody: it does not culminate in the thesis that justice consists in helping everyone, and not even in the thesis that it consists in helping all good men.[21] Justice is not beneficence. Perhaps Socrates means that there are human beings whom he cannot benefit: regarding fools only negative justice (abstention from harming them) is possible; justice consists in helping the wise and in harming no one. Remembering that according to Polemarchus' original claim his thesis is identical with his father's, one might say that justice consists in helping the wise by saying the truth and giving to them what belongs to them and in failing to do these things to the fools, to the madmen. However this may be, Socrates surely means also something much more immediately important. Polemarchus' thesis reflects the most potent opinion regarding justice—the opinion according to which justice means public-spiritedness or concern with the common good, full dedication to one's city as a particular city which as such is potentially the enemy of other cities, or patriotism. Justice thus understood consists indeed in helping one's friends, *i.e.* one's fellow citizens, and in hating one's enemies, *i.e.* the foreigners. Justice thus understood cannot be dispensed with in any city however just, for even the justest city is a city, a particular or closed or exclusive society. Therefore Socrates himself demands later on (375b–376e) that the guardians of the city be by nature friendly to their own people and harsh or nasty to strangers. He also demands that the non-austere poets, a great evil for the city, be sent away to other cities (398a5–b1). Above all, he demands that the citizens of the just city cease to regard all human beings as their brothers and limit the feelings and actions of fraternity to their fellow citizens alone (414d–e). Polemarchus' opinion properly understood is the only one among the generally known views of justice discussed in the first book of the *Republic* which is entirely preserved in the positive or constructive part of the work. This opinion, to repeat, is to the effect that justice is full dedication to the common good; it demands that one withhold nothing of his own from his city; it demands therefore by itself absolute communism.

The third and last opinion discussed in the first book of the *Republic* is the one maintained by Thrasymachus. The discussion with him forms by far the largest part of the first book, although not its central part. In a sense, however, it forms the center of the *Republic* as a whole, namely, if one divides the work in accordance with the change of Socrates' interlocutors: (1) Cephalus-Polemarchus

---

[21] Cf. Cicero, *Republic* I 28. Cf. Xenophon, *Memorabilia* IV 8.11 and I 6.5.

(father and son), (2) Thrasymachus, (3) Glaucon and Adeimantus (brother and brother); Thrasymachus stands alone as Socrates does but his aloneness resembles rather that of the impious Cyclops. Thrasymachus is the only speaker in the work who exhibits anger and behaves discourteously and even savagely: his entry into the debate is compared by so gentle a man as Socrates to a wild beast's hurling itself upon him and Polemarchus as if he were about to tear them to pieces—one might say, Thrasymachus behaves like a graceless hater of speeches whose only weapon is force and savagery (336b5–6; cf. 411e1 and context). It seems to be entirely fitting that the most savage man present should maintain the most savage thesis on justice. Thrasymachus contends that justice is the advantage of the stronger, that it is the other fellow's good, *i.e.* good only for the receiver and bad for the giver; so far from being an art, it is folly; accordingly he praises injustice. He is lawless and shameless in deed and in speech; he blushes only on account of the heat. And, needless at it may be to say so, he is greedy for money and prestige. One might say that he is Plato's version of the Unjust Speech in contrast to Socrates as his version of the Just Speech, with the understanding that whereas in the *Clouds* the Unjust Speech is victorious in speech, in the *Republic* the Just Speech is victorious in speech. One may go so far as to say that Thrasymachus presents Injustice incarnate, the tyrant, provided one is willing to admit that Polemarchus presents the democrat (327c7) and Cephalus the oligarch. But then one would have to explain why a tyrant should be as eager as Thrasymachus is to teach the principles of tyranny and thus to breed competitors for himself. In addition, if one contrasts the beginning of the Thrasymachus-section with its end (354a12–13), one observes that Socrates succeeds in taming Thrasymachus: Socrates could not have tamed Critias. But tameness is akin to justice (486b10–12): Socrates succeeds in making Thrasymachus somewhat just. He thus lays the foundation for his friendship with Thrasymachus, a friendship never preceded by enmity (498c9–d1). Plato makes it very easy for us to loathe Thrasymachus: for all ordinary purposes we ought to loathe people who act and speak like Thrasymachus and never to imitate their deeds and never to act according to their speeches. But there are other purposes to be considered. At any rate it is most important for the understanding of the *Republic* and generally that we should not behave toward Thrasymachus as Thrasymachus behaves, *i.e.* angrily, fanatically, or savagely.

If we look then without indignation at Thrasymachus' indignation, we must admit that his violent reaction to Socrates' conversation with Polemarchus is to some extent the reaction of common
sense. That conversation led up to the assertion that it is not good
for oneself to harm anyone or that justice is never harmful to anyone
including oneself. Since the city as city is a society which from time
to time must wage war, and war is inseparable from harming innocent people (471a–b), the unqualified condemnation of harming
human beings is tantamount to the condemnation of even the justest
city. This objection is indeed not raised by Thrasymachus but it is
implied in his thesis. That thesis proves to be only the consequence
of an opinion which is not only not manifestly savage but even
highly respectable. When Thrasymachus has become dumbfounded
for the first time by Socrates' reasoning, Polemarchus avails himself
of this opportunity to express his agreement with Socrates most
vigorously. Thereupon Clitophon, a companion of Thrasymachus
just as Polemarchus is a companion of Socrates (cf. also 336b7 and
340c2), rises in defense of Thrasymachus. In this way there begins
a short dialogue between Polemarchus and Clitophon, consisting
altogether of seven speeches. In the center of this intermezzo we
find Clitophon's statement that according to Thrasymachus justice
consists in obeying the rulers. But to obey the rulers means in the
first place to obey the laws laid down by the rulers (338d5–e6).
Thrasymachus' thesis is then that justice consists in obeying the law
or that the just is identical with the lawful or legal, or with what
the customs or laws of the city prescribe. This thesis is the most
obvious, the most natural, thesis regarding justice.[22] It deserves to
be noted that the most obvious view of justice is not explicitly
mentioned, let alone discussed at all in the *Republic*. One may say
that it is the thesis of the city itself: no city permits an appeal
from its laws. For even if a city admits that there is a law higher
than the law of the city, that higher law must be interpreted by
properly constituted authority which is either instituted by the city
or else constitutes a commonwealth comprising many cities in which
commonwealth the just is again the legal. If the just is then identical
with the legal, the source of justice is the will of the legislator. The
legislator in each city is the regime: the tyrant, the common people,
the men of excellence, and so on. Each regime lays down the laws

---

[22] *Republic* 359a4; *Gorgias* 504d1–3; Xenophon, *Memorabilia* IV 4.1, 12;
6.5–6; Aristotle, *Eth. Nic.* 1129a32–34.

with a view to its own preservation and well-being, to its own advantage. From this it follows that obedience to the laws or justice is not necessarily to the advantage of those who do not belong to the regime or of the ruled but may be bad for them. One might think that the regime could lay down the laws with a view to the common good of the rulers and the ruled. That common good would be good intrinsically, not merely by virtue of enactment or agreement; it would be what is by nature just; it would be right independent of, and higher than, what the city declares to be right; justice would not then be primarily and essentially legality—contrary to the thesis of the city. Since the thesis of the city excludes then a natural common good, that thesis leads to the conclusion that justice or obedience to the laws is necessarily to the advantage of the ruled and bad for them. And as for the rulers, justice simply does not exist; they are "sovereign." Justice is bad because it does not aim at a natural good which can only be an individual's good. The understanding required for taking care of one's own good is prudence. Prudence requires either that one disobey the laws whenever one can escape punishment—to that extent prudence is in need of forensic rhetoric—or else that one become a tyrant since only the tyrant can pursue his own good without any regard whatever for others. Thrasymachus' thesis—the thesis of "legal positivism"—is nothing less than the thesis of the city which thesis destroys itself.

Let us now reconsider the first two opinions. According to Cephalus' opinion, justice consists in giving, leaving, or restoring to everyone what he is entitled to, what belongs to him. But what belongs to a man is determined by the law. Justice in Cephalus' sense is then only a subdivision of justice in Thrasymachus' sense. (In Aristotelian terms, particular justice is implied in universal justice.) The first and the third opinions on justice belong together. The law determining what belongs to a man may be unwise, *i.e.* it may assign to a man what is not good for him; only wisdom, as distinguished from law, fulfills the function of justice, *i.e.* of assigning to each what is truly good for him, what is good for him by nature. But is this view of justice compatible with society? Polemarchus' view of justice, which does not imply the necessity of law, takes care of this difficulty: justice consists in helping one's friends as fellow citizens, in dedicating oneself to the common good. But is this view of justice compatible with concern for the natural good of each? The positive part of the *Republic* will have to show whether or how the two conflicting views of justice—which are reflected in the two views that justice is legality or law-abidingness[23] and that justice is dedication to the city—can be reconciled. Here we merely note that Polemarchus who had eventually abandoned his father's thesis also turns against Thrasymachus: on the primary level Polemarchus and Socrates belong together as defenders of the common good.

The brief dialogue between Polemarchus and Clitophon shows that the dialogue between Socrates and Thrasymachus, or at any rate its initial part, has the character of a lawsuit. The defendant is Socrates: Thrasymachus accuses Socrates of wrongdoing. It is a demand of justice that "the other party," *i.e.* Thrasymachus, also receive a fair hearing. Everyone listens to what Socrates tells us about Thrasymachus. But we must also pay attention to what Thrasymachus thinks of Socrates. Socrates thinks that Thrasymachus behaves like a wild beast; Socrates is entirely innocent and on the defensive. Thrasymachus has met Socrates before. His present exasperation is prepared by his experience in his earlier meeting or meetings with Socrates. He is sure that Socrates is ironic, *i.e.* a dissembler, a man who pretends to be ignorant while in fact he knows things very well; far from being ignorant and innocent he is clever and tricky; and he is ungrateful. The immoral Thrasymachus is morally indignant whereas moral Socrates is, or pretends to be, merely afraid. At any rate, after Thrasymachus' initial outburst Socrates offers an apology for any mistake he and Polemarchus may have committed. Thrasymachus in his turn behaves not merely like an accuser but like a man of the highest authority. He simply forbids Socrates to give certain answers to his questions. At a given moment he asks Socrates: "what in your estimate should be done to you?" The penalty which Socrates thereupon proposes is in fact a gain, a reward, for him. Thereupon Thrasymachus demands that Socrates should pay him money. When Socrates replies that he has no money, Glaucon steps forth and declares that "all of us will contribute for Socrates." The situation strikingly resembles the one on Socrates' day in court when he was accused by the city of Athens of having given a "forbidden answer"—an answer forbidden by the

---

[23] For the understanding of the connection between "law" and "the good of the individual," cf. *Minos* 317d3ff.

city of Athens—and when Glaucon's brother Plato among others vouched for a fine to be paid by Socrates. Thrasymachus acts like the city, he resembles the city, and this means according to a way of reasoning acceptable to both Socrates and Thrasymachus (350c7–8), Thrasymachus is the city. It is because he is the city that he maintains the thesis of the city regarding justice and that he is angry at Socrates for his implicit antagonism to the thesis of the city. But obviously Thrasymachus is not the city. He is only a caricature of the city, a distorted image of the city, a kind of imitation of the city: he imitates the city; he plays the city. He can play the city because he has something in common with the city. Being a rhetorician, he resembles the sophist, and the sophist *par excellence* is the city (492aff.; *Gorgias* 465c4–5). Thrasymachus' rhetoric was especially concerned with both arousing and appeasing the angry passions of the multitude, with both attacking a man's character and counteracting such attacks, as well as with play-acting as an ingredient of oratory.[24] When making his appearance in the *Republic*, Thrasymachus plays the angry city. It will become clear later in the *Republic* that anger is no mean part of the city.

That Thrasymachus' anger or spiritedness is not the core of his being but subordinate to his art becomes clear as his conversation with Socrates proceeds. Socrates draws his attention to the difficulty caused by the fact that the rulers who lay down the laws with exclusive regard to their own advantage may make mistakes. In that case they will command actions which are harmful to them and advantageous to their subjects; by acting justly, *i.e.* by obeying the laws, the subjects will then benefit themselves, or justice will be good. In other words, on Thrasymachus' hypothesis, the well-being of the subjects depends entirely on the folly of the rulers. When this difficulty is pointed out to him, Thrasymachus declares after some hesitation due to his slow comprehension that the rulers are not rulers if and when they make mistakes: the ruler in the strict sense is infallible, just as the other possessors of knowledge, the craftsmen and the wise in the strict sense, are infallible. It is this Thrasymachean notion of "the knower in the strict sense" transformed with the help of Socrates into that of "the artisan in the strict sense" which Socrates uses with great felicity against Thrasymachus. For the artisan in the strict sense proves to be concerned,

---

[24] *Phaedrus* 267c7–d2; Aristotle, *Rhetoric* 1404a13.

not with his own advantage, but with the advantage of the others whom he serves: the shoemaker makes shoes for others and only accidentally for himself; the physician prescribes things to his patients with a view to their advantage; hence, if ruling is, as Thrasymachus admitted, something like an art, the rulers serve the ruled, *i.e.* rule for the advantage of the ruled. The artisan in the strict sense is infallible, *i.e.* does his job well, and he is only concerned with the well-being of others. This however means that art strictly understood is justice—justice in deed and not merely justice in intention as law-abidingness is. "Art is justice"—this proposition reflects the Socratic assertion that virtue is knowledge. The suggestion emerging from Socrates' discussion with Thrasymachus leads to the conclusion that the just city will be an association in which everyone is an artisan in the strict sense, a city of craftsmen or artificers, of men (and women) each of whom has a single job which he does well and with full dedication, *i.e.* without minding his own advantage, only for the good of others or for the common good. This conclusion pervades the whole teaching of the *Republic*. The city constructed therein as a model is based on the principle "one man one job" or "each should mind his own business." The soldiers in it are "artificers" of the freedom of the city (395c); the philosophers in it are "'artificers" of the whole common virtue (500d); there is an "artificer" of heaven (530a); even God is presented as an artisan—as the artificer even of the eternal ideas (507c, 597). It is because citizenship in the just city is craftsmanship of one kind or another, and the seat of craft or art is in the soul and not in the body, that the difference between the two sexes loses its importance, or the equality of the two sexes is established (452c–455a; cf. 452a). The best city is an association of artisans: it is not an association of gentlemen who "mind their own business" in the sense that they lead a retired or private life (496d6), nor an association of the fathers.

Thrasymachus could have avoided his downfall if he had left matters at the common sense view according to which rulers are of course fallible (340c1–5) or if he had said that all laws are framed by the rulers with exclusive regard to their apparent (and not necessarily true) advantage. Yet since he is or rather plays the city, his choice of the alternative which proves fatal to him was inevitable. If the just is to remain the legal, if there is to be no appeal from the laws and the rulers, the rulers must be infallible;

*79*

if the laws are bad for the subjects, the laws will lose all respect-
ability if they are not at least good for the rulers. This however
means that the laws owe their dignity to an art; that art may even
make the laws superfluous as is indicated by the facts that according to Thrasymachus the "lawgiver" may be a tyrant, *i.e.* a ruler
who according to a common view rules without laws, and that the
rule exercised by the arts is as such absolute rule (*Statesman* 293a6–
c4). Not law but art is productive of justice. Art takes the place of
law. Yet the time when Thrasymachus could play the city has gone.
Since in addition we know that he is not a noble man, we are
entitled to suspect that he made his fatal choice with a view to his
own advantage. He was a famous teacher of rhetoric. Hence, incidentally, he is the only man professing an art who speaks in the
*Republic*. The art of persuasion is necessary for persuading rulers,
and especially ruling assemblies, at least ostensibly of their true
advantage. Even the rulers themselves need the art of persuasion
in order to persuade their subjects that the laws which are framed
with exclusive regard to the benefit of the rulers serve the benefit
of the subjects. Thrasymachus' own art stands and falls by the view
that prudence is of the utmost importance for ruling. The clearest
expression of this view is the proposition that the ruler who makes
mistakes is not a ruler at all. To praise art is conducive to Thrasymachus' private good.

If art as essentially serving others is just and if Thrasymachus is
the only artisan present, it follows that Socrates has beaten Thrasymachus soundly but must tacitly admit that Thrasymachus is against
his will and without his knowledge the justest man present. Let us
then consider his downfall somewhat more closely. One may say
that that downfall is caused not by a stringent refutation nor by an
accidental slip on his part, but by the conflict between his depreciation of justice and the implication of his art: there is some truth
to the view that art is justice. Against this one could say—and as a
matter of fact Thrasymachus himself says—that Socrates' conclusion,
according to which no ruler or other artisan ever considers his own
advantage, is very simple-minded. As regards the artisans proper
they consider of course the compensation which they receive for
their work. It may be true that to the extent to which the physician
is concerned with what is characteristically called his honorarium,
he does not exercise the art of medicine, but the art of money-
making; but since what is true of the physician is true of the shoe-

maker and of any other craftsman as well, one would have to say
that the only universal art, the art accompanying all arts, the art
of arts, is the art of money-making; one must therefore further say
that serving others or being just becomes good for the artisan (the
giver) only through his practicing the art of money-making or that
no man is just for the sake of justice or that no one likes justice as
such. Differently stated, Socrates and Polemarchus sought in vain
for the art which is justice; in the meantime we have seen that art
as art is just; justice is not one art among many but pervades all
arts; but the only art pervading all arts is the art of money-making;
as a matter of fact, we call an artisan just with a view less to his
exercise of his art than to his conduct regarding the compensation
which he demands for his work; but the art of money-making as
distinguished from the arts proper is surely not essentially just:
many men who are most proficient in money-making are not just;
hence the essentially just arts are ultimately in the service of an art
which is not essentially just. Thrasymachus' view, according to
which the private good is supreme, triumphs.

But the most devastating argument against Socrates is supplied
by the arts which are manifestly devoted to the most ruthless and
calculating exploitation of the ruled by the rulers. Such an art is
the art of the shepherd—the art wisely chosen by Thrasymachus in
order to destroy Socrates' argument, especially since kings and other
rulers had been compared to shepherds from the oldest times. The
shepherd is surely concerned with the well-being of his flock—so
that the sheep may supply men with the juiciest lamb chops. If we
are not fooled by the touching picture of the shepherd gathering or
nursing a lost or ailing lamb, we see that in the last analysis the
shepherds are exclusively concerned with the good of the owners
and of the shepherds (343b). But—and here Thrasymachus' triumph seems to turn into his final defeat—there is obviously a difference between the owners and the shepherds: the juiciest lamb chops
are for the owner and not for the shepherd, unless the shepherd is
dishonest. Now, the position of Thrasymachus or of any man of his
kind with regard to both rulers and ruled is precisely that of the
shepherd with regard to both the owner and the sheep: Thrasymachus can derive benefit from his art, from the assistance which
he gives to the rulers (regardless of whether they are tyrants, the
common people, or the men of excellence), only if he is loyal to
them, if he does his job for them well, if he keeps his part of the

√ bargain, if he is just. Contrary to his assertion he is compelled to grant that a man's justice is salutary, not only to others, and especially to the rulers, but also to himself. What is true of the helpers of rulers is true of the rulers themselves and all other human beings (including tyrants and gangsters) who need the help of other men in their enterprises however unjust: no association can last if it does not practice justice among its members (351c7–d3). This however amounts to an admission that justice may be a mere means, if an indispensable means, for injustice: for the shearing and eating of the sheep. Justice consists in helping one's friends and harming one's enemies. The common good of the city is not fundamentally different from the common good of a gang of robbers. The art of arts is not the art of money-making but the art of war. As for Thrasymachus' art, he himself cannot think of it as the art of arts or of himself as the ruler tyrannical or non-tyrannical (344c7–8). Yet this rehabilitation of Polemarchus' view proves to have been achieved on the Thrasymachean ground: the common good is derived from the private good via calculation. Not Thrasymachus' principle but his reasoning has proved to be defective.

In replying to Thrasymachus' argument which is based on the example of the art of the shepherd, Socrates again has recourse to the notion of "art in the strict sense." He is now silent about the infallibility of art but speaks more emphatically than before (341d5) of the fact that the arts proper become beneficial to the artisan only through his practicing the art of money-making which he now calls the wage-earning or mercenary art. Denying Thrasymachus' assertion that the rulers like to rule, he asserts that if Thrasymachus were right, the rulers would not demand, as they do, wages for ruling, for the ruling of men means service to them, *i.e.* concerning oneself with other men's good and every sensible man would prefer being benefited by others to benefiting others and thus being inconvenienced (346e9, 347d2–8). Hitherto it seemed that Socrates, the friend of justice, was in favor of sacrificing the private good, including one's mere convenience, to the common good. Now it seems that he adopts Thrasymachus' principle: no one likes to serve or help others or to act justly unless it is made profitable to him; the wise man seeks only his own good, not the other man's good; justice in itself is bad. Let us remind ourselves here of the fact that Socrates had never said that justice consists in helping everyone √ regardless of whether he is one's friend or one's enemy or whether he is good or bad. The difference between Thrasymachus and Socrates is then merely this: according to Thrasymachus, justice is an unnecessary evil whereas according to Socrates it is a necessary evil. This terrible result is by no means sufficiently counteracted by the exchange between Socrates and Glaucon which takes place at this point. As a matter of fact, what Socrates says to Glaucon suggests this result as much as it contradicts it. It is therefore necessary for Socrates to prove immediately afterward that justice is good. He proves this in three arguments addressed to Thrasymachus. The arguments are far from conclusive. They are defective on account of the procedure followed, a procedure proposed by Socrates, approved by Glaucon and imposed on Thrasymachus. It demands that instead of "counting and measuring" they should argue on the basis of premises on which they agree, and in particular of the premise that if something is similar to X, it is X (348a7–b7; 350c7–8, d4–5; 476c6–7), to say nothing of the fact that Socrates' refutation of Thrasymachus' assertion that no one likes to rule leaves something to be desired (347b8–e2). The only argument of a different kind, of not so "simple" a kind (351a6–7) is the central one which establishes that no society however unjust can last if it does not practice justice among its members. When Socrates has completed the proof of the goodness of justice, he frankly states that the proof is radically inadequate: he has proved that justice is good without knowing what justice is. Superficially this means that the three views of justice proposed successively by Cephalus, Polemarchus, and Thrasymachus have been refuted and no other view has been tested or even stated. Yet through the refutation of the three views and the reflection about them it has become clear, not perhaps what justice is but what the problem of justice is. Justice has proved to be the art which on the one hand assigns to every citizen what is good for his soul and which on the other hand determines the common good of the city. Hence Socrates' attempt to prove that justice is good without having previously settled what justice is, is not absurd, for it has been settled that justice is one of the two things mentioned. There would be no difficulty if one could be certain that the common good were identical or at least in harmony with the good of all individuals. It is because we cannot yet be certain of this harmony that we cannot yet say with definiteness that justice is good. It is the tension within justice which gives rise to the question of whether justice is good or bad—of whether the primary consideration is the common good or the individual's own good.

When Thrasymachus begins to speak, he behaves according to Socrates' lively description like a raving beast; by the end of the first book he has become completely tame. He has been tamed by Socrates: the action of the first book consists in a marvelous victory of Socrates. As we have seen, that action is also a disgraceful defeat of Socrates as the defender of justice. It almost goes without saying that Thrasymachus has in no way become convinced by Socrates of the goodness of justice. This goes far toward explaining Thrasymachus' taming: while his reasoning proves to be poor, his principle remains victorious. He must have found no small comfort in the observation that Socrates' reasoning was on the whole not superior to his, although he must have been impressed both by the cleverness with which Socrates argued badly on purpose and the superior frankness with which he admitted at the end the weakness of his proof. Yet all this implies that Socrates has succeeded perfectly in establishing his ascendancy over Thrasymachus; from now on Thrasymachus will not only no longer try to teach—he will not even be a speaker any more. On the other hand he shows by the fact that he stays on for many hours unrelieved by sights, food or drink, to say nothing of satisfactions of his vanity (344d1), that he has become a willing listener, a subordinate of Socrates. From the beginning he regarded his art as ministerial to rulers and hence he regarded himself as ministerial. His art consists in gratifying rulers and especially ruling multitudes. His opening statements in which he imitated the city revealed him as a man willing and able to gratify the city. He gradually came to see that by gratifying the political multitude he would not gratify the multitude assembled in Polemarchus' house. At least the vocal majority of the latter multitude is clearly on Socrates' side.[25] While Thrasymachus is more outspoken and less easily restrained than Polus in the *Gorgias*, he is less daring, less outspoken than Callicles, and this is surely connected with the fact that he is not an Athenian citizen.[26] From a certain moment on he shows a curious hesitation to become identified with the thesis which he propounds. Given this restraint,

---

[25] 337d10, 345a1–2. Cf. 350e6; 351c6, d7; 352b4; 354a10–11 with *Gorgias* 462d5.

[26] Cf. 348e5–349a2 with *Gorgias* 474c4–d2, 482d7–e5, and 487a7–b1.

the discussion between him and Socrates is in a sense a joke (349a6–b1). We may say that in the conversation between Socrates and Thrasymachus, justice is treated in a bantering and hence unjust manner. This is not altogether surprising since Thrasymachus, in contradistinction to the characters in the *Euthyphro* and the *Laches* for instance, does not take seriously the virtue under discussion; he does take seriously his art. In all these matters we must never forget the rhetoric used by Socrates in his description of Thrasymachus; it is very easy to read his discussion with Thrasymachus in the light of that description. The powerful effect of that description illustrates beautifully the virtues of the narrated dialogue.

What Socrates does in the Thrasymachus section would be inexcusable if he had not done it in order to provoke the passionate reaction of Glaucon, a reaction which he presents as entirely unexpected. According to his presentation Glaucon, who was responsible for Socrates' staying in the Piraeus (not to say for his descending to the Piraeus), is responsible also for the bulk of the *Republic*, for the elaboration of the best city. With Glaucon's entry, which is immediately followed by the entry of his brother Adeimantus, the discussion changes its character profoundly. It becomes altogether Athenian. In contradistinction to the three non-Athenians with whom Socrates conversed in the first book, Glaucon and Adeimantus are not tainted by the slightest defect of manners. They fulfill to a considerable degree the conditions stated by Aristotle in his *Ethics* which participants in discussions of noble things must fulfill. They belong by nature to a nobler polity than the characters of the first book, who belong respectively to oligarchy, democracy, and tyranny. They belong at the very least to timocracy, the regime dedicated to honor. Being an intelligent lover of justice, Glaucon is thoroughly displeased with Socrates' sham refutation of Thrasymachus' assertion that injustice is preferable to justice or that justice taken by itself is an evil, if a necessary evil: Socrates had merely charmed Thrasymachus. Being courageous and high-minded, loathing the very suggestion of a calculated and calculating justice, he wishes to hear Socrates praise justice as choiceworthy for its own sake without any regard to its consequences or purposes. Thus while Socrates is responsible for the fact that justice is the theme of the conversation, Glaucon is responsible for the manner in which it is treated. In order to hear a solid praise of justice itself, he presents a solid blame of it, a blame which could serve as the model for the praise.

It is obvious that he is dissatisfied not only with Socrates' refutation of Thrasymachus but with Thrasymachus' statement of the case for injustice as well. He would not have been able to surpass Thrasymachus if he were not thoroughly familiar with the view propounded by Thrasymachus; that view is not peculiar to Thrasymachus but held by "the many," by "ten thousand others." Glaucon believes in justice; this authorizes him as it were to attack justice in the most vigorous manner. For an unjust man would not attack justice; he would prefer that the others remain the dupes of the belief in justice so that they might become his dupes. A just man on the other hand would never attack justice unless to provoke the praise of justice. Glaucon's dissatisfaction with Thrasymachus' attack on justice is justified. Thrasymachus had started from the law and the city as already established: he had taken them for granted. He had remained within the limits of "opinion." He had not gone back to "nature." This was due to his concern with his art and hence with art as such. When developing Thrasymachus' notion of "art strictly understood," Socrates speaks with Thrasymachus' entire approval of the self-sufficiency of art, of every art, as contrasted with the lack of self-sufficiency of the things with which art is concerned; he contrasts the goodness of the art of medicine e.g. with the badness of the human body; he also says that the art of medicine is related to the human body as sight is to the eyes. Elaborating a Thrasymachean suggestion, Socrates almost contrasts the goodness of art with the badness of nature. (Cf. 341c4–342d7 with 373d1–2, 405aff. and *Protagoras* 321c–e.) Glaucon on the other hand in praising injustice goes back to nature as good. But how does he know what injustice and hence justice is? He assumes that he can answer the question of what justice is by answering the question of how justice came into being: the What or the nature of justice is identical with its coming-into-being. Yet the origin of justice proves to be the goodness of doing injustice and the badness of suffering injustice. One can overcome this difficulty by saying that by nature everyone is concerned only with his own good and wholly unconcerned with anyone else's good to the point that he has no hesitation whatever to harm his fellows in any way conducive to his own good. Since all men act according to nature, they all bring about a situation which is unbearable for most of them; the majority, i.e. the weaklings, figure out that every one of them would be better off if they agreed among themselves not to harm one another. Thus they

*86*

began to lay down laws; thus justice arose. Yet what is true of the majority of men is not true of him who is "truly a man" who can take care of himself and who is better off if he does not submit to law or convention. But even the others do violence to their nature by submitting to law and injustice; they submit only from fear of the evil consequences of injustice, of consequences which presuppose the detection of injustice. Hence the perfectly unjust man whose injustice remains completely concealed, who is therefore reputed to be perfectly just, leads the happiest life, whereas the perfectly just man whose justice remains completely unknown, who has the reputation of being completely unjust, leads the most miserable life. (This implies that Thrasymachus is not a completely unjust man.) Therefore since, as Glaucon hopes, justice is choiceworthy for its own sake, he demands from Socrates in effect that he show that the life of the just man who lives and dies in the utmost misery and infamy is better than the life of the unjust man who lives and dies in abounding happiness and glory.

Glaucon agrees then with Thrasymachus in holding that justice is legality. But he makes this view more precise: justice is respect of the legally established equality which supersedes the contradictory natural inequality. Accordingly he denies that justice is the advantage of the stronger; according to him, justice is the advantage of the weaker.[27] When asserting that justice is the advantage of the stronger, Thrasymachus did not think of the naturally stronger (he is not concerned with nature but with art) but of the factually stronger, and, as he knew, the many who are by nature weak, may by banding together become stronger than those by nature strong (*Gorgias* 488c–e). We may therefore say that Thrasymachus' view is truer, more sober, more pedestrian than Glaucon's view. The same holds true of the most important difference between Glaucon and Thrasymachus. Glaucon denies that anyone is genuinely just, whereas Thrasymachus does not have the slightest doubt that there are many just men whom he despises indeed as simpletons. Glaucon is concerned with genuine justice, whereas Thrasymachus is satisfied with overt behavior. Glaucon looks into the hearts, and if someone would say that one cannot look into all men's hearts, we shall limit ourselves to saying that Glaucon has looked into his own heart and has found there injustice struggling manfully with his good breeding

---

[27] 347d8–e2; cf. Adeimantus' agreement with Thrasymachus (367c2–5).

(cf. 619b7–d1). He looks for a man who is truly just. In order to see him or rather in order to show that no one is truly just, he is compelled to make use of fiction based on myth (359d5–8); he has to assume that the impossible is possible. In order to understand the relation between the genuinely and purely just man and the genuinely and purely unjust man, he is compelled to become an "imitative" artisan (361d4–6), who presents as possible what is by nature impossible. All this is necessary in order to give Socrates a model for his praise of justice as choiceworthy for its own sake. From this we understand Glaucon's most radical deviation from Thrasymachus. In the discussion with Thrasymachus the issue had become blurred to some extent by the suggestion that there is a kinship between justice and art. Glaucon makes the issue manifest by comparing the perfectly unjust man to the perfect artisan who distinguishes clearly between what is possible and what is impossible for his art, whereas he considers the perfectly just man as a simple man who has no quality other than justice: he goes so far as to use some Aeschylean verses in which the just and pious man is described as shrewd and as having a fertile mind for describing the perfectly unjust man.[28] Perhaps he thought that his restatement makes the thought more conformable to the spirit of the Marathon fighter Aeschylus. Glaucon's perfectly just man is divorced from art and from nature: he is altogether a piece of fiction.

The view which Glaucon maintains in common with Thrasymachus implies that there is an insoluble conflict between the good of the individual and the common good. Hobbes, starting from a similar premise, reached the opposite conclusion because he denied that any good which any individual can possibly enjoy is as great as the evil which threatens him in the absence of society, peace, or the common good. Glaucon in contradistinction to Thrasymachus points to this consideration (358e4–5) but he also refers to the fundamental difference, denied by Hobbes, between the many who are by nature weak, and the few who are by nature strong. Glaucon thus rejoins Thrasymachus in holding that the good life is the tyrannical life, the exploitation, more or less concealed, of society or convention for one's own benefit alone, *i.e.* for the only natural good.

---

[28] 360e7–361a1; 361b2–6, c3; 362a8–b1, b7–8; Aeschylus, *Seven Against Thebes* 590–610.

The refutation of this Unjust Speech which Hobbes attempted[29] on the basis of natural equality was attempted by Socrates on the basis of natural inequality: precisely natural inequality properly understood supplies the refutation of the tyrannical life. Hobbes however cannot consistently maintain the distinction between the tyrant and the king. As for the view which Glaucon implicitly opposes to Thrasymachus' view, it cannot but remind us of Kant's view—of Kant's moving description of the simple man who has no quality other than the good will, the only thing of absolute worth. The opening statement of his *Foundations of the Metaphysics of Morals* makes it clear that morality as he understands it is more akin to justice than to any other virtue. Morality as Kant understands it is as much divorced from art and nature as justice is according to Glaucon: the moral laws are not natural laws nor technical rules. The fate of Glaucon's view in the *Republic* foreshadows the fate of Kant's moral philosophy. What Glaucon intends is however better indicated by "honor" than by "the good will." When the signers of the Declaration of Independence say: "we mutually pledge to each other our Lives, our Fortunes, and our sacred Honor," they mean that they are resolved to forsake their lives and fortunes, but to maintain their honor: honor shines most clearly when everything else is sacrificed for its sake, including life, the matter of the first natural right mentioned in the Declaration of Independence. While honor or justice presupposes life and both are meant to serve life, they are nevertheless higher in rank than life.[30] It is this seeming paradox to which Glaucon draws our attention in his description of the perfectly just man. Within the *Republic* this thought is prepared by the notion of "art in the strict sense," *i.e.* by the divorce of art from the advantage of the artisan and the implied depreciation of nature.

Glaucon's demand on Socrates is strongly supported by his brother Adeimantus. It becomes clear from Adeimantus' speech that Glaucon's view according to which justice must be choice-worthy entirely for its own sake is altogether novel: the decay of justice is as old as the human race. Glaucon's blame of justice had insensibly shifted into a praise of justice. Adeimantus finds that

---

[29] *Leviathan* ch. 15 (p. 94 Blackwell's Political Texts ed.).
[30] Cicero, *De Finibus* III 20–22.

Glaucon had omitted the most important point. Adeimantus' speech is less a blame of justice than a blame of the common, nay, universal praise of justice by which justice is praised with exclusive regard to its consequences and hence as intrinsically bad. In Adeimantus' opinion Glaucon had not sufficiently stressed the recourse to the gods in the common praise, and especially in the poets' praise, of justice: justice is good because it is rewarded by the gods and injustice is bad because it is punished by them. Adeimantus demands then that the genuine praise of justice exclude divine punishment and reward; the genuine praise of justice surely requires the banishment of the poets. There is yet another kind of speech about justice and injustice which is also proffered both privately and by the poets. Moderation and justice are universally praised as indeed noble but hard and toilsome, *i.e.* as noble by convention and unpleasant and hence bad by nature. Adeimantus demands then that the genuine praise of justice present justice as intrinsically pleasant and easy (364a2–4, c6–d3; cf. 357b5–8 and 358a). Yet the strangest ones of the second kind of speech are those which say that the gods send misery to many good men and felicity to many bad ones, *i.e.* that the gods are responsible for the toilsome character of justice and the easy character of injustice. Adeimantus demands then that the genuine praise of justice exclude not only divine punishments and rewards but any divine action on men; and if it should prove hard to assert that the gods do not act on men while being aware of men, that the genuine praise of justice exclude divine knowledge of human things. At any rate, the hitherto universal praise of justice supplies the strongest incentive to injustice if injustice disguises itself successfully as justice. Such injustice is not an easy thing; it is in its way as difficult as justice is according to the old view; it is not possible without art, the art of rhetoric; but it is the only way toward felicity (cf. 365c7–d6 with 364a2–4). Precisely on the basis of the still universally or almost universally held beliefs, the argument for injustice is so powerful that only two kinds of men are voluntarily just: those who, thanks to a divine nature, feel disgust at acting unjustly and those who, having acquired knowledge, abstain from acting unjustly; neither of these two kinds of men will be angry at the unjust, although the former feel disgust at the thought that they themselves could act unjustly (366c3–d3).

The speeches of the two brothers are in character. Glaucon is characterized by manliness and impetuosity rather than by moderation and quietness and the opposite is true of Adeimantus ("the fearless one"). Accordingly Glaucon sees the splendor of justice in its toilsomeness whereas Adeimantus sees it rather in its pleasantness and ease and in its freedom from anger. Glaucon's just man is purely just—he has no quality other than justice and in particular no art; he does not even remotely remind of the philosopher. Adeimantus' just man on the other hand may be a man of knowledge. Adeimantus is more sober than Glaucon. Glaucon's speech makes use of poetry; Adeimantus' speech is so to speak nothing but an indictment of poetry. In order to discover what justice is, Socrates will have to weave together the courageous and the moderate, the suggestions peculiar to Glaucon and the suggestions peculiar to Adeimantus. He is able to do this to the extent to which the difference between the two brothers is less great than their agreement. They agree in their demand on Socrates that he praise justice as choiceworthy for its own sake, or pleasant, or even by itself sufficient to make a man perfectly happy in the midst of what is ordinarily believed to be the most extreme misery. In making this demand they establish the standard by which we must judge Socrates' praise of justice; they thus force us to investigate whether or to what extent Socrates has proved in the *Republic* that justice has the characteristics mentioned.

Socrates declares himself to be unable to defend justice against the two brothers' attack (368b4–7, 362d7–9) but he undoubtedly replies to it at very great length. The very least he will have to do is to show why he cannot comply fully with Glaucon's demand. In order to understand his procedure, we must remind ourselves again of the result of the first book. Justice came to sight as the art of assigning to each what is good for his soul and as the art of discerning and procuring the common good. Justice thus understood is not found in any city; it therefore becomes necessary to found a city in which justice as defined can be practiced. The difficulty is whether assigning to each what is good for him is the same as, or at least compatible with, procuring the common good. The difficulty would disappear if the common good were identical with the private good of each, and this would be possible if there were no essential difference, but only a quantitive difference, between the city and the individual, or if there were a strict parallel between the city and the individual. Assuming such a parallel Socrates turns first to investigating justice in the city and more particularly to the coming-into-being of the city which is accompanied by the coming-into-being of the city's justice and injustice, *i.e.* to the coming-into-being of the city out of the pre-political individuals. This procedure may be said to have been imposed on him by Glaucon. Glaucon had identified the What or the essence of justice with its coming-into-being; justice appeared to be preceded by contract and law, and hence by the city, which in its turn appeared to be preceded by individuals each of whom was concerned exclusively with his own advantage. That Socrates too should start from the individual concerned exclusively with his own good, is intelligible also directly on the basis of the result of the first book.

Nevertheless one cannot help wondering why Socrates is at all concerned with the coming-into-being of justice or why he does not limit himself to grasping the What, the essence, the idea of justice; for surely Socrates, in contradistinction to Glaucon, was incapable of identifying the What of a thing with its coming-into-being. By looking at the idea of justice which is of course the same regardless of whether an individual or a city participates in it, just as the idea of the equal is the same regardless of whether two pebbles or two mountains are equal, he could have avoided many difficulties. When investigating any of the other virtues in the other dialogues, he does not even dream of investigating the coming-into-being of beings which participate in these virtues. Socrates starts from "justice in the city" instead of from "justice in the individual" because the former is written in larger letters than the latter. But since the city possesses courage, moderation, and wisdom as well, he should have started his investigations of these virtues in the dialogues devoted to them also by considering these virtues as virtues of the city. Could this be the reason why the investigations of the *Euthyphro,* the *Laches,* the *Charmides,* and so on do not lead to a positive result? Socrates' procedure in the *Republic* can perhaps be explained as follows: there is a particularly close connection between justice and the city and while there is surely an idea of justice, there is perhaps no idea of the city. For there are not ideas of "everything." The eternal and unchangeable ideas are distinguished from the particular things which come into being and perish, and which are what they are by virtue of their participating in the idea in question; the particular things contain then something which cannot be traced to the ideas, which accounts for their belonging to the sphere of becoming as distinguished from being and in particular why they participate in ideas as distinguished from being ideas. Perhaps the city belongs so radically to the sphere of becoming that there cannot be an idea of the city. Aristotle says that Plato recognized ideas only of natural beings.[31] Perhaps Plato did not regard the city as a natural being. Yet if there is a strict parallel between the city and the human individual, the city would seem to be a natural being. Surely by asserting that parallel, Socrates contradicts Glaucon's thesis which may be said to be to the effect that the city is against nature. On the other hand, by putting such an emphasis on the coming-into-being of the city, Socrates compels us to raise the question which we have raised.

The city does not come into being like a natural being; it is founded by Socrates together with Glaucon and Adeimantus (369a5–6, c9–10). But in contradistinction to all other known cities it will be according to nature. Prior to their turning to the founding of the city Glaucon and Adeimantus had taken the side of injustice. At the moment they begin to act as founders they take the side of justice. This radical change, this transformation, is not due to any seduction or charm practiced by Socrates, nor does it constitute a genuine conversion. Taking the side of injustice means praising and choosing the tyrannical life, being a tyrant, being dedicated to nothing but one's greatest power and honor. But the honor of a tyrant who exploits a city which is the work of others is petty compared with the honor of the man who founds a city, who, for the sake of his glory alone, must be concerned with founding the most perfect city or must dedicate himself entirely to the service of the city. The "logic" of injustice leads from the small-time criminal via the tyrant to the immortal founder. Glaucon and Adeimantus cooperating with Socrates in founding the best city remind one of the young tyrant mentioned in the *Laws* (709e6–710b3; cf. *Republic* 487a) who does not possess justice and cooperates with the wise legislator.

The founding of the good city takes place in three stages: the founding of the healthy city called the city of pigs, the founding of the purified city or the city of the armed camp, and the founding of the City of Beauty or the city ruled by the philosophers.

The city has its origin in human needs: every human being, just or unjust, is in need of many things and is at least for this reason

---

[31] *Metaphysics* 991b6–7, 1070a18–20.

in need of other human beings. By starting from the self-interest of each we arrive at the necessity of the city and therewith of the common good for the sake of each man's own good (369c7, 370a3–4). By identifying to some extent the question of justice with the question of the city and by tracing the city to man's needs, Socrates indicates that it is impossible to praise justice without regard to the function or consequence of justice. The fundamental phenomenon is not, as Glaucon had asserted, the desire to have more than others but the desire for the necessities of life; the desire to have more is secondary. The healthy city satisfies properly the primary needs, the needs of the body. This proper satisfaction requires that everyone work for his living in such a way that he exercises only one art. This is in accordance with nature: men differ from one another by nature or different men are gifted for different ends, and the nature of the work to be done requires this "specialization." When everyone dedicates himself to a single art, Glaucon's and Adeimantus' conflicting views of the just man are reconciled: the just man is simple and the just man is a man of knowledge (397e). As a consequence everyone does almost all his work for others but also the others work for him. All will exchange with one another their products as their products: there will be private property; by working for the advantage of others everyone will work for his own advantage. Since everyone will exercise the art for which he is best fitted by nature, the burden will be easier on everyone. The healthy city is a happy city; it knows no poverty, no coercion or government, no war, and no eating of animals. It is happy in such a way that every member of it is happy: it does not need government because there is perfect harmony between everyone's service and his reward; no one encroaches on anyone else. It does not need government because everyone chooses by himself the art for which he is best fitted: everyone takes to his particular trade as a duck takes to water; there is perfect harmony between natural gifts and preferences. There is also perfect harmony between what is good for the individual (his choosing the art for which he is best fitted by nature) and what is good for the city: nature has so arranged things that there is no surplus of blacksmiths or deficit of shoemakers. The healthy city is happy because it is just and it is just because it is happy. It is just without anyone concerning himself with justice; it is just by nature. The healthy city is altogether natural; it is little in need of medicine because in the healthy city the bodies are not as bad as they were supposed to be in the conversation with Thrasymachus (341e4–6, 373d1–3). In the healthy city justice is free from any tincture of self-sacrifice: justice is easy and pleasant. Justice is easy and pleasant because no one has to concern himself with the common good and to dedicate himself to it; the only action which could look like concern with the common good, the restriction of the number of children (372b8–c1),will be effected by everyone thinking of his own good. The healthy city complies with the demand of Adeimantus. It complies to some extent with Adeimantus' character.[32] It is Adeimantus' city. But it is wholly unacceptable to his brother. It does not satisfy Glaucon's need for luxury, and in the first place for meat. (He did not get the promised dinner.) But we could greatly underestimate him if we were to believe him. He does not lie of course, but he is not fully aware of what induces him to rebel against the healthy city. The healthy city may be just in a sense but it surely lacks virtue or excellence (cf. 372b7–8 with 607a4): such justice as it possesses is not virtue. Glaucon is characterized by the fact that he cannot distinguish between his desire for dinner and his desire for virtue. (He is the one who calls the healthy city the city of pigs. In this respect too he does not quite know what he says. The healthy city is literally a city without pigs. Cf 370d–e and 373c.) Virtue is impossible without toil, effort or repression of the evil in oneself. In the healthy city evil is only dormant. Death is mentioned only when the transition from the healthy city to the next stage has already begun (372d). Because virtue is impossible in the healthy city, the healthy city is impossible. The healthy city or any other form of anarchic society would be possible if men could remain innocent; but it is of the essence of innocence that it is easily lost; men can be just only through knowledge. "Self-realization" is not essentially in harmony with sociability.

Socrates calls the healthy city the true city or simply the city (372e6–7, 374a5, 433a2–6). It is the city *par excellence* for more than one reason, one reason being that it exhibits the fundamental character of the best city. When Socrates speaks about the primary needs which bring men together, he mentions food, housing, and clothing but is silent about procreation. He speaks only of those natural needs which are satisfied by means of arts as distinguished

---

[32] Consider Adeimantus' most lengthy reply in this context (371c5–d3: the need for shopkeepers) with Socrates' reply (e5–6: "as I believe").

from that natural need which is satisfied naturally. He abstracts from procreation in order to be able to understand the city as an association of artisans or in order to effect as complete a coincidence as possible between the city and the arts. The city and the arts belong together. Socrates seems to agree with the Bible in so far as the Bible traces the city as well as the arts to one and the same origin.[33] At any rate, we are forced to reconsider the natural character of the healthy city. The care for men which the description of the healthy city ascribes to nature goes much beyond what nature ever provides. It could be ascribed only to the gods. No wonder that the citizens of the healthy city sing hymns to the gods. All the more remarkable is the silence of Socrates and Adeimantus about the gods' efficacy in the healthy city.

Before the purified city can emerge or rather be established, the healthy city must have decayed. Its decay is brought about by the emancipation of the desire for unnecessary things, *i.e.* for things which are not necessary for the well-being of the body. Thus the luxurious or feverish city emerges, the city characterized by striving for unlimited acquisition of wealth. One can expect that in such a city the individuals will no longer exercise the single art for which each is fitted by nature, but any art, genuine or spurious, or combination of arts which is most lucrative or that there will no longer be a strict correspondence between service and reward; hence there will be dissatisfaction and conflicts and therefore need for government which will restore justice; hence there will be need for something else which was also entirely absent from the healthy city, *i.e.* the education at least of the rulers and more particularly education to justice. Justice will no longer be effective naturally. This is reflected in the conversation: whereas in the description of the healthy city Socrates and his interlocutors were onlookers of the coming-into-being of the city, they must now become founders, men responsible for the effectiveness of justice (cf. 374e6–9 with 369c9–10; 378e7–379a1). There will also be need for additional territory and hence there will be war, war of aggression. Building on the principle "one man one art," Socrates demands that the army consist of men who have no other art than the art of war. It appears that the art of the warrior or guardian is by far superior to the other arts. Hitherto it looked as if all arts were of equal rank and the only

---

[33] Cf. also Sophocles, *Antigone* 332ff. with 786ff.

universal art or the only art accompanying all arts was the art of money-making (342a–c, 346c). Now we receive the first glimpse of the true order of arts: that order is hierarchic; the universal art is the highest art, the art directing all other arts which as such cannot be practiced by the practitioners of arts other than the highest; in particular, it cannot be practiced by anyone practicing the money-making art. The art of arts will prove to be philosophy. For the time being we are merely told that the warrior must have a nature resembling the nature of that philosophic beast, the dog. For the warriors must be spirited and hence irascible and harsh on the one hand and gentle on the other, since they must possess disinterested dislike for foreigners and disinterested liking for their fellow citizens. The men possessing such special natures need in addition a special education. With a view to their work they need training in the art of war, of guarding the city. But this is not the education with which Socrates is much concerned. We recall that the art of the keeper proved to be identical with the art of the thief. The education of the guardians must make sure that they will not practice thievery and the like except perhaps against a foreign enemy. The warriors will be by nature the best fighters and in addition they will be the only ones armed and trained in arms: they will inevitably be the sole possessors of political power. Besides, the age of innocence having gone, evil will be rampant in the city and therefore also in the warriors. The education which the warriors more than anyone else need is therefore education in civic virtue. This is again reflected in the conversation. The one who rebelled against the healthy city was Glaucon; his rebellion was prompted by his desire for luxury, for "having more," for the thrills of war and destruction (cf. 471b6–c1). He is now compelled by Socrates to accept the complete divorce of the profession of arms from all luxury and gain (374a3): the spirit of luxury and gain is replaced by the spirit of discipline and selfless service. Glaucon's education in this respect is part of the education to moderation which is effected by the conversation reported in the *Republic* as a whole.

The education of the warriors in civic virtue is "music" education, education through poetry and music. Not all poetry and music is apt to make men good citizens in general and good warriors in particular. Therefore the poetry and music not conducive to the acquisition of the virtues in question must be banished from the city. The specific pleasure which poetry affords can be tolerated only when it is conducive to the noble, to nobility of character. The austerity of this demand is entirely agreeable to Adeimantus who is now again Socrates' interlocutor. Socrates himself regards that demand as provisional; the whole discussion partakes of the character of myth.[34] The first place is occupied by education to piety. Piety requires that only the right kind of stories about the gods be told, not the kind told by the greatest poets. To indicate the right kind Socrates lays down two laws regarding what Adeimantus calls "theology." For the proper understanding of that theology one must consider the context. The theology is to serve as model for the untrue stories to be told to little children (377c7–d1 and a). As we know, untrue stories are needed not only for little children but also for the grown-up citizens of the good city, but it is probably best if they are imbued with these stories from the earliest possible moment. There was no need for untrue stories in the city of pigs. This may have been one reason why Socrates called it "the true city," i.e. the truthful city. At any rate, the conversation between Socrates and Adeimantus about the theology shifts insensibly from the demand for noble lies about the gods to the demand for the truth about the gods. The speakers start from the implicit premise that there are gods, or that there is a god and that they know what a god is. The difficulty can be illustrated by an example. Socrates asks Adeimantus whether the god would lie or say the untruth because of his ignorance of ancient things and Adeimantus replies that this would be ridiculous (382d6–8). But why is it ridiculous in Adeimantus' view? Because the gods must know best their own affairs, as Timaeus suggests (Timaeus 40d3–41a5)? It is true that Timaeus makes a distinction between the visible gods who revolve manifestly and those gods who manifest themselves so far as they choose, between the cosmic gods and the Olympian gods, and that no such distinction is made in the theology of the Republic where only the Olympian gods are identified. But precisely this fact shows the "mythical" character of the theology or the gravity of the failure to raise and answer the question "what is a god?" or "who are the gods?" Other Socratic utterances might enable one to ascertain Socrates' answer, but they are of no use for ascertaining Adeimantus' answer and therewith for gauging how deep the agreement is which Socrates and Adeimantus achieve. They surely agree as to this, that

---

[34] 376d9, 387b3–4, 388e2–4, 389a7, 390a5, 396c10, 397d6–e2, 398a8.

the gods are superhuman beings, that they are of superhuman goodness or perfection (381c1–3). That the god is good is even the
thesis of the first theological law. From this it follows that the god
is not the cause of all things but only of the good ones. This amounts
to saying that the god is just: the first theological law applies to the
god the result of the conversation with Polemarchus according to
which justice consists in helping the friends, *i.e.* sensible men and
in not harming anyone.[35] The explicit difficulty concerns exclusively
the other theological law which asserts the simplicity of the god and
which is to some extent a mere corollary of the first. The second law
has two implications: (1) the god does not change his looks or form
(*eidos* or *idea*), *i.e.* he does not take on a variety of shapes or
undergo changes of his form; (2) the gods do not deceive or lie. In
contradistinction to the first law, the second law is not immediately
evident to Adeimantus; this is true especially of the second implication (380a7, 381e11, 382a3). Adeimantus obviously sees no difficulty in maintaining simultaneously that the gods are good and that
they lie: the gods possess all virtues, hence also justice, and justice
sometimes requires lying; as Socrates makes clear partly in this context and partly shortly afterwards,[36] rulers must lie for the benefit
of their subjects; if the gods are just or rulers, it would seem that
they must lie. Adeimantus' resistance is then due to his concern with
justice as distinguished from love of truth (382a4–10) or philosophy.
He resists the dogma stating the simplicity of the gods because he
is more willing than his brother to grant that justice is akin to
knowledge or art rather than it is essentially simplicity. His resistance is not altogether in harmony with the implications of his long
speech near the beginning of the second book.[37] This is not surprising: he still has much to learn. After all, he does not yet know what
justice is. Somewhat later in the conversation Socrates suggests that
justice is a specifically human virtue (392a3–c3), perhaps because
justice is rooted in the fact that every human being lacks self-
sufficiency and hence is ordered toward the city (369b5–7) and
therefore that man is essentially "erotic" whereas the gods are self-

---

[35] 382d11–e3, 378b2–3, 380b1. Polemarchus and Adeimantus appear together: 327c1; cf. 449b1–7.

[36] 382c6ff., 389b2–d6; cf. the conditional and partly metrical clause in
389b2–4.

[37] The core of the difficulty is indicated in 366c7 as one sees if one considers the fact that the gods themselves must have divine natures.

sufficient and hence free from *eros*. *Eros* and justice would thus seem to have the same root.

The education of the warriors as envisaged by Socrates is education to almost all virtues. Piety, courage, moderation, and justice are clearly recognizable as goals of this education, whereas wisdom is replaced by truthfulness and rejection of love of laughter. The discussion of how to educate the warriors to justice is postponed on the ground that the interlocutors do not yet know what justice is.[38] This ground is rather specious, for they can hardly be said to know what the other virtues are either. We see the true ground when we pay attention to the fact that as the conversation turns to music proper, the music and erotic Glaucon who makes his re-entry laughingly again takes the place of his brother (398c7, e1; 402e2). Generally speaking, Glaucon is the interlocutor of Socrates in the *Republic* whenever the highest themes are discussed. It is in a conversation with Glaucon that Socrates makes clear the ultimate end of the education of the warriors. That ultimate end proves to be *eros* of the beautiful or noble. That *eros* is linked especially to courage and above all to moderation or seemliness.[39] Justice in the narrow sense may be said to flow from moderation or from the proper combination of moderation and courage. Socrates thus makes silently clear the difference between the gang of robbers and the good city: these kinds of society differ essentially because the armed and ruling part of the good city is animated by the *eros* for everything beautiful and graceful. The difference is not to be sought in the fact that the good city is guided in its relations to other cities, Greek or barbarian, by considerations of justice: the size of the territory of the good city is determined by that city's own moderate needs and by nothing else (423a5–c1; cf. 422d1–7); the relation of the city to the other cities belongs to the province of wisdom rather than of justice (428d2–3); the good city is not a part of a community of cities or is not dedicated to the common good of that community or does not serve other cities. Therefore, if the parallel between the city and the individual is to be preserved, one must at least try to understand the virtues of the individual in terms of virtues other than justice. It is in connection with this experiment that *eros* of the

---

* Cf. 395c4–5 and 427e10–11 with 386a1–6; 388e5; 389b2, d7; 392a8–c5.
* 399c3, e11; 401a5–8; 402c2–4; 403c4–8; 410a8–9; e10; 411c4ff. (376e2–10); 416d8–e1.

beautiful provisionally takes the place of justice. One might say that in this stage the situation in the good city is exactly the reverse of the situation in the healthy city.

While the parallel between the city and the individual is thus surreptitiously established, it is surreptitiously brought into question. In order to be as good as possible, the city must be united or one as much as possible and therefore the individual must be one as much as possible: every citizen must devote himself single-mindedly to a single art (423d3–6). Justice is simplicity. Hence education must be simple: the simple gymnastic and the simple music is to be preferred to the composite, "sophisticated," or complex forms (404b5, 7, e4–5; 410a8–9). But man is a dual being, consisting of body and soul: in order to become an educated warrior, one must therefore practice the two arts (411e4) of gymnastic and music.[40] This dualism is illustrated by the radical difference discussed in this context between the physician, the healer of the body, and the judge, the healer of the soul. It goes without saying that music itself consists of two arts, poetry and music in the narrow sense, to say nothing of the art of reading and writing (402b3). If Asclepius' sons combine the two heterogeneous arts of medicine and war (408a1–2), one begins to wonder whether the strict separation of the men devoting themselves to the art of war from all other artisans (374a3–d6) is Socrates' last word. Perhaps it is also not as impossible as Socrates here suggests for the same man to be a good comic poet and a good tragic poet, especially since we learn from the context that the man of noble simplicity who for the sake of this simplicity would never imitate a lower man, might nevertheless do this in jest: the dualism of play and seriousness warns us against too simple an understanding of simplicity. Such a simple understanding is however most simply prevented by the recollection of the fact that the rulers of the best city must combine the two heterogeneous activities of the philosopher on the one hand and of the king on the other.

The difference between justice and the *eros* of the beautiful which is the end of the warriors' education comes out in Socrates' discussion of the rulers. The rulers must be taken from among the elite of the warriors. In addition to possessing the art of guarding

---

[40] Cf. the different meaning of "unmixed" in 410d3 and 412a4 on the one hand and in 397d2 (cf. e1–2) on the other.

the citizens, the rulers must possess the quality of caring for the city or of loving the city; this love (*philia*) is not *eros*. As we recall, the art of guarding is in itself also the art of thieving. A man is most likely to love that whose interest he believes to be identical with his own interest or whose happiness he believes to be the condition of his own happiness (412c5–d8). The love which is demanded of the rulers is then neither spontaneous nor disinterested in the sense that the good ruler would love the city without any regard to his own interest; the love expected of him is a calculating kind of love. Justice as dedication to the common good is neither art nor *eros*; it does not appear to be choiceworthy for its own sake. Caring for one's city is one thing; undergoing the hardships of ruling the city, *i.e.* of serving the city, is another thing. This explains why Socrates demands that the good rulers be honored both while they are alive and after their death (414a1–4; cf. 347d4–8). Yet this incentive cannot affect the ruled. It is therefore with special regard to the ruled and more precisely to the soldiers, the strongest part of the city, that Socrates introduces at this point the noble lie *par excellence;* that noble lie is to bring about the maximum of caring for the city and for one another on the part of the ruled (415d3–4). The good city is not possible then without a fundamental falsehood; it cannot exist in the element of truth, of nature. The noble lie consists of two parts. The first part is meant to make the citizens forget the truth about their education or the true character of their becoming citizens out of mere human beings or out of what one may call natural human beings.[41] It surely is meant to blur the distinction between nature and art and between nature and convention. It demands that the citizens regard themselves as children of one and the same mother and nurse, the earth, and hence as brothers, but in such a way that the earth is to be identified with a part of the earth, with the particular land or territory belonging to the particular city in question: the fraternity of all human beings is to be replaced by the fraternity of all fellow citizens. The second part of the noble lie qualifies this qualified fraternity by the fundamental inequality of the brothers; while the fraternity is traced to the earth, the inequality is traced to the god. If the god is the cause of all good things (380c8–9), inequality would seem to be a good thing. The god did not however create the brothers unequal by arbitrary decision, as it

---

[41] Consider Rousseau, *Du Contrat Social* II 7 ("Du Législateur").

were choosing some for rule and others for subjection; he merely sanctioned a natural difference or put a stamp on it. One might expect that the god would at least guarantee what nature does not guarantee, namely, that the rulers generate only rulers, the soldiers only soldiers, and the farmers and craftsmen only farmers and craftsmen; but the god limits himself to demanding that the ignoble sons of noble fathers be relegated to a lower class and vice versa, *i.e.* that the natural order be respected without mercy. The division of the human race into independent self-sufficient cities is not simply natural; the order of rank within the city would be simply natural if it were divinely sanctioned with sufficient force. It is the second part of the noble lie which, by adding divine sanctions to the natural hierarchy, supplies the required incentive for the soldiers to obey the rulers and thus to serve the city wholeheartedly. Yet unless one ascribes a weight not warranted by the text to the divine sanction mentioned, one must admit that the suggested incentive is not sufficient. It is for this reason that Socrates introduces at this point the institution of communism: the incentive to justice still being insufficient, the opportunity for injustice must be removed. In the extremely brief discussion of communism regarding property the emphasis is on "housing": there will be no hiding places. Everyone is compelled always to live, if not in the open, at least within easy inspection: everyone may enter everyone else's dwelling at will. As reward for their service to the craftsmen proper the soldiers will not receive money of any kind but only a sufficient amount of food and of the other necessities. In the city of the armed camp there does not exist that approximation to the ring of Gyges which is the private home: no one can be happy through injustice because injustice, in order to be successful, requires a secrecy which is no longer possible.

In the good city as hitherto described justice then still depends on the lack of opportunity for injustice, as it does necessarily according to Glaucon's charge in his long speech; we have not yet come face to face with genuine justice. Hence, according to Glaucon's hope, we have not yet come face to face with genuine happiness. In other words, the coincidence of self-interest and the interest of the others or of the city, which was lost with the decay of the healthy city, has not yet been restored at least as far as the soldiers are concerned. The common people are the sheep, the soldiers are the dogs, and the rulers are the shepherds (416a2–7). But

*103*

who are the owners? Who benefits from the whole enterprise? Who is made happy by it? No wonder that at the beginning of the fourth book the quiet and somewhat pedestrian Adeimantus, who is entirely oblivious of the joys of war and does not discern any peaceful activity of the soldiers which would be choiceworthy for its own sake, lodges an accusation against Socrates on behalf of the soldiers, the true owners of the city (419a2–4). Socrates defends himself as follows: we are concerned with the happiness of the city rather than with the happiness of any one section of it; we gave to each section that degree of happiness which is compatible with its specific service to the city or with its justice; we gave to each section of the city that degree of happiness which that section's nature requires or permits. But the section consists of individuals. It is not clear whether it is sufficient for the individual's happiness that the section to which he belongs is as happy as its political function permits, whether his happiness coincides with his complete dedication to the happiness of the city or with his justice, or whether he can reach a higher degree of happiness by being unjust. We must see whether it has become clear by the time that they begin to answer the question of whether genuine justice or genuine injustice is required for happiness (427d5–7).

Just as Glaucon had opposed the healthy city because its citizens lack the pleasures of the table, and not because they lack virtue, Adeimantus opposes the city of the armed camp because its citizens lack wealth, and not because they lack genuine justice. The incompleteness of the argument is matched by the incompleteness of the training of the interlocutors. The cure for the desire for the pleasures of the table was found in moderation. The cure for the desire for wealth must be found in justice. If the latter cure has been found by the time that they begin to answer the question of whether genuine justice is required for happiness, it was found much more easily than the former cure. The reason would be that wealth is much more political than the sensual pleasures: the city as city cannot eat and drink whereas it can own property. After Socrates has completed his defense against Adeimantus' charge, Adeimantus states the case for wealth, not indeed of the individuals, but of the city which needs wealth for waging war (422a4–7, b9, d8–e2). Through refuting that case Socrates completely overcomes Adeimantus' resistance to the city of the armed camp and therewith, it seems, completes the case for genuine justice. According to Socrates, one substitute for wealth will be the policy of the good city to ally itself with the many poor in enemy cities against the few rich in them (423a3–5; cf. 471b2). But this is not the strongest medicine which the sternly anti-democratic Adeimantus, who is so averse to innovation (424d3–e4), is forced by Socrates to take. Socrates avails himself of the present opportunity to slip in the demand for communism regarding women and children. Even the necessity of innovation regarding songs (as distinguished from innovation regarding kinds of songs) (424c1–5) is imposed on Adeimantus. His accusation of Socrates had shown that the previously suggested safeguards are insufficient or that still more radical deviations from custom than hitherto stated are needed: the purgation of the feverish city requires the complete subversion of the city as hitherto known; it requires an act of what is thought to be the greatest injustice (cf. 426b9–c2). This radical change does not lose its character by the fact that the first, the most important, and the most resplendent legal establishments of the good city, i.e. those concerning divine worship, are left to the decision of the ancestral interpreter, i.e. to the god who is the ancestral interpreter regarding such matters for all human beings: to the Delphic Apollo, for if Apollo were only a Greek god, he could not perform this function for a city which is to be not only Greek but good as well.

After the founding of the good city is completed, Socrates and his friends turn to seeking where in it are justice and injustice and whether the man who is to be happy must possess justice or injustice. They surely succeed in stating what justice is. This is perhaps the strangest happening in the whole *Republic*. That Platonic dialogue which is devoted to the subject of justice answers the question of what justice is long before the first half of the work is finished, long before the most important facts without the consideration of which the essence of justice cannot be possibly determined in an adequate manner, have come to light, let alone have been duly considered. No wonder that the definition of justice at which the *Republic* arrives determines at most the genus to which justice belongs but not its specific difference (cf. 433a3). One cannot help contrasting the *Republic* with the other dialogues which raise the question of what a given virtue is; those other dialogues do not answer the question with which they deal; they are aporetic dialogues. The *Republic* appears to be a dialogue in which the truth is declared, a dogmatic dialogue. But since that truth is set forth on the basis of strikingly deficient evidence, one is compelled to say that the *Republic* is in fact as aporetic as the so-called aporetic dialogues. Why did Plato proceed in this manner in the dialogue treating justice as distinguished from the dialogues treating the other virtues? Justice, we may say, is the universal virtue, the virtue most obviously related to the city. The theme of the *Republic* is political in more than one sense, and the political questions of great urgency do not permit delay: the question of justice must be answered by all means even if all the evidence needed for an adequate answer is not yet in. The *Laches* begins with a question which is much more practical than the question "what is justice?", with the question of whether a certain kind of fighting is good or bad in combat. Since the military experts disagree, Socrates enters the discussion and shows, in a manner which at any rate in the eyes of those present is unobjectionable, that the question cannot be answered before they know what courage is; the discussion of what courage is does not lead to a result and hence the answer to the initial practical question is postponed indefinitely or rather the initial practical question is completely lost sight of. That question could safely be forgotten because it was neither very important nor very urgent; otherwise it would have been settled by the authority in charge without waiting for an adequate answer to the question of what courage is, and rightly so because there is no necessary connection between the two questions. Although the *Laches* leaves unanswered the question of what courage is, a careful reading of the dialogue would show that it answers that question at least as well as the *Republic* answers the question of what justice is. The distinction between aporetic dialogues and dialogues which convey a teaching is deceptive. To avoid deception, one would have to consider whether or not all dialogues which convey a teaching, and especially those in which Socrates is the chief speaker, are not carried on under a pressure comparable to the pressure operative in the *Republic*. For instance, the conversation which is reported in the *Phaedo* had to be completed because it takes place on the day of Socrates' death. As for the *Banquet*, one must not forget that the teaching conveyed therein is ascribed by Socrates to Diotima.

The premature investigation of what justice is becomes possible because the interlocutors accept Socrates' claim that the founding of the good city has been completed: can anything be lacking after the first, the most important, and the most resplendent things, *i.e.* the crowning things, have been provided for? Thereupon Socrates demands from them with some justice that they should seek where in that city is justice and where in it is injustice. Yet Glaucon forces him, by reminding him of his promise to come to the assistance of justice, to participate, nay, to lead in that search. But the interlocutors are not aware that Socrates has changed the terms of his commitment or commission. He was supposed to prove that justice is choiceworthy for its own sake and not merely on account of its consequences, but he now declares the question to be whether in order to be happy a man must possess justice or injustice: justice may be an indispensable condition for happiness without being choiceworthy for its own sake, while being necessary only as a means or while being a necessary evil. Yet while the question of whether justice is good even in this restricted sense is said to be still entirely open, Socrates says immediately afterward that if the city which they have founded in speech is good, it must possess all virtues and justice among them, *i.e.* he takes it for granted that justice is good, or begs the decisive question. These moves succeed because Glaucon does not have a clear grasp of the issue; he is a well-wisher of justice but he is also perplexed by the speeches of the detractors of justice; he would like to believe that justice is the highest thing but he is aware of other things which do not seem to be lower than justice. Therefore when Socrates does not turn immediately to the search for justice but discusses first the other virtues, Glaucon's concern with the other virtues is sufficiently great to prevent him from protesting against Socrates' roundabout procedure (cf. 430d4–e1). One is not unjust to anyone if one notes that the beginning of the discussion of justice itself strangely lacks simplicity, and that justice seemed to be akin to simplicity.

Socrates and Glaucon look first for the three virtues other than justice. In the city which is founded according to nature, wisdom resides in the rulers and only in the rulers, for the wise men are by nature the smallest part of any city and it would not be good for the city if they were not at its helm. In the good city courage resides in the warriors, for political courage, as distinguished from brutish fearlessness, arises only through education in those by nature fitted for that courage. To find moderation is not quite so easy. If it is self-control regarding pleasures and desires, it is also the preserve of the rulers and warriors (431b9–d3). Yet it can also be understood to be the control of what is by nature worse by what is by nature better, *i.e.* that through which the whole is in harmony, or the agreement of the naturally superior and the naturally inferior as to which of the two ought to rule in the city; moderation thus understood pervades all parts of the good city. Even so, moderation lacks the simplicity and univocity of wisdom and of courage. Since controlling and being controlled differ, the moderation of the upper class differs from the moderation of the lower class. While Socrates and Glaucon find the three first virtues in the good city with ease, it is difficult for them to find justice in it; it seems to reside in a place difficult of access and lying in deep shadows; in fact, however, it was tumbling about their feet; they missed it because they looked for it far off. The difficulty of discovering justice in contradistinction to the other virtues reflects the fact that the education to justice in contradistinction to the other virtues has not been discussed. Justice proves to be the principle which guided the foundation of the good city from the very beginning, which was already effective in the healthy city although incompletely and which is, as we know, not yet completely effective in the city of the armed camp. Justice consists in everyone's doing the one thing pertaining to the city for which his nature is best fitted or simply in everyone's minding his own business: it is by virtue of justice thus understood that the three other virtues are virtues (433a–b). More precisely, a city is just if each of its three parts (the money-makers, the soldiers, and the rulers) does its own work and only its own work. Justice is then like moderation and unlike wisdom and courage not the preserve of a single part but required of every part. Hence justice, like moderation, has a different character in each of the three classes. One must assume, for instance, that the justice of the wise rulers is tinged by their wisdom (to say nothing of their peculiar incentive to justice) and the justice of the money-makers is colored by their vulgarity, for if even the courage of the warriors is only political or civic courage and not courage pure and simple (430c; cf. *Phaedo* 82a), it stands to reason that their justice too—to say nothing at all of the justice of the money-makers—will not be justice pure and simple. The courage of the warriors is not courage pure and simple because it is essentially dependent on law (cf. 429c7 with 412e6–8 and 413c5–7) or because they lack the highest responsibility. In order to discover justice pure and simple, it becomes necessary then to consider justice in the individual human being. This consideration would be easiest if justice in the individual were identical with justice in the city; this would require that the individual or rather his soul consist of the same three kinds of "natures" as the city. We note that the parallel between the city and the individual by which the good city stands or falls, demands the abstraction from the body (cf. the transition from the individual to the soul in 434d–435c). A provisional consideration of the soul seems to establish the requirement mentioned: the soul contains desire, spiritedness or anger (440a5, c2), and reason, just as the city consists of the money-makers, the warriors, and the rulers. Hence we may conclude that a man is just if each of these three parts of the soul does its own work and only its own work, *i.e.* if his soul is in a state of health. But if justice is health of the soul and conversely injustice is disease of the soul, it is obvious that justice is good and injustice is bad, regardless of whether or not one is known to be just or unjust (444d–445b). A man is just if the rational part of his soul is wise and rules (441e) and if the spirited part, being the subject and ally of the rational part, assists it in controlling the multitude of desires which become almost inevitably desires for more and ever more money. This means however that only the man in whom reason properly cultivated rules the two other parts properly cultivated, *i.e.* only the wise man, can be truly just (cf. 442c); the soul cannot be healthy if one of its parts, and especially its best part is atrophied. No wonder then that the just man eventually proves to be identical with the philosopher (580d–583b). And the philosopher can be just without being a member of the just city. The money-makers and the warriors are not truly just because their justice derives exclusively from habituation of one kind or another as distinguished from philosophy; hence in the deepest recesses of their souls they long for tyranny, *i.e.* for complete injustice (619b–d). We see then how right Socrates was when he expected to find injustice in the good city (427d). This is not to deny of course that as members of the good city the non-philosophers would act much more justly than they do as members of the actual cities.

The justice of those who are not wise appears in a different light in the consideration of justice in the city on the one hand and in the consideration of justice in the soul on the other. This fact shows that the parallel between the city and the soul is misleading. That parallel is defective because the definition of justice which supports it is defective. Justice is said to consist in each part of the city or of the soul "doing the work for which it is best fitted by nature" or in a "kind" of this; a part of the city or of the soul is said to be just if it does its work or minds its own business "in a certain manner." The indefiniteness is removed if one replaces "in a certain manner" by "in the best manner" or simply by "well" (433a–b, 443c4–d7; Aristotle, *Eth. Nic.* 1098a7–12). If each part of the city does its work well, and hence has the virtue or virtues belonging to it, the city is wise, courageous, and moderate and therewith perfectly good: it does not need justice in addition. The case of the individual is different. If he is wise, courageous, and moderate, he is not yet perfectly good; for his goodness toward his fellows, his willingness to help them, to care for them, or to serve them (412d13), as distinguished from unwillingness to harm them, does not follow from his possessing the three first virtues. The three first virtues are sufficient for the city because the city is self-sufficient, and they are insufficient for the individual because the individual is not self-sufficient. It is because justice as a distinct virtue is superfluous in the case of the good city that Socrates and Glaucon have difficulty in seeing it when they look for it.

The parallel between the city and the soul requires that just as in the city the warriors occupy a higher rank than the money-makers, in the soul spiritedness occupy a higher rank than desire (440e2–7). It is very plausible that those who uphold the city against foreign and domestic enemies and who have received a music education should be more highly respected than those who lack public responsibility as well as music education. But it is much less plausible that spiritedness as such should be higher in rank than desire as such. It is true that spiritedness includes a large variety of phenomena ranging from the most noble indignation about injustice, turpitude, and meanness down to the anger of a spoiled child who resents being deprived of anything, however bad, that he desires (cf. 441a7–b2). But it is also clear that the same holds of desire: one kind of desire is *eros*, which ranges in its healthy forms from the longing for immortality through offspring via the longing for immortality through fame to the longing for immortality through participation by knowledge in the things which are unchangeable in every respect. The assertion that spiritedness as such is higher in rank than desire as such is then questionable. Although or because Glaucon denies it with an oath, spiritedness does conspire with desire against reason (440b4–8). Let us also never forget that while there is a philosophic *eros*, there is no philosophic indignation, desire for victory, or anger. (Consider 536b8–c7.) The parallel of the city and the soul is based on a deliberate abstraction from *eros,* an abstraction characteristic of the *Republic.* This abstraction shows itself most strikingly in two facts: when Socrates mentions the fundamental needs which give rise to human society, he is silent about the need for procreation, and when he describes the tyrant, he presents him as *Eros* incarnate (573b–e, 574d–575a). This is to say nothing of the fact that the *Republic* almost opens with a curse on *eros* (329b6–d1). In the thematic discussion of the respective rank of spiritedness and desire, Socrates is silent about *eros.*[42] It seems that there is a tension between *eros* and the city and hence between *eros* and justice: only through the depreciation of *eros* can the city come into its own. *Eros* obeys its own laws, not the laws of the city however good; lovers are not necessarily fellow citizens (or fellow party-members); in the good city *eros* is simply subjected to the requirements of the city: only those are permitted to join each other for procreation who promise to bring forth the right kind of offspring. The abolition of privacy is a blow struck at *eros.* The city is not an erotic association although in a way it presupposes erotic associations. There is not an erotic class of the city as there are classes of rulers, warriors, and money-makers. The city does not procreate as it deliberates, wages wars, and owns property. As far as possible, patriotism, dedication to the common good, justice, must take the place of *eros,* and patriotism has a closer kinship to spiritedness, eagerness to fight, "waspishness," indignation, and anger than to *eros.* Both the erotic association and the political association are exclusive, but they are exclusive in different ways: the lovers seclude themselves from the others (from "the world") without opposition to the others or hate of the others, but the city cannot be said to seclude itself from "the world": it separates itself from others by opposing or resisting them; the opposition of "We and They" is essential to the political association. The superiority of spiritedness to desire seems to be shown by the fact that every act of human spiritedness seems to include a sense that one is in the right (440c). A considerable part

---

[42] Cf. 439d6. Cf. the similar procedure in the *Timaeus* where the thesis asserting the superiority of spiritedness to desire is repeated with the consequence that original man, man as he left the hands of his Maker, is (*sit venia verbo*) a sexless male; cf. 69d–71a and 72e–73a with 91a–d; cf. also 88a8–b2.

of the acts of justice are acts of punishment, and punishment is, to say the least, assisted by anger.[43] Anger is so much concerned with right that it treats even lifeless things as if they could do wrong; spiritedness is more apt to "personify" its objects than desire (cf. 440a1–3; 469e1–2). But whether this fact establishes a simple superiority of spiritedness to desire depends on what we have to think about the worth of "personification." The *Republic* supplies food for thought on this subject especially through the presentation of Glaucon, the most spirited speaker in the work, who as Spiritedness incarnate comes to the assistance of Reason in the founding of the just city. What was said about the abstraction from *eros* in the *Republic* is not contradicted by the fact that the education of the warriors is meant to culminate in the *eros* of the beautiful; that *eros* points to the philosophic *eros*, the *eros* peculiar to the philosophers (501d2), which becomes quest for knowledge of the idea of the good, an idea higher than the idea of justice. The *Republic* could unqualifiedly abstract from *eros* only if it could abstract from philosophy. But there is a tension between philosophy and the city; on the level of this tension, the tension between *eros* and justice recurs. The *Republic* claims that the tension between philosophy and the city would be overcome if the philosophers become kings. We must investigate whether it is in fact overcome. We are guided toward this investigation by that qualified abstraction from *eros* which we have pointed out.

The good city is characterized above all by the rule of those best in philosophy and with regard to war (543a5)—of those who come closest to the virgin goddess Athena (*Timaeus* 24c7–d1), to a goddess who, in addition, was not formed in a womb. The good city is therefore characterized by the pre-eminence of reason and spiritedness as distinguished from *eros* in the primary sense. Prior to the emergence of philosophy the good city is characterized by the facts that it attributes a higher rank to spiritedness than to desire and that it is a city of artisans. There is a connection between these two facts. The arts are unerotic. They are unerotic because they are concerned with producing useful things, *i.e.* particular goods (428d12–e1), or means, whereas *eros* tends toward the complete good. Yet because of their partial character the arts are ministerial to the art of arts and call for it. The art of arts, *i.e.*

---

[43] Cf. *Laws* 731b3–d5.

philosophy, is concerned with the complete good simply, "the idea of the good." Just as art, *eros* points to philosophy as to its highest form. Toward philosophy, art and *eros*, the most pedestrian or utilitarian and the least utilitarian, manifestly converge. That spiritedness should also tend toward philosophy is, to say the least, less manifest.[44]

The founding of the good city started from the fact that men are by nature different and this proved to mean that they are by nature of unequal rank. They are unequal in the first place with regard to their abilities to acquire virtue. The inequality which is due to nature is increased and deepened by the different kinds of education or habituation and the different ways of life (communistic or non-communistic) which the different parts of the good city enjoy. As a result, the good city comes to resemble a caste society. A Platonic character who hears the account of the good city of the *Republic* is reminded by it of the caste system established in ancient Egypt, although it is quite clear that in Egypt the rulers were priests and not philosophers (*Timaeus* 24a–b). Yet in the good city of the *Republic*, not descent but everyone's natural gifts determine to which class he will belong. But this leads to a difficulty. The members of the upper class which lives communistically are not supposed to know who their natural parents are, for they are supposed to regard all men and women belonging to the older generation of the upper class as their parents. On the other hand, the gifted children of the non-communist lower class are to be transferred to the upper class (and vice versa); since their superior gifts are not necessarily recognizable at the moment of their birth, they may come to know their natural parents and even become attached to them; this would seem to unfit them for transfer to the upper class. There are three ways in which this difficulty can be overcome. The first is to make post-natal selection superfluous by guaranteeing the desired result through the right selection of parents, and this means of course of upper-class parents: every child of the properly chosen parents is fit to belong to the upper class. This is the solution underlying Socrates' discussion of the nuptial number (546c6–d3). The second way is to extend communism and —considering the connection between way of life and education—

---

[44] This difficulty is adumbrated most impressively at the end of the *Laws* (963e). Cf. the preceding note.

music education to the lower class (401b–c, 421e–422d, 460a, 543a). According to Aristotle (*Politics* 1264a13–17) Socrates has left it undecided whether in the good city absolute communism is limited to the upper class or extends also to the lower class. To leave this question undecided would be in agreement with Socrates' professed low opinion of the importance of the lower class (421a, 434a). The ambiguity regarding music education is due in other words to the anticipatory comparison of music education with the highest education, compared with which the difference between the education of the warriors and that of the money-makers becomes insignificant. Yet from any point of view but the highest that difference is of course very important. One must not forget that the class of money-makers, to say the least, contains those who lack good natures but are curable so that they do not have to be killed (410a1–4, 456d8–10). Accordingly Socrates alludes to the need for untrue stories to be addressed, not to the warriors, but to those insensitive to the beautiful or to honor, *i.e.* to the need for terrifying or punitive lies (386c1, 387b4–c3), for the multitude wholly deprived of political power would seem to be in the greatest need of incentives for obeying the rulers wholeheartedly. There can then be only little doubt that Socrates wishes to limit communism and music education to the upper class (398b2–4, 415eff., 431b4–d3). Therefore, in order to remove the difficulty under discussion, he can hardly avoid making an individual's belonging to the upper or lower class hereditary and thus violating one of the most elementary principles of justice. Apart from this, one may wonder whether a perfectly clear line between the gifted and those not gifted for the profession of warriors can be drawn, hence whether a perfectly just assignment of the individuals to the upper or lower class is possible, and hence whether the good city can be simply just (cf. 427d). In addition, if communism is limited to the upper class, there will be privacy both in the money-making class and among the philosophers as philosophers, for there may very well be only a single philosopher in the city and surely never a herd or a platoon: the warriors are the only class which is entirely political or public or entirely dedicated to the city; the warriors alone therefore present the clearest case of the just life in one sense of the word "just."

It is necessary to understand why communism is limited to the upper class or what the natural obstacle to communism is. That which is by nature private or a man's own is the body and only the body (464d; cf. *Laws* 739c). The most complete communism would therefore require complete abstraction from the body. The approximation to communism pure and simple which is demanded in the *Republic*, and which we have called absolute communism, requires an approximation to the complete abstraction from the body. The needs or desires of the body induce men to extend the sphere of the private, of what is each man's own, as far as they can. This most powerful striving is countered by music education which brings about moderation, *i.e.* by a most severe training of the soul of which, it seems, only a minority of men is capable. Yet this kind of education does not extirpate the natural desire of each for things (and human beings) of his own: the warriors will not accept absolute communism if they are not subject to the philosophers. It thus becomes clear that the striving for one's own is countered ultimately only by philosophy, by the quest for truth which as such cannot be anyone's private possession. Whereas the private *par excellence* is the body, the common *par excellence* is the mind, the pure mind, rather than the soul in general, for only pure thoughts can be simply identical and known to be simply identical in different individuals. The superiority of communism to non-communism as taught in the *Republic* is intelligible only as a reflection of the superiority of philosophy to non-philosophy. Yet while philosophy is the most common, it is also, as was indicated in the preceding paragraph, the most private. While in one respect the warriors' life is the just life *par excellence*, in another respect only the philosopher's life is just. The distinction between two meanings of justice which is implied cannot become clear before one has understood the teaching of the *Republic* regarding the relation of philosophy and the city. We must therefore make a new beginning.

At the end of the fourth book it looks as if Socrates had completed the task which Glaucon and Adeimantus had imposed on him, for he had shown that justice as health of the soul is desirable not only because of its consequences but above all for its own sake. But then, at the beginning of the fifth book, we are suddenly confronted by a new beginning, by the repetition of a scene which had occurred at the very beginning. Both at the very beginning and at the beginning of the fifth book (and nowhere else), Socrates' companions make a decision, nay, take a vote, and Socrates, who had no share in the decision, obeys it (cf. 449b–450a with 327c–328b3). Socrates' companions behave in both cases like a city (an assembly

of citizens), if of the smallest possible city (369d11–12). But there
is this decisive difference between the two scenes: whereas Thrasymachus was absent from the first scene, he has become a member
of the city in the second scene. It would seem that the foundation
of the good city requires that Thrasymachus be converted into
one of its citizens.

At the beginning of the fifth book Socrates' companions force
him to take up the subject of communism in regard to women and
children. They do not object to the proposal itself in the way in
which Adeimantus had objected to the communism regarding property at the beginning of the fourth book, for even Adeimantus is no
longer the same man he was at that time. They only wish to know
the precise manner in which communism regarding women and
children is to be managed. Socrates replaces the question raised by
these more incisive questions: (1) is that communism possible?
(2) is it desirable? It appears that communism regarding women
is the consequence or the presupposition of the equality of the two
sexes concerning the work they must do: the city cannot afford to
lose half of its adult population from its working and fighting force,
and there is no essential difference regarding natural gifts for the
various arts between men and women. The demand for equality
of the two sexes requires a complete upheaval of custom, an upheaval which is here presented less as shocking than as laughable;
the demand is justified on the ground that only the useful is fair
or noble and that only what is bad, *i.e.* against nature, is laughable;
the customary difference of conduct between the two sexes is rejected as being against nature, and the revolutionary change suggested is meant to bring about the order according to nature
(456c1–3). For justice requires that every human being should
practice the art for which he or she is fitted by nature, regardless
of what custom or convention may dictate. Socrates shows first that
the equality of the two sexes is possible, *i.e.* in agreement with the
nature of the two sexes as their nature appears when viewed with
regard to its aptitude for the practice of the various arts, and then
that it is desirable. In proving the possibility he explicitly abstracts
from the difference between the sexes in regard to procreation. As
we must repeat, this means that that argument of the *Republic* as a
whole, according to which the city is a community of male and
female artisans, abstracts to the highest degree possible from that
activity essential to the city which takes place "by nature" and not

"by art"; it means at the same time that it abstracts from the most important bodily difference within the human race, *i.e.* it abstracts as much as possible from the body: the difference between men and women is treated as if it were comparable to the difference between bald and long-haired men (454c–e). Socrates turns then to the communism regarding women and children and shows that it is desirable because it would make the city more "one" and hence more perfect than a city consisting of separate families would be: the city should be as similar as possible to a single human being, or to a single living body (462c10–d7, 464b2), *i.e.* to a natural being. The political argument which is directed toward the greatest possible unity of the city conceals the trans-political argument which is directed toward the naturalness of the city. The abolition of the family does not mean of course the introduction of license or promiscuity; it means the most severe regulation of sexual intercourse from the point of view of what is useful for the city or what is required for the common good. The consideration of the useful, one might say, supersedes the consideration of the sacred (458e4): human males and females are to be copulated with exclusive regard to the production of the best offspring in the spirit in which the breeders of dogs, birds, and horses proceed; the claims of *eros* are simply silenced; the new order naturally affects the customary prohibitions against incest, the most sacred rules of customary justice (cf. 461b–e). In the new scheme no one will know any more his natural parents, children, brothers and sisters but everyone will *regard* all men and women of the older generation as his fathers and mothers, of his own generation as his brothers and sisters, and of the younger generation as his children (463c). This means however that the city constructed according to nature lives in a most important respect more according to convention than according to nature. For this reason we are disappointed to see that while Socrates takes up the question of whether communism regarding women and children is possible, he drops it immediately (466d6ff.). It looks as if it were too much even for Socrates to prove that possibility, given the fact that men seem to desire naturally to have children of their own (cf. 330c3–4; 467a10–b1). Since the institution in question is indispensable for the good city, Socrates thus leaves open the question of the possibility of the good city, *i.e.* of the just city, as such. And this happens to his listeners, and to the readers of the *Republic*, after they have brought the greatest sacrifices—such as the sacrifice of *eros* as well as of the family—for the sake of justice.

Socrates is not for long allowed to escape from his awesome duty to answer the question of the possibility of the just city. The manly or rather spirited Glaucon compels him to face that question. Perhaps we should say that by apparently escaping to the subject of war—a subject both easier in itself and more attractive to Glaucon than the communism regarding women and children—yet treating that subject according to the stern demands of justice and thus depriving it of much of its attractiveness, he compels Glaucon to compel him to return to the fundamental question. Perhaps we should also say that Socrates does not truly run away from the subject of communism regarding women and children or of the equality of the two sexes by turning to the subject of war, since the only relevant difference between the two sexes was said to be that men are stronger than women (451e1-2, 455e1-2, 456a10-11, 457a9-10), a difference most relevant for fighting, and the death of female fighters is a graver loss for the city than the death of male fighters given the different function of the two sexes in procreation; besides, war may be said to prepare the abolition of the family. Be this as it may, the question to which they return is not the same which they left. The question which they left was whether the good city is possible in the sense that it is in agreement with human nature. The question to which they return is whether the good city is possible in the sense that it can be brought into being by the transformation of an actual city. The latter question might be thought to presuppose the affirmative answer to the first question, but this is not quite correct. As we learn now, our whole effort to find out what justice is (so that we will be enabled to see how it is related to happiness) was a quest for "justice itself" as a "pattern." By seeking for justice as a pattern we imply that the just man and the just city will not be perfectly just but will indeed approximate justice itself with particular closeness (472a–b): only justice itself is perfectly just (479a; cf. 538cff.). We thus learn that not even the characteristic institutions of the good city (absolute communism, equality of the sexes, and the rule of philosophers) are simply just. Justice itself is not "possible" in the sense that it is capable of coming into being because it is always without being capable of undergoing any change whatever. Justice is a "form" or an "idea," one of many "ideas." Ideas are the only things which strictly speaking "are," *i.e.* are without any admixture of non-being; they are beyond all becoming and whatever is becoming is between being and non-being. Since the ideas are the only things which are beyond all change, they are in a sense the cause of all change. For instance, the idea of justice is the cause of anything (human beings, cities, laws, commands, actions) having become just. They are self-subsisting beings which subsist always. They are of the utmost splendor. For instance, the idea of justice is perfectly just. But this splendor escapes the eyes of the body. The ideas are "visible" only to the eye of the mind, and the mind as mind perceives nothing but ideas. Yet, as is indicated by the facts that there are many ideas and that the mind which perceives the ideas is radically different from the ideas themselves, there must be something higher than the ideas: the idea of the good, which is in a sense the cause of all ideas as well as of the mind perceiving them (517c1–5). Plato and Aristotle agree that in the highest, the perfect knower and the perfect known must be united; but whereas according to Aristotle the highest is knowledge or thought thinking itself, according to Plato the highest is beyond the difference between knower and known or is not a thinking being. It also becomes questionable whether the highest as Plato understands it is still properly called an idea; Socrates uses "the idea of the good" and "the good" synonymously (505a2–b3). It is only through the perception of the good on the part of properly equipped human beings that the good city can come into being and subsist for a while.

The doctrine of ideas which Socrates expounds to his interlocutors is very hard to understand; to begin with, it is utterly incredible, not to say that it appears to be fantastic. Hitherto we had been given to understand that justice is fundamentally a certain character of the human soul or of the city, *i.e.* something which is not self-subsisting. Now we are asked to believe that it is self-subsisting, being at home as it were in an entirely different place from human beings and everything else participating in justice (cf. 509d1–510a7; *Phaedrus* 247c3). No one has ever succeeded in giving a satisfactory or clear account of this doctrine of ideas. It is possible however to define rather precisely the central difficulty. "Idea" means primarily the looks or shape of a thing; it means then a kind or class of things which are united by the fact that they all possess the same looks, the same character or power, or the same "nature"; therewith it means the class-character or the nature of the things belonging to the class in question: the idea of a thing is that which we seek when we try to find out the "What" or the "nature" of a thing or a class of things. The connection between "idea" and "nature" appears in the *Republic* from the facts that "the idea of justice" is called "that which is just by nature" (501b2) and the ideas in contradistinction to the things which are not ideas are said to be "in nature" (597b5–e4). This does not explain however why the ideas are presented as "separated" from the things which are what they are by participating in an idea, or, in other words, why "dogness" (the class character of dogs) should be "the true dog." It seems that two kinds of phenomena lend support to Socrates' assertion. In the first place, the mathematical things as such can never be found among sensible things; no line drawn on sand or paper is a line as meant by the mathematician. Secondly and above all, what we mean by justice and kindred things is not as such in its purity or perfection necessarily found in human beings or societies; it rather seems that what is meant by justice transcends everything which men ever achieve; precisely the justest men were and are the ones most aware of the shortcomings of their justice. Socrates seems to say that what is patently true of mathematical things and of the virtues is true universally: there is an idea of the bed or of the table as of the circle and of justice. Now while it is obviously reasonable to say that a perfect circle or perfect justice transcends everything which can be seen, it is hard to say that a perfect bed is something on which no man can ever rest or that a perfect howl is completely inaudible. However this may be, Glaucon and Adeimantus accept this doctrine of ideas with relative ease. They surely have heard of the ideas, even of the idea of the good, many times before. This does not guarantee however that they have a genuine understanding of that doctrine.[45] Yet they have heard still more frequently, and in a way they know, that there are gods like *Dike* (536b3; cf. 487a6), or *Nike* who is not this victory or that victory, nor this or that statue of *Nike*, but one and the same self-subsisting being which is in a sense the cause of every victory and which is of unbelievable splendor. More generally, Glaucon and Adeimantus know that there are gods —self-subsisting beings which are the cause of everything good, which are of unbelievable splendor, and which cannot be apprehended by the senses since they never change their "form" (cf.

---

[45] 505a2–3, 507a8–9, 509a6–8, 532d2–5, 533a1–2, 596a5–9, 597a8–9.

379a–b and 380dff.). This is not to deny that there is a profound difference between the gods as understood in the theology of the *Republic* and the ideas. It is merely to assert that those who have come to accept that theology are best prepared for accepting the doctrine of ideas. The movement to which the reader of the *Republic* is exposed leads from the city as the association of the fathers who are subject to the law and ultimately to the gods toward the city as an association of artisans who are subject to the philosophers and ultimately to the ideas.

We must now return to the question of the possibility of the just city. We have learned that justice is not "possible" in the sense that it can come into being. We learn immediately afterwards that not only justice itself but also the just city is not "possible" in the sense indicated. This does not mean that the just city as meant and as outlined in the *Republic* is an idea like justice itself and still less that it is an ideal: "ideal" is not a Platonic term. The just city is not a self-subsisting being like the idea of justice, located so to speak in a super-heavenly place. Its status is rather like that of a perfectly beautiful human being as painted which is only by virtue of the painter's painting; it is akin to that of Glaucon's statues of the perfectly just man who is thought to be perfectly unjust and of the perfectly unjust man who is thought to be perfectly just; more precisely, the just city is only "in speech": it "is" only by virtue of having been figured out with a view to justice itself or to what is by nature right on the one hand and the human all too human on the other. Although the just city is of decidedly lower rank than justice itself, even the just city as a pattern is not capable of coming into being as it has been blueprinted; only approximations to it can be expected in cities which are in deed and not merely in speech (472b1–473b3; cf. 500c2–501c9 with 484c6–d3 and 592b2–3). It is not clear what this means. Does it mean that the best possible solution will be a compromise so that we must become reconciled to a certain degree of private property (*e.g.* that we must permit every soldier to keep his shoes and the like as long as he lives) and a certain degree of inequality of the sexes (*e.g.* that certain military and administrative functions will remain a preserve of the male warriors)? There is no reason to suppose that this is what Socrates meant. In the light of the succeeding part of the conversation the following suggestion would seem to be plausible. The assertion according to which the just city cannot come into being as blueprinted is provisional or prepares the assertion according to which the just city, while capable of coming into being as blueprinted, is very unlikely to do so. At any rate immediately after having declared that only an approximation to the good city can reasonably be expected, Socrates raises the question, Which feasible change in the actual cities would be the necessary and sufficient condition of their transformation into good cities. His answer is that that condition is the "coincidence" of political power and philosophy: the philosophers must rule as kings or the kings must genuinely and adequately philosophize. That coincidence will bring about "the cessation of evil," *i.e.* both private and public happiness (473c11–e5). No less than this must be possible if justice as full dedication to the city is to be choiceworthy for its own sake; this condition can be fulfilled only if the city is of consummate goodness, *i.e.* such as to bring about the happiness of "the human race." One even begins to wonder whether the coincidence of philosophy and political power is not only the necessary but the sufficient condition of universal happiness, *i.e.* whether absolute communism and the equality of the sexes are still at all necessary. Socrates' answer is not altogether surprising. If justice is giving or leaving to each what is good for his soul but what is good for the soul is the virtues, it follows that no man can be truly just who does not know "the virtues themselves" or generally the ideas, or who is not a philosopher.

By answering the question of how the good city is possible, Socrates introduces philosophy as a theme of the *Republic*. This means that in the *Republic* philosophy is not introduced as the end of man but as a means for realizing justice and therefore the just city, the city as armed camp which is characterized by absolute communism and equality of the sexes in the upper class, the class of warriors. Since the rule of philosophers is not introduced as an ingredient of the just city but only as a means for its realization, Aristotle legitimately disregards this institution in his critical analysis of the *Republic*. Philosophy is introduced in the context of the question of the possibility, as distinguished from the question of the desirability, of the city of the armed camp. The question of possibility—of what is conformable to nature and in particular to the nature of man—did not arise in regard to the healthy city. The question of possibility came to the fore only at the beginning of the fifth book as a consequence of an intervention initiated by Polemarchus. The two earlier comparable interventions—that of Glaucon after the description of the healthy city and that of Adeimantus after the abolition of private property and of privacy altogether— were limited to the question of desirability: Polemarchus is more important for the action of the *Republic* than one might desire.[46] He supplies an indispensable corrective to the action of the two brothers and especially of Glaucon. As a remote consequence of Polemarchus' action Socrates succeeds in reducing the question of the possibility of the just city to the question of the possibility of the coincidence of philosophy and political power. That such a coincidence should be possible is to begin with most incredible: everyone can see that the philosophers are useless, if not even harmful, in politics. Socrates, who had experiences of his own with his own city—experiences to be crowned by his capital punishment—regards this accusation of the philosophers as well-founded, although in need of deeper exploration. He traces the antagonism of the cities to the philosophers primarily to the cities: the present cities, *i.e.* the cities not ruled by philosophers, are like assemblies of madmen which corrupt most of those fit to become philosophers, and to which those who have succeeded against all odds in becoming philosophers rightly turn their backs in disgust. But Socrates is far from absolving the philosophers altogether. Only a radical change on the part of both the cities and the philosophers can bring about that harmony between them for which they seem to be meant by nature. The change consists precisely in this, that the cities become willing to be ruled by philosophers and the philosophers become willing to rule the cities. This coincidence of philosophy and political power is very difficult to achieve, very improbable, but not impossible. To bring about the needed change on the part of the city, of the non-philosophers or the multitude, the right kind of persuasion is necessary and sufficient. The right kind of persuasion is supplied by the art of persuasion, the art of Thrasymachus, directed by the philosopher and in the service of philosophy. No wonder then that in this context Socrates declares that he and Thrasymachus have just become friends, having not been enemies before either. The multitude of the non-philosophers is good-natured and therefore persuadable. Without "Thrasymachus" there will never be a just city. We are compelled to expel Homer and Sophocles but we must invite Thrasymachus. Thrasymachus justly occu-

---

[46] Cf. Socrates' praise of Polemarchus in the *Phaedrus* 257b3–4.

pies the central place among the interlocutors of the *Republic*, the place between the pair consisting of the father and the son and the pair consisting of the brothers. Socrates and Thrasymachus "have just become friends" because Socrates had just said that in order to escape destruction, the city must not permit philosophizing, and especially that philosophizing which is concerned with "speeches," to the young, *i.e.* the gravest kind of "corrupting the young"; Adeimantus believes that Thrasymachus will be passionately opposed to this proposal; but Socrates who knows better holds that by making that proposal he has become the friend of Thrasymachus who is or plays the city. After having become the friend of Thrasymachus, Socrates turns to vindicating the many against the charge that they cannot be persuaded of the worth of philosophy or to taming the many (497d8–498d4, 499d8–500a8, 501c4–502a4). His success with the many however is not genuine since they are not present or since the many whom he tames are not the many in deed but only the many in speech; he lacks the art of taming the many in deed which is only the reverse side of the art of arousing the many to anger, that single art which is the art of Thrasymachus. The many will have to be addressed by Thrasymachus and he who has listened to Socrates will succeed.

But if this is so why did not the philosophers of old, to say nothing of Socrates himself, succeed in persuading the multitude, directly or through such intermediaries as Thrasymachus, of the supremacy of philosophy and the philosophers and thus bring about the rule of the philosophers and therewith the salvation and the happiness of their cities? Strange as it may sound, in this part of the conversation it appears easier to persuade the multitude to accept the rule of the philosophers than to persuade the philosophers to rule the multitude: the philosophers cannot be persuaded, they can only be compelled to rule the cities (499b–c, 500d4–5, 520a–d, 521b7, 539e2–3). Only the non-philosophers could compel the philosophers to take care of the city. But, given the prejudice against the philosophers, this compulsion will not be forthcoming if the philosophers do not in the first place persuade the non-philosophers to compel the philosophers to rule over them, and this persuasion will not be forthcoming, given the philosophers' unwillingness to rule. We arrive then at the conclusion that the just city is not possible because of the philosophers' unwillingness to rule.

Why are the philosophers unwilling to rule? Being dominated

by the desire, the *eros*, for knowledge as the one thing needful, or knowing that philosophy is the most pleasant and blessed possession, the philosophers have no leisure for looking down at human affairs, let alone for taking care of them. They believe that while still alive they are already firmly settled far away from their cities in the "Islands of the Blessed." Hence only compulsion could induce them to take part in public life in the just city, *i.e.* in the city which regards the proper upbringing of the philosophers as its most important task. Having perceived the truly grand, the philosophers regard the human things as paltry. Their very justice—their abstaining from wronging their fellow human beings—flows from contempt for the things for which the non-philosophers hotly contest. They know that the life not dedicated to philosophy and therefore even political life at its best is like life in a cave, so much so that the city can be identified with the Cave.[47] The cave-dwellers, *i.e.* the non-philosophers, see only the shadows of artifacts (514b–515c). That is to say, whatever they perceive they understand in the light of opinions sanctified by the fiat of legislators, regarding the just and noble things, *i.e.* of fabricated or conventional opinions, and they do not know that these their most cherished convictions possess no higher status than that of opinions. For if even the best city stands or falls by a fundamental falsehood, albeit a noble falsehood, it can be expected that the opinions on which the imperfect cities rest or in which they believe will not be true, to say the least. Precisely the best of the non-philosophers, the good citizens, are passionately attached to these opinions and therefore passionately opposed to philosophy (517a) which is the attempt to go beyond opinion toward knowledge: the multitude is not as persuadable by the philosophers as we sanguinely assumed in an earlier part of the argument. This is the true reason why the coincidence of philosophy and political power is extremely improbable: philosophy and the city tend away from one another in opposite directions.

The difficulty of overcoming the natural tension between the city and the philosophers induces Socrates to turn from the question whether the just city is "possible" in the sense of being conformable to human nature, to the question of whether the just city is "possible" in the sense of being capable of being brought to light by the transformation of an actual city. The first question, understood

---

[47] 485b, 486a–b, 496c6, 499c1, 501d1–5, 517c7–9, 519c2–d7, 539e.

in contradistinction to the second, points to the question whether the just city could not come into being through the settling together of men who were before wholly unassociated. To this question Socrates tacitly gives a negative answer by turning to the question of whether the just city could be brought into being by the transformation of an actual city. The good city cannot be brought to light out of human beings who have not yet undergone any human discipline, out of "primitives" or "stupid animals" or "savages" cruel or gentle—the good city cannot be brought to light out of the healthy city of the *Republic;* the potential members of the good city must already have acquired the rudiments of civilized life; the process of long duration during which pre-political men become political men cannot be the work of the founder or legislator of the good city but is presupposed by him (cf. 376e2–4). But on the other hand, if the potential good city must be an old city, its citizens will have become thoroughly moulded by the imperfect laws or customs of their city, hallowed by antiquity, and will have become passionately attached to them. Socrates is therefore compelled to revise his original suggestion according to which the rule of the philosophers is the necessary and sufficient condition for the coming into being of the just city. Whereas he had originally suggested that the good city will come into being if the philosophers become kings, he finally suggests that the good city will come into being if, when the philosophers have become kings, they expel everyone older than ten from the city, *i.e.* separate the children completely from their parents and their parents' ways and bring them up in the entirely novel ways of the good city (540d–541b; cf. 499b; 501a,e). By taking over a city, the philosophers make sure that their subjects will not be savages; by expelling everyone older than ten, they make sure that their subjects will not be enslaved by any traditional civility. The solution is elegant but it leaves one wondering how the philosophers can compel everyone older than ten to obey submissively the command decreeing the expulsion and the separation, since they cannot yet have trained a warrior class absolutely obedient to them. This is not to deny that Socrates could have persuaded many fine young men, and not a few old ones, not indeed to leave the city and to live in the fields, but to believe that the multitude could be, not indeed compelled, but persuaded by the philosophers to leave their city and their children to the philosophers and to live in the fields so that justice will be done.

The just city is then impossible. It is impossible because it is against nature. It is against nature that there should ever be a "cessation of evils," "for it is necessary that there should always be something opposed to the good, and evil necessarily wanders about the mortal nature and the region here."[48] It is against nature that rhetoric should have the power ascribed to it: that it should be able to overcome the resistance rooted in men's love of their own and ultimately in the body; as Aristotle puts it, the soul can rule the body only despotically, not by persuasion; the *Republic* repeats, in order to overcome it, the error of the sophists regarding the power of speech. The just city is against nature because the equality of the sexes and absolute communism are against nature. It holds no attraction for anyone except for such lovers of justice as are willing to destroy the family as something essentially conventional and to exchange it for a society in which no one knows of parents, children, and brothers and sisters who are not conventional. The *Republic* would not be the work which it is if this kind of lover of justice were not the most outstanding kind in the practically most important sense of justice. Or to state this in a manner which is perhaps more easily intelligible today, the *Republic* conveys the broadest and deepest analysis of political idealism ever made.

That part of the *Republic* which deals with philosophy is the most important part of the book. Accordingly it transmits the answer to the question regarding justice to the extent to which that answer is given in the *Republic*. The just man, we recall, is the man in whom each part of the soul does its work well. But only in the philosopher does the best part of the soul, reason, do its work well, and this is not possible if the two other parts of the soul do not do their work well also: the philosopher is necessarily by nature both courageous and moderate (487a2–5). Only the philosopher can be truly just. But the work with which the philosopher is concerned above everything else is intrinsically attractive and in fact the most pleasant work, regardless of what consequences it may entail (583a). Hence only in philosophy do justice and happiness coincide. In other words, the philosopher is the only individual who is just in the sense in which the city can be just: he is self-sufficient, truly free, or his life is as little devoted to the service of other individuals as the life of the city is devoted to the service of other cities. But

---

[48] *Theaetetus* 176a5–8; cf. *Laws* 896e4–6.

the philosopher in the good city is just also in the sense that he serves his fellow men, his fellow citizens, his city, or that he obeys the law. That is to say, the philosopher is just also in the sense in which all members of the just city, and in a way all just members of any city, regardless of whether they are philosophers or not, are just. Yet justice in this second sense is not intrinsically attractive or choiceworthy for its own sake but is good only with a view to its consequences; or it is not noble but necessary: the philosopher serves the city, even the good city, not, as he seeks the truth, from natural inclination, from *eros*, but under compulsion (519e–520b; 540b4–5, e1–2). Justice in the first sense may be said to be the advantage of the stronger, *i.e.* of the most superior man, and justice in the second sense the advantage of the weaker, *i.e.* of the inferior men. It should not be necessary but it is necessary to add that compulsion does not cease to be compulsion if it is self-compulsion.[49] According to a notion of justice which is more common than the one referred to in Socrates' definition, justice consists in not harming others; justice thus understood proves to be in the highest case merely a concomitant of the philosopher's greatness of soul. But if justice is taken in the larger sense according to which it consists in giving to each what is good for his soul, one must distinguish between the cases in which such giving is intrinsically attractive to the giver (these will be the cases of the potential philosophers) and those in which it is merely a duty or compulsory. This distinction, incidentally, underlies the difference between the voluntary conversations of Socrates (the conversations which he spontaneously seeks) and the compulsory ones (those which he cannot with propriety avoid). The clear distinction between the justice which is choiceworthy for its own sake wholly regardless of its consequences, and identical with philosophy, and the justice which is merely necessary, and identical in the highest imaginable case with the rule of the philosopher, is rendered possible by the abstraction from *eros* which is characteristic of the *Republic*—an abstraction which is also effective in the simile of the Cave in so far as that simile presents the ascent from the cave to the light of the sun as entirely compulsory (515c5–516a1). For one might well say that there is no reason why the philosopher should not engage in political activity out of that kind of love of one's own which is patriotism.[50]

---

[49] Kant, *Metaphysik der Sitten*, Einleitung zur Tugendlehre I and II.

[50] Consider *Apology of Socrates* 30a3–4.

By the end of the seventh book justice has come to sight fully. Socrates has performed the duty laid upon him by Glaucon and Adeimantus to show that justice is choiceworthy for its own sake, regardless of its consequences, and therefore that it is unqualifiedly preferable to injustice. Nevertheless the conversation continues, for it seems that our clear grasp of justice does not include a clear grasp of injustice but must be supplemented by a clear grasp of the wholly unjust city and the wholly unjust man: only after we have seen the wholly unjust city and the wholly unjust man with the same clarity with which we have seen the wholly just city and the wholly just man will we be able to judge whether we ought to follow Socrates' friend Thrasymachus who chooses injustice or Socrates himself who chooses justice (545a2–b2; cf. 498c9–d1). This in turn requires that the fiction of the possibility of the just city be maintained. As a matter of fact, the *Republic* never abandons the fiction that the just city as a society of human beings, as distinguished from a society of gods or sons of gods (*Laws* 739b–e), is possible. When Socrates turns to the study of injustice, it even becomes necessary for him to reaffirm this fiction with greater force than ever before. The unjust city will be uglier, more condemnable, more deserving indignation in proportion as the just city will be more possible. Anger, indignation (Adeimantus' favorite passion—cf. 426e4 with 366c6–7), spiritedness could never come into their own if the just city were not possible. Or inversely, exaltation of spiritedness is the inevitable by-product of the utopia—of the belief that the cessation of evils is possible—taken seriously; the belief that all evil is due to human fault (cf. 379c5–7 and 617e4–5) makes man infinitely responsible; it leads to the consequence that not only vice but all evil is voluntary. But the possibility of the just city will remain doubtful if the just city was never actual. Accordingly Socrates asserts now that the just city was once actual. More precisely, he makes the Muses assert it or rather imply it. The assertion that the just city was once actual, that it was actual in the beginning is, as one might say, a mythical assertion which agrees with the mythical premise that the best is the oldest. Socrates asserts then through the mouth of the Muses that the good city was actual in the beginning, prior to the emergence of evil, *i.e.* of the inferior kind of city (547b): the inferior cities are decayed forms of the good city, soiled fragments of the pure city which was entire; hence, the nearer in time a kind of inferior city is to the just city, the better it is, or vice versa. It is more proper to speak of the good and inferior regimes than of the good and inferior cities (cf. the transition from "cities" to "regimes" in 543c7ff.). According to Socrates, there are five kinds of regime worth mentioning: (1) kingship or aristocracy, (2) timocracy, (3) oligarchy, (4) democracy, and (5) tyranny. The descending order of regimes is modelled on Hesiod's descending order of the five races of men: the races of gold, of silver, of bronze, the divine race of heroes, the race of iron (546e–547a; Hesiod, *Works and Days* 106ff.). We see at once that the Platonic equivalent of Hesiod's divine race of heroes is democracy. We shall have to find the reason for this seemingly strange correspondence.

The *Republic* is based on the assumption that there is a strict parallel between the city and the soul. Accordingly Socrates asserts that just as there are five kinds of regimes, there are five kinds of characters of men. The distinction which for a short while was popular in present-day political science between the authoritarian and the democratic "personalities," as corresponding to the distinction between authoritarian and democratic societies, was a dim and crude reflection of Socrates' distinction between the kingly or aristocratic, the timocratic, the oligarchic, the democratic, and the tyrannical souls or men, as corresponding to the aristocratic, timocratic, oligarchic, democratic, and tyrannical regimes. In this connection one might mention that in describing the regimes Socrates does not speak of "ideologies" belonging to them; he is concerned with the character of each kind of regime and with the end which it manifestly and knowingly pursues as well as with the political justification of the end in question in contradistinction to any transpolitical justification stemming from cosmology, theology, metaphysics, philosophy of history, or myth. In his study of the inferior regimes he examines in each case first the regime and then the corresponding individual. He presents both the regime and the corresponding individual as coming into being out of the preceding one. We shall consider here only his account of democracy because of its crucial importance for the argument of the *Republic*. Democracy arises from oligarchy which in its turn arises from timocracy, the rule of insufficiently music warriors who are characterized by the supremacy of spiritedness. Oligarchy is the first regime in which desire is supreme. In oligarchy the ruling desire is that for wealth or money or unlimited acquisitiveness. The oligarchic man is thrifty and industrious, controls all desires other than the desire for money, lacks education and possesses a superficial honesty derivative from the crudest self-interest. Oligarchy gives to each the unqualified right to dispose of his property as he sees fit. It thus renders inevitable the emergence of "drones," *i.e.* of members of the ruling class who are either burdened with debt or already bankrupt and hence disfranchised—of beggars who hanker after their squandered fortunes and hope to restore their fortunes and political power through a change of regime. Besides, the correct oligarchs themselves, being both rich and unconcerned with virtue and honor, render themselves and especially their sons fat, spoiled, and soft. They thus become despised by the lean and tough poor. Democracy comes into being when the poor, having become aware of their superiority to the rich and perhaps led by some drones who act as traitors to their class and possess skills which ordinarily only members of a ruling class possess, at an opportune moment make themselves masters of the city by defeating the rich, killing and exiling some of them and permitting the rest to live with them in possession of full citizen rights. Democracy itself is characterized by freedom which includes the right to say and do whatever one wishes: everyone can follow the way of life which pleases him most. Hence democracy is the regime which fosters the greatest variety: every way of life, every regime can be found in it. Hence, we must understand, democracy is the only regime other than the best in which the philosopher can lead his peculiar way of life without being disturbed: it is for this reason that with some exaggeration one can compare democracy to Hesiod's age of the divine race of heroes which comes closer to the golden age than any other. Plato himself called the Athenian democracy, looking back on it from the rule of the Thirty Tyrants, "golden" (*Seventh Letter* 324d7–8). Since democracy, in contradistinction to the three other bad regimes, is both bad and permissive, it is that regime in which the frank quest for the best regime is at home: the action of the *Republic* takes place under a democracy. Certainly in a democracy the citizen who is a philosopher is under no compulsion to participate in political life or to hold office. One is thus led to wonder why Socrates did not assign to democracy the highest place among the inferior regimes or rather the highest place simply, seeing that the best regime is not possible. One could say that he showed his preference for democracy by deed: by spending his whole life in democratic Athens, by fighting for her in her wars and by dying in obedience to her laws. However this may be, he surely did not prefer democracy to all other regimes in speech. The reason is that, being a just man in more than one sense, he thought of the well-being not merely of the philosophers but of the non-philosophers as well, and he held that democracy is not designed for inducing the non-philosophers to attempt to become as good as they possibly can, for the end of democracy is not virtue but freedom, i.e. the freedom to live either nobly or basely according to one's liking. Therefore he assigns to democracy a rank even lower than to oligarchy since oligarchy requires some kind of restraint whereas democracy, as he presents it, abhors every kind of restraint. One could say that, adapting himself to his subject matter, he abandons all restraint when speaking of the regime which loathes restraint. In a democracy, he asserts, no one is compelled to rule or to be ruled, if he does not like it; he can live at peace while his city is at war; sentence to capital punishment does not have the slightest consequence for the condemned man: he is not even jailed; the order of rulers and ruled is completely reversed: the father behaves as if he were a boy and the son neither respects nor fears the father, the teacher fears his pupils while the pupils pay no attention to the teacher, and there is complete equality of the sexes; even horses and donkeys no longer step aside when encountering human beings. Plato writes as if the Athenian democracy had not carried out Socrates' execution, and Socrates speaks as if the Athenian democracy had not engaged in an orgy of bloody persecution of guilty and innocent alike when the Hermes statues were mutilated at the beginning of the Sicilian expedition.[51] Socrates' exaggeration of the licentious mildness of classical democracy is matched by an almost equally strong exaggeration of the intemperance of democratic man. He could indeed not avoid the latter exaggeration if he did not wish to deviate from the procedure which he follows in his discussion of the inferior regimes. That procedure—a consequence of the parallel between the city and the individual—consists in understanding the man corresponding to an inferior regime as the son of a father corresponding to the preceding regime. Hence the democratic man comes to sight as the son of an oligarchic father, as the degenerate son of a wealthy father who is concerned with nothing but making money: the democratic man is a drone, the fat, soft, and prodigal

---

[51] Thucydides VI 27–29, 53–61.

playboy, the Lotus-eater who, assigning a kind of equality to equal and unequal things, lives one day in complete surrender to the lowest desires and the next day ascetically, or who according to Marx's ideal "goes hunting in the morning, fishing in the afternoon, raises cattle in the evening, devotes himself to philosophy after dinner,"[52] i.e. does at all times what he happens to like; the democratic man is not the lean, tough and thrifty peasant or craftsman who has a single job (cf. 564c9–565b1, 575c). Socrates' deliberately exaggerated blame of democracy becomes intelligible to some extent once one considers its immediate addressee, the austere Adeimantus, who is not a friend of laughter and who had been the addressee of the austere discussion of poetry in the section on the education of the warriors: by his exaggerated blame of democracy Socrates lends words to Adeimantus' "dream" of democracy (cf. 563d2 with 389a7). One must also not forget that the sanguine account of the multitude, which was provisionally required in order to prove the harmony between the city and philosophy, is in need of being redressed; the exaggerated blame of democracy reminds us again of the disharmony between philosophy and the people.

After Socrates has brought to light the entirely unjust regime and the entirely unjust man and then compared the life of the entirely unjust man with that of the perfectly just man, it becomes clear beyond the shadow of a doubt that justice is preferable to injustice. Nevertheless the conversation continues. Socrates suddenly returns to the subject of poetry, a subject which had already been discussed at great length when the education of the warriors was being considered. We must try to understand this apparently unmotivated return. In an explicit digression from the discussion of tyranny, Socrates had noted that the poets praise tyrants and are honored by tyrants (and also by democracy) whereas they are not honored by the three better regimes (568a8–d4). Tyranny and democracy are characterized by the surrender to the sensual desires, including the most lawless ones. The tyrant is *Eros* incarnate. And the poets sing the praise of *Eros*. They pay very great attention and homage precisely to that phenomenon from which Socrates abstracts in the *Republic* to the best of his powers. The poets therefore foster injustice. So does Thrasymachus. Therefore, just as in spite of this Socrates could become a friend of Thrasymachus, there is no reason

---

[52] *Die deutsche Ideologie* (Berlin: Dietz Verlag, 1955) 30.

why he could not be a friend of the poets and especially of Homer. Perhaps Socrates needs the poets in order to restore, on another occasion, the dignity of *eros*: the *Banquet*, the only Platonic dialogue in which Socrates is shown to converse with poets, is devoted entirely to the praise of *eros*.

When using the fate of Thrasymachus in the *Republic* as a key to the truth about poetry, we are mindful of the kinship between rhetoric and poetry as indicated in the *Gorgias* (502b1–d9). But we must not overlook the difference between rhetoric and poetry. There are two kinds of rhetoric, the erotic rhetoric described in the *Phaedrus*, of which Socrates was a master and which is surely not represented by Thrasymachus, and the other kind which is represented by Thrasymachus. That other kind consists of three forms: forensic, deliberative, and epideictic. The *Apology of Socrates* is a piece of forensic rhetoric, while in the *Menexenus* Socrates plays with epideictic rhetoric. Socrates does not engage in deliberative rhetoric, *i.e.* in political rhetoric proper. The closest approximation to deliberative rhetoric in the *Corpus Platonicum* would seem to be Pausanias' speech in the *Banquet* in which the speaker proposes a change, favorable to lovers, in the Athenian law regarding *eros*.

The foundation for the return to poetry in the tenth book was laid at the very beginning of the discussion of the inferior regimes and the inferior souls. The transition from the best regime to the inferior regimes was explicitly ascribed to the Muses speaking "tragically," and the transition from the best man to the inferior men has in fact a slightly "comical" character (545d7–e3, 549c2–e2): poetry takes the lead when the descent from the highest theme— justice understood as philosophy—begins. The return to poetry, which is preceded by the account of the inferior regimes and the inferior souls, is followed by a discussion of "the greatest rewards for virtue," *i.e.* the rewards not inherent in justice or philosophy as such (608c, 614a). The second discussion of poetry constitutes the center of that part of the *Republic* in which the conversation descends from the highest theme. This cannot be surprising, for philosophy as quest for the truth is the highest activity of man and poetry is not concerned with the truth.

In the first discussion of poetry, which preceded by a long time the introduction of philosophy as a theme, poetry's unconcern with the truth was its chief recommendation, for at that time it was untruth that was needed (377a1–6). The most excellent poets were expelled from the city, not because they teach untruth but because they teach the wrong kind of untruth. But in the meantime it has become clear that only the life of the philosophizing man in so far as he philosophizes is the just life, and that life, so far from needing untruth, utterly rejects it (485c3–d5). The progress from the city, even the best city, to the philosopher requires, it seems, a progress from the qualified acceptance of poetry to its unqualified rejection.

In the light of philosophy poetry reveals itself as the imitation of imitations of the truth, *i.e.* of the ideas. The contemplation of the ideas is the activity of the philosopher, the imitation of the ideas is the activity of the ordinary artisan, and the imitation of the works of artisans is the activity of the poets and other "imitative" artisans. To begin with, Socrates presents the order of rank in these terms: the maker of the ideas (*e.g.* of the idea of the bed) is the god, the maker of the imitation (of the bed which can be used) is the artisan, and the maker of the imitation of the imitation (of the painting of a bed) is the imitative artisan. In the repetition he states the order of rank in these terms: first the user, then the artisan, and finally the imitative artisan. The idea of the bed, we shall then say, resides in the user who determines the "form" of the bed with a view to the end for which it is to be used. The user is then the one who possesses the highest or most authoritative knowledge: the highest knowledge is not that of any artisan as such at all; the poet who stands at the opposite pole from the user does not possess any knowledge, not even right opinion (601c6–602b11). The preference given to the arts proper which are concerned with the useful rather than with a certain kind of the beautifully pleasant (389e12–390a5) is in agreement with the notion that the good city is a city of artisans or with the abstraction from *eros*. Nor shall we overlook the fact that the order of rank referred to in the first half of the tenth book abstracts from the warriors: it looks as if the healthy city, which did not know warriors or imitative artisans (373b5–7), were to be restored with its natural head—the philosophers—added to it. In order to understand Socrates' seemingly outrageous judgment on poetry, one must first identify the artisans whose work the poet imitates. The poets' themes are above all human beings as referred to virtue and vice; the poets see the human things in the light of virtue; but the virtue toward which they look is an imperfect and even distorted image of virtue (598e1–2, 599c6–d3, 600e4–5). The artisan whom the poet imitates is the non-philosophic legislator who is himself an imperfect imitator of virtue (cf. 501b and 514b4–515a3). In particular, justice as understood by the city is necessarily the work of the legislator, for the just as understood by the city is the legal. No one expressed Socrates' suggestion more clearly than Nietzsche who said that "the poets were always the valets of some morality."[53] But according to the French saying, for a valet there is no hero: are the poets (at least those who are not entirely stupid) not aware of the secret weaknesses of their heroes? This is indeed the case according to Socrates. The poets bring to light, for instance, the full force of the grief which a man feels for the loss of someone dear to him—of a feeling to which a respectable man would not give adequate utterance except when he is alone because its adequate utterance in the presence of others is not becoming and lawful: the poets bring to light that in our nature which the law forcibly restrains (603e3–604b8, 606a3–607a9). The poets as spokesmen of the passions oppose the legislator as spokesman of reason. Yet the non-philosophic legislator is not unqualifiedly the spokesman of reason; his laws are very far from being simply the dictates of reason. The poets have a broader view of human life as the conflict between passion and reason (390d1–6) than do the legislators; they show the limitations of law. But if this is so, if the poets are perhaps the men who understand best the nature of the passions which the law should restrain, they are very far from being merely the servants of the legislators but also the men from whom the prudent legislator will learn. The genuine "quarrel between philosophy and poetry" (607b5–6) concerns, from the philosopher's point of view, not the worth of poetry as such, but the order of rank of philosophy and poetry. According to Socrates, poetry is legitimate only as ministerial to the "user" *par excellence,* to the king (597e7) who is the philosopher, and not as autonomous. For autonomous poetry presents human life as autonomous, *i.e.* not as directed toward the philosophic life, and it therefore never presents the philosophic life except in its distortion by comedy; hence autonomous poetry (regardless of whether it is dramatic or not) is necessarily either tragedy or comedy (or some mixture of both) since the non-philosophic life has either no way out of its fundamental difficulty or else only an inept one. But ministerial poetry presents the non-philosophic life as ministerial to the philosophic life and therefore,

---

[53] *The Gay Science* nr. 1.

above all, the philosophic life itself (cf. 604e). The greatest example of ministerial poetry is the Platonic dialogue.

The *Republic* ends with a discussion of the greatest rewards for justice and the greatest punishments for injustice. The discussion consists of three parts: (1) proof of the immortality of the soul; (2) the divine and human rewards and punishments while man is alive; (3) the rewards and punishments after death. The central part is silent about philosophy: rewards for justice and punishments for injustice during life are needed for the non-philosophers whose justice does not have the intrinsic attractiveness which the justice peculiar to the philosophers has. No one who has understood the dual meaning of justice can fail to see the necessity of Socrates' "Philistine" utterance on the earthly rewards which the just, generally speaking, receive (613d, c4). Socrates, who knew Glaucon, is a better judge of what is good for Glaucon than any reader of the *Republic*, and surely than the modern "idealists" who shudder in a thoroughly unmanly way at the thought that men who are pillars of a stable society through their uprightness, which indeed must not be entirely divorced from ability or artfulness, are likely to be rewarded by their society. This thought is an indispensable corrective to Glaucon's exaggerated statement in his long speech about the extreme sufferings of the genuinely just man: Glaucon could not have known what a genuinely just man is. It cannot be the duty of a genuinely just man like Socrates to drive weaker men to despair of the possibility of some order and decency in human affairs, and least of all those who, by virtue of their inclinations, their descent, and their abilities, may have some public responsibility. For Glaucon it is more than enough that he will remember for the rest of his days and perhaps transmit to others the many grand and perplexing sights which Socrates has conjured for his benefit in that memorable night in the Piraeus. The account of the rewards and punishments after death is given in the form of a myth. The myth is not baseless since it is based on a proof of the immortality of the souls. The soul cannot be immortal if it is composed of many things unless the composition is most perfect. But the soul as we know it from our experience lacks that perfect harmony. In order to find out the truth, one would have to recover by reasoning the original or true nature of the soul (611b–612a). This reasoning is not achieved in the *Republic*. That is to say, Socrates proves the immortality of the soul without having brought to light the nature of the soul. The situation at the end of the *Republic* corresponds precisely to the situation at the end of the first book, where Socrates makes clear that he has proved that justice is salutary without knowing the What or nature of justice. The discussion following the first book does bring to light the nature of justice as the right order of the soul, yet how can one know the right order of the soul if one does not know the nature of the soul? Let us remember here again the fact that the parallel between soul and city, which is the premise of the doctrine of the soul stated in the *Republic*, is evidently questionable and even untenable. The *Republic* cannot bring to light the nature of the soul because it abstracts from the body and from *eros;* by abstracting from the body and *eros*, the *Republic* in fact abstracts from the soul; the *Republic* abstracts from nature; this abstraction is necessary if justice as full dedication to the common good of a particular city is to be praised as choiceworthy for its own sake; and why this praise is necessary, should not be in need of an argument. If we are concerned with finding out precisely what justice is, we must take "another longer way around" in our study of the soul than the way which is taken in the *Republic* (504b; cf. 506d). This does not mean that what we learn from the *Republic* about justice is not true or is altogether provisional. The first book surely does not teach what justice is, and yet by presenting Socrates' taming of Thrasymachus as an act of justice, it lets us see justice. The teaching of the *Republic* regarding justice can be true although it is not complete, in so far as the nature of justice depends decisively on the nature of the city—for even the trans-political cannot be understood as such except if the city is understood—and the city is completely intelligible because its limits can be made perfectly manifest: to see these limits, one need not have answered the question regarding the whole; it is sufficient for the purpose to have raised the question regarding the whole. The *Republic* then indeed makes clear what justice is. As Cicero has observed, the *Republic* does not bring to light the best possible regime but rather the nature of political things[54]—the nature of the city. Socrates makes clear in the *Republic* of what character the city would have to be in order to satisfy the highest need of man. By letting us see that the city constructed in accordance with this requirement is not possible, he lets us see the essential limits, the nature, of the city.

---

[54] *De republica* II 52.

*Chapter III*

# ON THUCYDIDES' WAR OF
# THE PELOPONNESIANS AND
# THE ATHENIANS

## 1. *Political Philosophy and Political History*

In turning from Aristotle and Plato to Thucydides, we seem to enter an entirely different world. This is no longer the world of political philosophy, of the quest for the best regime which is possible, although it never was, is, or will be actual, for the shining and pure temple built on a noble elevation, far away from vulgar clamor and everything else disharmonious. Seen in the light of the best polity, of the truly just order, of justice or philosophy, political life or political greatness loses much, if not all, of its charm; only the charm of the greatness of the founder and legislator seems to survive the severest of all tests. When we open Thucydides' pages, we become at once immersed in political life at its most intense, in bloody war both foreign and civil, in life and death struggles. Thucydides sees political life in its own light; he does not transcend it; he does not stand above the turmoil but in the midst of it; he takes seriously political life as it is; he knows only of actual cities, statesmen, commanders of armies and navies, citizens and demagogues as distinguished from founders and legislators; he presents to us political life in its harsh grandeur, ruggedness, and even squalor. It suffices to remember how Socrates on the one hand and Thucydides on the other speak of Themistocles and Pericles, and how Plato on the one hand and Thucydides on the other present Nicias. Thucydides sympathizes and makes us sympathize with political greatness as displayed in fighting for freedom and in the founding, ruling, and expanding of empires. The loudest event that takes place in the Platonic dialogues is the drunken Alcibiades' irruption into a banquet of his friends. Thucydides lets us hear the

delirious hopes at the beginning of the Sicilian expedition and the
indescribable anguish in the quarries of Syracuse. He looks at political things not only in the same direction as the citizen or statesman
but also within the same horizon. And yet he is not simply a political man. We indicate the difference between Thucydides and the
political man as such by calling Thucydides, as tradition bids us do,
a historian.

However profound the difference between Plato and Thucydides
may be, their teachings are not necessarily incompatible; they may
supplement one another. Thucydides' theme is the greatest war
known to him, the greatest "motion." The best city described in the
*Republic* (and in the *Politics*) is at rest. But in the sequel to the
*Republic* Socrates expresses the desire to see the best city "in motion," *i.e.* at war; "the best city in motion" is the necessary sequel
to the speech on the best city. Socrates feels unable to praise
properly, to present properly the best city in motion.[1] The philosopher's speech on the best city requires a supplement which the
philosopher cannot give. The description of the best city which
avoids everything accidental deals with a nameless city and nameless men living in an indeterminate place and at an indeterminate
time (cf. *Republic* 499c8–d1). Yet a war can only be a war between
this particular city and other particular cities, under these or these
leaders, at this or that time. Socrates seems to call for the assistance
of a man like Thucydides who could supplement political philosophy or complete it. As it happens, Critias, one of Socrates' three
interlocutors, had heard as a child from his very old grandfather
who had heard it from his father who had heard it from his kinsman
and close friend Solon who had heard it from an Egyptian priest
that in very ancient times Athens, being then a supremely excellent
city, waged war against Atlantis, an unbelievably large island in
the west; the people of Atlantis, led by their kings—men of mar-
vellously great power—attempted to enslave Athens and the rest
of Greece and all countries bordering on the Mediterranean; but
Athens, partly as leader of the Greeks and partly acting alone when
the others had deserted her, defeated the assailants and thus saved
all Mediterranean peoples from enslavement. It is this truthful
speech, not a fictitious myth (*Timaeus* 26e4–5), which is to be the
supplement to Socrates' account of the best city. It reminds of

---

[1] *Timaeus* 19b3–d2, 20b3.

Thucydides' work not only because it is an account of "the greatest motion" but because the Atlantic war reminds of the Peloponnesian war or more precisely of the Sicilian part of that war; the Atlantic war reminds of the Sicilian expedition while surpassing it infinitely. It surpasses it in the first place by the gigantic size both of the island in the west and of its armed host. It surpasses it above all by its glory: whereas the Athenians' unjust attack on the island in the west ended in ignominious defeat, the Athenians' just defense of all Greece and everything near to Greece against the unjustly attacking men of the island in the west ended in most glorious victory. The victory over Atlantis by far surpasses in magnitude and in glory the combined actual victory in the Persian war and the hoped-for victory in the Sicilian expedition. It looks as if some Critias had attempted to surpass Critias' competitor Alcibiades by a speech infinitely surpassing Alcibiades' deeds and plans which in themselves were already almost incredible. This however seems only to confirm the first impression of the relation between Plato and Thucydides: the Peloponnesian war was waged by an Athens which was informed by a regime regarded as defective by both Thucydides and Plato and which was known to them through their seeing it; the Atlantic war was waged by an Athens which was informed by a superlatively good regime and which is known only through the report of an Egyptian priest. Nevertheless there is one point of no small importance in which the two thinkers agree. Plato did not permit his Critias to describe Athens' superlative glory: he did not wish to allow an Athenian to praise Athens. Thucydides, the historian, was indeed compelled to permit his Pericles to praise Athens. But he did his best to prevent Pericles' Funeral Speech from being mistaken for his own praise of Athens.

Whichever way we turn, we seem to be compelled to fall back on the trite assertion that Thucydides is distinguished from Plato by the fact that he is a historian. To understand him as a historian is particularly easy for us, the sons of the age of historicism. There even seems to be a particularly close kinship between the "scientific history" of the nineteenth and twentieth centuries and Thucydides' thought; as a matter of fact, Thucydides has been called a "scientific historian." But the differences between Thucydides and the scientific historians are immense. In the first place, Thucydides limits himself severely to military and diplomatic history and at most to political history; while he does not ignore the "economic factor," he says amazingly little about it; he says next to nothing regarding cultural, religious, or intellectual history. Secondly, his work is meant to be a possession for all times, whereas the works of the scientific historians do not seriously claim to be "definitive." Thirdly, Thucydides does not merely narrate and explain actions and quote official documents but he inserts speeches, composed by him, of the actors. Yet Thucydides may be a historian without being a historian in the modern sense. What then is a historian in the pre-modern sense? According to Aristotle, the historian presents what has happened whereas the poet presents the kind of things that might happen: "therefore poetry is more philosophic and more serious than history, for poetry states rather the universals, history however states the singulars."[2] Poetry is between history and philosophy: history and philosophy stand at opposite poles; history is simply unphilosophic or pre-philosophic; it deals with individuals (individual human beings, individual cities, individual kingdoms or empires, individual confederations); whereas philosophy deals with the species as species, history does not even let us see the species in the individuals and through them as poetry does. Philosophy, for instance, deals with war as such, or the city as such, whereas Thucydides deals only with the war between the Peloponnesians and the Athenians. Aristotle thus shows implicitly that there is no opposition between philosophy and history, as little as there is between philosophy and poetry. But the question is whether Thucydides is a historian in Aristotle's sense. Occasionally Thucydides seems to suggest that he is a historian in that sense. The notion of history implied in the passage in question (I 97.2) may be stated as follows: it is desirable and even necessary that we should have at our disposal a continuous, reliable, and clear account of what men and cities did and suffered at all times, the account of each time being written by a contemporary. Yet Thucydides suggests this notion of history in order to explain or to excuse a seemingly unnecessary digression from his work; he does not suggest this notion when stating the reason why he wrote his work. Seen within the context of his whole work, that suggestion reads like a rejection of the view of history which it conveys. The reason why he rejects that view is not difficult to discern. When he explains why he wrote his account of the Peloponnesian war, he stresses the unique importance of that event. The vulgar notion, pre-modern or modern,

---

[2] *Poetics* 1451a36–b11.

of history does not make sufficient allowance for the difference between the important and the unimportant.

Above all, Thucydides surely lets us see the universal in the individual event which he narrates and through it: it is for this reason that his work is meant to be a possession for all times. On the basis of the Aristotelian remark one is therefore compelled to say that Thucydides is not a historian simply but a historian-poet; he does in the element of prose what the poets do in the element of poetry. Yet he is as little a historian-poet as he is a historian simply. While he states explicitly what he regards as his task, he does not state explicitly what he regards as the task of the historian. As a matter of fact, in contradistinction to Herodotus he never speaks of "history"; this fact alone could make one hesitate to call him a historian. He does state what he regards as the characteristic of the poets: the poets present things as bigger and grander than they are (I 21.1 and 10.1) whereas he presents them exactly as they are. The decisive reason why we must abandon the attempt to understand Thucydides in the light of the Aristotelian distinction is that that distinction presupposes philosophy and we have no right to assume that philosophy is present in Thucydides or for Thucydides. Perhaps Thucydides' "quest for the truth" (I 20.3) antedates essentially, *i.e.* not temporally, the distinction between history and philosophy. His work is meant to be a possession for all times because it enables those who will read it in future times to know the truth not only regarding the past, *i.e.* the Peloponnesian war and "the old things" preceding it (cf. I 1.3 beg.), but regarding their own times as well (I 22.4); the toil which Thucydides has invested in discovering the truth about the Peloponnesian war (and "the old things") will dispense those readers from investing a comparable toil in understanding the events of their times; his work presents the results of a kind of inquiry (or of "history") which makes that kind of inquiry superfluous. If we may use the Aristotelian distinction once more, Thucydides has discovered in the "singulars" of his time (and of "the old things") the "universal." It is not altogether misleading to refer to the Platonic parallel: Plato too can be said to have discovered in a singular event—in the singular life of Socrates—the universal and thus to have become able to present the universal through presenting a singular.

At the time when the tradition stemming from Aristotle was being decisively shaken, Hobbes turned from Aristotle to Thucydides. He too understood Thucydides as a historian as distinguished from a philosopher. But he understood the relation between the historian and the philosopher differently than did Aristotle. The philosopher's part is "the open conveyance of precepts" whereas history is "merely narrative." History too then conveys precepts; to take the most important example, according to Hobbes, Thucydides' work teaches the superiority of monarchy to any other form of government but especially to democracy. Yet at any rate in a good history "the narrative doth secretly instruct the reader, and more effectually than can possibly be done by precept." To support his assertion that Thucydides instructs his readers secretly, Hobbes adduces the judgments of Justus Lipsius and, above all, of Marcellinus: "Marcellinus saith, he was obscure on purpose; that the common people might not understand him. And not unlikely; for a wise man should so write (though in words understood by all men), that wise men only should be able to commend him." Since Thucydides is "the most politic historiographer that ever writ," his reader "may from the narrations draw out lessons to himself": Thucydides does not draw out the lessons. Hobbes sees then the characteristic difference between the historian (or at any rate the most politic historian) and the philosopher in the fact that the historian presents the universals silently. He takes it for granted that the speeches which Thucydides has inserted do not convey the instruction in question; the speeches are "of the contexture of the narrative."[3] This implies that no sentiment expressed in a speech of a Thucydidean character can be as such ascribed to Thucydides. This iron rule is not qualified but merely rendered more precise by the following corollary: the fact that a Thucydidean character expresses a given view proves that that view was known to Thucydides; it may therefore be used for completing a view stated by Thucydides himself if the former view is evidently implied in the latter view. Far from impairing Thucydides' reticence, the speeches only increase it. Since he is so reticent regarding the universals and the speeches are so rich in pithily and forcefully expressed statements regarding them, he as it were seduces the readers into taking these statements as expressing his own view. The temptation becomes almost irresistible when the speakers express views which no intelligent or decent man seems able to gainsay.

---

[3] Hobbes, *English Works* (ed. Molesworth) VIII, pp. viii, xvi–xvii, xxii, xxix, and xxxii. Cf. *Opera Latina* (ed. Molesworth) I, pp. lxxxviii and xiii–xiv.

If Thucydides is as reticent as Hobbes's suggestive remarks may induce us to think, it seems to be well-nigh impossible to establish Thucydides' teaching with any degree of certainty. Hobbes held that Thucydides, "as he was of regal descent, so he best approved of the regal government."[4] Hardly anyone living today would agree with this judgment. Today not a few people believe that Thucydides, far from being simply opposed to democracy, was in sympathy with the imperialism which went with the Athenian democracy or that he believed in "power politics"; accordingly they hold that Thucydides' comprehensive view is stated by the Athenians in their dialogue with the Melians. This interpretation is indeed rendered possible by Thucydides' reticence, by his failure to pass judgment on that dialogue. Yet the same silence would justify also the opposite interpretation. The contemporary interpreters of Thucydides who are perceptive note the presence in his thought of that which transcends "power politics," of what one may call the human or the humane. But if one addresses to Thucydides the question of how the power political and the humane are reconciled with one another, one receives no answer from him.[5]

After one has recovered from one's first impression, one is amazed to see how many and how important judgments Thucydides makes explicitly, in his own name. These judgments form the only legitimate starting point for the understanding of his teaching.

## 2. *The Case for Sparta: Moderation and the Divine Law*

Thucydides' first explicit judgment is to the effect that the war between the Peloponnesians and the Athenians was greater than the earlier wars. In order to prove this assertion, he must show "the weakness of the ancients." He thus deprives antiquity of the splendor which, it seems, was the work of the poets who celebrated antiquity. While following the way from ancient weakness to present strength, he sketches the emergence of the protagonists of the present war, of Athens and Sparta. Because of the poverty of the soil of their country which therefore was not desired by others, the Athenians were left in peace and thus their city grew to some greatness much earlier than Sparta. The Athenians were the first who, relaxing the ancient, barbaric style of life, turned toward

---

[4] *English Works* VIII, p. xvii.
[5] Karl Reinhardt, *Vermächtnis der Antike* (Göttingen, 1960) 216–217.

rather luxurious practices. Yet the Spartans were the first to introduce a style of life which is peculiarly Greek, a style of republican
simplicity and equality, a mean between barbaric penury and barbaric pomp. Accordingly, Sparta has enjoyed order and freedom
from a very old time without interruption; her regime has remained
the same during the preceding 400 years; her regime is then the
oldest of the present Greek regimes; her regime, *i.e.* not war, was
and is the source of her outstanding power. Sparta liberated Greece
from the rule of tyrants and, above all, she was the leader of the
Greeks in the Persian war. Sparta's power is greater than her "looks"
might seem to bear out: hers is a solid power. The connection
between Sparta's power and her regime to which Thucydides draws
our attention near the beginning of his book is brought out most
clearly in what he says about Sparta near the end: the Spartans,
above all others of whom Thucydides had any direct knowledge,
succeeded in being prosperous and moderate at the same time.
The Athenians became moderate and established a moderate
regime induced by disaster, when they were cast down by fright.
The Spartans on the other hand were moderate also in prosperity
thanks to their stable and moderate regime which bred moderation.[6]
Thucydides' taste is the same as that of Plato and Aristotle.

Someone might say that Sparta's superiority with regard to
republican virtue, political stability, and moderation is only the
reverse side of her inferiority in other, perhaps more important
respects, for instance regarding imperial greatness and brilliance.
This objection receives apparent support from Thucydides' final
judgment on the manner of the two antagonists: the Athenians were
militarily superior to the Spartans because they were quick and
enterprising whereas the Spartans were slow and unwilling to dare
(VIII 96.5). Considering the kinship between slowness, caution,
circumspection, and moderation,[7] the judgment could be thought to
imply that moderation is a defect in war. But even in this respect
moderation is not unqualifiedly a defect; after all, the Spartans won
the war. However this may be, we surely must find out what Thucydides thinks of the status of moderation simply.

Thucydides reveals his taste most explicitly and most comprehensively in his reflections on how the civil wars which occurred in

---

[6] I 2.5–6, 6.3–5, 10.2–3, 13.1, 15.2, 18.1–2, VIII 1, 24.4, 96–97.
[7] Plato, *Charmides* 159bff.

the Greek cities during the Peloponnesian war affected the manners of judging and of acting (III 82–83). These manners became altogether depraved. The depravation showed itself in the abandonment of the customary praising and blaming as well as of the customary ways of acting. It consisted in the complete triumph of the spirit of daring and its kin over that of moderation and its kin. Men came to praise the most reckless daring, quickness, anger, revenge, distrust, secrecy, and fraud, and to blame moderation, caution, trust, good-naturedness, open and frank dealings; what was called manliness took the place of moderation. The decay in speech and in deed of moderation was accompanied by the decay of respect for law, not only for the laws laid down by men but for the divine law as well,[8] and for right and the benefit of the city as distinguished from the benefit of one's faction (be it the many or the few). Moderation, justice, and piety belong together; their enemy calls itself daring and shrewdness or intelligence. While not every civil war is a consequence of foreign war and not every foreign war culminates in civil war, there is nevertheless a kinship between war and civil war: both cities and individuals have better thoughts in peace and when things go well than in war; war is a violent teacher, *i.e.* a teacher of violence by violence, which strengthens the angry passions not indeed of all men but of most; war is an intermediate stage between peace and civil war. This means that moderation, justice, and piety and the praise of these ways of conduct are at home in the city at peace rather than in the city at war. From all this it would seem to follow that the fully developed contrast between Sparta and Athens is that between the city at peace and the city in the grip of civil war. It would seem to follow more particularly that a good regime (like the Spartan) is averse to war and will avoid every war which can be avoided. Above all, it would seem to follow that even if moderation should be a handicap in war, its superiority to its opposite will not become doubtful.

The depravation caused by civil war, that man-made plague,

---

[8] The divine law is preceded in the context (III 82.6) by kinship (the family) and the established laws (the city); the order appears to be one of ascent. Here Thucydides no longer speaks of the change in the meaning of words (*ibid.* 4–5); he does not mean that in civil war kinship, etc., are no longer called kinship, etc., but that they are no longer held in high esteem. As a consequence, he does not tell us what piety (*ibid.* 8) is called after it has fallen into contempt.

resembles the depravation caused by the plague proper. The over-whelming force of the plague, the universal insecurity brought about general lawlessness, the surrender to the pleasures of the moment. Neither fear of the gods or piety nor human law restrained anyone. The distinction between the pleasant and the noble collapsed: the noble was sacrificed to the pleasant (II 52.3, 53). Depravation is, above all, the destruction of moderation.

Thucydides' favorable judgment on Sparta—a judgment whose major premise is the goodness of moderation, justice, and piety—is reflected in some of the speeches which he has inserted. The judgments of his speakers cannot be identical with his own since the speakers are not simply concerned with the truth but with the interests of their city or faction. The Corinthian's first speech in Sparta (I 68–71) is meant to incite the Spartans to go to war at once against Athens. In order to show the Spartans the magnitude of the danger threatening them at the hands of the Athenians and also to explain the Spartans' seeming inability to comprehend that danger, they contrast the Spartan character with the Athenian. The characteristic Spartan qualities are said to be these: moderation, tranquillity or restfulness, satisfaction with what they possess, hence clinging to immutable laws and aversion to being away from home, old-fashionedness, reliability, and trust among themselves coupled with distrust of foreigners and hence neglect, even betrayal, of their allies, hesitation, slowness, lack of inventiveness, no trust even in the safest calculations, apprehensiveness. The Athenian manner is the opposite: always restless, innovating, quick to invent and to execute, daring beyond their power, full of hope, and so on. The Spartans will have to change their manners and to assimilate themselves to the Athenians in order to overcome the danger. The Athenians who reply to the Corinthians (I 72–78) wish to induce the Spartans to remain at rest and to deliberate slowly. They wish then to induce the Spartans to continue in their manner which proved to be so conducive to Athens' increase. Accordingly they must show that the difference between Athens and Sparta is not as radical, as dangerous to Sparta, as the Corinthians had asserted. They do this partly by being silent about that difference and partly by stating generally that the Athenian manner is not different from the manner common to all men (and hence also to the Spartans): the difference is due only to the difference of circumstances. They are almost silent about the possibility that the difference of circumstances might have brought about the very difference of manner which is stressed by Thucydides himself, by the Corinthians and above all by Pericles in his Funeral Speech. They do say that the primary motive for Athenian expansion was fear or concern with security. Yet even they speak with pride of the singular daring and intelligence to which Athens owes her greatness. The Spartan king Archidamus who was reputed to be both intelligent and moderate wishes to preserve the peace (I 79–85). He recommends tranquil and slow deliberation. He is therefore compelled to defend the Spartan manner which according to the Corinthians has brought Sparta into grave danger. At the same time he must, just as the Athenians and for the same reason, minimize the difference between the Spartan and the Athenian manner. This Spartan, we may say, is compelled to praise the Spartan manner in a Spartan manner. His speech breathes sober apprehension regarding the proposed war or the absence of all hope except regarding the possibility of reaching some peaceful agreement with Athens; that hope is based on the possibility that the Athenians might prefer in the Spartan manner the tranquil possession of what they have to the risks of war. He asserts that the Spartan qualities to which the Corinthians objected are the cause of Spartan freedom and her outstanding renown. Moderation guarantees against insolent pride in success and against abjectness in disaster. It makes the Spartans wise in counsel and brave in battle, for it is akin to reverance or sense of shame which in its turn is akin to bravery, and it makes them submit to the superior wisdom of the laws.

Even if Thucydides would have agreed with Archidamus in every other point, he disagreed with his appraisal of the situation. According to Thucydides, the Spartans who were so averse to taking risks and so slow to go to war were compelled by the Athenians to go to war against the Athenians. Thucydides agrees then in effect with the harsh and unpleasant Spartan ephor who opposed Archidamus' peaceable counsel in the Spartan assembly; Thucydides does not say that Archidamus had in fact good judgment but merely that he was reputed to have good judgment (I 23.6, 84, 88, 118.2). If we take into consideration the connection between moderation, reverence for antiquity, and above all for the divine law, we are not surprised to learn that when the Spartans sent to Delphi to ask the god whether they should go to war against Athens, he assured them of victory if they would wage that war with all their might, and told them in addition that he himself would help them, called or uncalled (I 118.3). And the Spartans won the war.

If we take into consideration the connection between moderation, gentleness, justice, and the divine law, we understand not only Thucydides' admiration for the Spartan manner, but above all his humanity which might seem to come to sight only on the margin of a power-political text but which is more likely to point to the boundary or limit separating lawful and unlawful politics. He reveals his compassion for the victims of angry passion or even murderous savagery most clearly when he speaks of the lamentable disaster which befell Mycalessus, a small town possessing a large school for children—of the senseless and cowardly butchery of women, children, and beasts (VII 29.4–5, 30.3). He reveals himself above all in his remark about the fate of Nicias: Nicias deserved least of all Greeks of Thucydides' time his disastrous end because of his full dedication, guided and inspired by law, to the practice of excellence (VII 86.5; cf. 77.2–3). As Thucydides narrates in the same context, Nicias' fellow commander Demosthenes came to a no less disastrous end. But—this is implied in his judgment on Nicias—Demosthenes' fate was not so entirely undeserved as that of Nicias, since Demosthenes was not as fully dedicated to law-bred virtue. The connection, expected by Thucydides, between the dedication, guided by law and surely also by divine law, to virtue and a good end, between desert and fate, points to the rule of just gods.

After Thucydides had completed the proof of his assertion that the ancients were weak and in addition had spoken of his manner of treating both the ancient things and the Peloponnesian war itself, he adds a chapter (I 23) which concludes his Introduction in an apparently strange way. The chapter ceases to appear strange if one reads it by itself with a view to the question of how it might be a fitting conclusion to the Introduction, and if one keeps in mind the message conveyed by Thucydides' most comprehensive judgments. The chapter consists of two parts, the first proving again the superiority of the Peloponnesian war to all earlier wars and the second dealing with the causes of the Peloponnesian war. In the first part Thucydides proves the superiority of the Peloponnesian war to the Persian war which was the greatest of the earlier deeds and therewith to all earlier wars by showing that the Peloponnesian war surpassed the Persian war in regard to human sufferings. These sufferings were caused partly by men and partly by what we are tempted to call natural catastrophes: earthquakes, eclipses of the sun, droughts and as their consequence famines, and last but not least the plague. It is at least as proper to speak of sufferings inflicted by human beings on the one hand and of "demonic (divine) things" on the other (II 64.2). The four demonic things independent of one another which Thucydides mentions might remind one of the four elements.[9] Eclipses of the sun are indeed not disasters but they may well be thought to announce disasters. The connection between the disasters of human origin and the other kind of disasters would then be supplied by divine rule: the gods punished Greece for the fratricidal war,[10] and they punished especially those Greeks who were responsible for the war. Accordingly, Thucydides turns immediately to the question of who was responsible for the war. His answer is that the Athenians forced the Spartans into war. The plague smote the Athenians and not the Spartans. Was it not Apollo who sent the plague which smote the Athenians (II 54.4–5)? The majority of the Greeks sympathized with the Spartans who appeared to be the liberators of Greece from Athenian tyranny (II 8.4–5). At any rate if one remembers what Thucydides had said earlier in praise of Sparta as distinguished from Athens, one will cease to find the concluding chapter of the Introduction disconcerting.

By starting from the most comprehensive judgments made by Thucydides himself we arrive at the conclusion that this great Athenian preferred the Spartan manner to the Athenian manner. This in itself is not paradoxical: there is no necessity that a man, and especially a great man, should identify himself with what prevails or what is most highly esteemed in his place of birth or with the ancestral. The judgments from which we have started are much less resplendent than the praise of Athens in the Funeral Speech, but the Funeral Speech expresses the sentiments of Pericles and not those of Thucydides. It is not Thucydides' fault if his readers are more impressed by the brilliant than by the unobtrusive. It is one of the differences between Sparta and Athens that no Spartan could

---

[9] Cf. Lucretius VI 1096ff.

[10] Aristophanes, *Peace* 204ff. Cf. the sequence of topics in III 86–89: a small Athenian expedition to Sicily; the plague smites the Athenians for the second time, and earthquakes; Aeolus and Hephaestus; the Spartans regarding an earthquake as an ill omen fail to invade Attica; natural consequences of earthquakes. The preceding section (III 69–85) dealing with the civil war (in Corcyra) is the only one in which "the divine law" is mentioned.

praise Sparta as well as Pericles praised Athens: Spartans were less eloquent or more laconic than the Athenians (cf. IV 84.2). On the other hand, no non-Spartan had a reason for praising Sparta as unqualifiedly as Pericles praised Athens, for all non-Spartans who were not enemies of Sparta, requesting Sparta's grudgingly given help, were compelled to express their dissatisfaction with the Spartan manner. Pericles' Funeral Speech, however, precisely serves the purpose of making everyone who listens—Athenian or foreigner —most satisfied with the Athenian manner and Athenian policy. All this goes to show that the absence of a praise of Sparta which is comparable in power to the praise of Athens in the Funeral Speech, does not prove that in Thucydides' view Sparta did not deserve higher praise than Athens. Thucydides does praise Pericles. But this praise is perfectly compatible with preferring Sparta to Pericles and his Athens. Pericles was by far superior to his successors by his ability to guide Athens safely in peace and through the war; Athens reached her greatest power under his rule (II 65.5–13). Yet Thucydides does not say of Periclean Athens as he says of Sparta that it succeeded in combining prosperity with moderation and still less that Athens succeeded in this thanks to Pericles. He does not even mention moderation (*sophrosyne*) in his eulogy of Pericles. Nor does his Pericles ever in any of his three speeches mention moderation. This revealing silence is not rendered ambiguous by the fact that both Cleon and the Athenian ambassadors to Melos use that word, for it is a sign of Pericles' superiority to his successors that he knows what he is talking about. The Funeral Speech, pronounced in obedience to a law, opens with a blame of that very law: Pericles lacks the moderation which prevents a man from regarding himself as wiser than the law (II 35; cf. I 84.3). This is to say nothing of the link between Pericles' speeches and the famous or infamous dialogue of the Athenians with the Melians in which the existence of a divine law limiting the desire for expansion is openly denied; Pericles admits without hesitation the quasi-tyrannical character of his Athens' rule over her subject cities (II 63.2; V 104–105.2). The Funeral Speech as a whole is a praise of the Athenian manner in contradistinction especially to the Spartan manner—of daring, permissiveness, and hope as opposed to caution, sternness, and fear. The fact that under Pericles, or thanks to Pericles, Athens became most powerful does not prove that under him, or thanks to him, it became "best." The polity established in 411 appeared to Thucydides to be the best that Athens had in his lifetime (VIII 97.2). The Periclean regime—a democracy in name but in fact the rule of the first man (II 65.9)—was inferior. It indeed saved democracy from itself and increased Athens' power and splendor beyond anything achieved earlier but it had to rely constitutionally on elusive chance: on the presence of a Pericles. A sound regime is one in which a fairly large group united by civic virtue of a fairly high level rules in broad daylight, in its own right. However great Pericles' merits may have been, his rule is inseparable from the Athenian democracy; it belongs to the Athenian democracy; the judgment on Pericles' rule must not be made in oblivion of the unsolid character of its foundation. A sound regime is a moderate regime dedicated to moderation.

All this is in accordance with our first impression according to which Thucydides' horizon is the horizon of the city. Every human being and every society is what it is by virtue of the highest to which it looks up. The city, if it is healthy, looks up, not to the laws which it can unmake as it made them, but to the unwritten laws, the divine law, the gods of the city. The city must transcend itself. The city can disregard the divine law; it can become guilty of *hybris* by deed and by speech: the Funeral Speech is followed by the plague, and the dialogue with the Melians is followed by the disaster in Sicily. This would seem to be the most comprehensive instruction which Thucydides silently conveys, the silent character of the conveyance being required by the chaste character of his piety.[11] If this is so, we shall cease to wonder why he is so silent about economic and cultural matters. Such matters were less important to him than, for instance, which army was in the possession of the battlefield after a battle; this was ultimately due to the fact that burial of one's dead is a most sacred duty; the army which had to abandon the battlefield was compelled to ask the enemy for permission to gather their dead and thus formally to concede defeat; this was a further reason why possession of the battlefield was so important.[12] When Thucydides fails to mention "the doubling or trebling of the tribute [of Athens' allies] in 425"—"the most notable omission in his narrative" from the point of view of the modern historian[13]—this may well be due to the fact that for Thucydides

---

[11] Cf. Classen-Steup, *Thukydides* I (4th ed.; Berlin, 1897) pp. xliv–xlvi.

[12] Cf. IV 44 with Plutarch, *Nicias* 6.5–6.

[13] A.W. Gomme, *A Historical Commentary on Thucydides*, I (Oxford, 1945) 26.

and for the cities, the payment of tribute as such, *i.e.* impairment of freedom, was much more important than the amount of the tribute; what is most important for the city is its freedom, the freedom endangered by the tyrant city of Athens: Sparta did not impose tribute on her allies but only her regime so favorable to stable freedom or an approximation to her regime (I 19). The general conclusion which we have drawn from Thucydides' explicit statements surely goes beyond these statements: we shall have to reconsider, in the light of the evidence supplied especially by his silence, our tentative suggestion as to what in his view transcends the city. Wherever that reconsideration will lead us, it cannot make doubtful the fact that the most important consideration concerns that which transcends the city or which is higher than the city; it does not concern things which are simply subordinate to the city.

### 3. *The Case for Athens: Daring, Progress, and the Arts*

The first subject of our reconsideration must be Thucydides' initial judgment according to which the Peloponnesian war was greater than the earlier wars, that it was the most memorable war. He selected this war not only because he happened to be contemporary with it but because he regarded it as singularly memorable. The greatness of this war is therefore not only the reason for the selection of his theme but is itself a theme, an important ingredient in his account of the war: one does not know the truth about the Peloponnesian war if one does not know that it was the greatest war. The proof of the initial assertion seems to be supplied by the few lines in which Thucydides shows that the Peloponnesian war surpassed by far the Persian war by virtue of the sufferings which it caused. But perhaps there was another war which caused greater sufferings than the Persian war. And perhaps the greatness of a war is not merely established by the amount of suffering which it causes. The fact that an author as terse as Thucydides wrote about nineteen chapters in order to prove his contention that the Peloponnesian war was the greatest or most memorable war shows that that war had another competitor than the Persian war. That competitor was the Trojan war. A generation after him, Isocrates still maintained the view that the Trojan war was the greatest war.[14]

---

[14] *Panathenaicus* 76–83; *Helen* 49.

The Peloponnesian war was the greatest motion because it affected all Greece and a part of the barbarians, "so to speak the largest part of mankind."[15] It was, so to speak, the first universal motion. It was the most memorable war because it was memorable, so to speak, to all men. Its universality is not impaired by the fact that not all barbarians were affected by it; it is sufficiently guaranteed by the fact that all Greece and some barbarians were affected by it because of the special importance of the Greeks for the Greek Thucydides. For the Peloponnesian war to be the greatest motion, it is of decisive importance that the Greeks, *i.e.* the leading Greek cities, were at their peak when the war began: the Peloponnesian war is the climactic war. Being both universal and climactic, it is the complete war, the absolute war. It is *the* war, war writ large:[16] the universal character of war will be more visible, and there will be more of war in the greatest war than in any other, smaller war. The Peloponnesian war is that singular event which reveals fully, in an unsurpassable manner, for all times, the nature of war.

Thucydides is under an obligation to prove his contention that the Peloponnesian war is the absolute war, the universal and climactic war. The universal war requires communication among all cities and, so to speak, among all countries, especially communication overseas; it presupposes the existence of powerful and wealthy cities. He must then prove that these requirements were fulfilled to a much lesser degree in the past than in his own time; he must show "the weakness of the ancients" (I 3.1). He matches his suggestion regarding the universality of the war ("so to speak the largest part of mankind") by a suggestion regarding the most ancient antiquity (as distinguished from the most ancient antiquity of which one knows by tradition—cf. I 4 beg.), regarding the simply first things. He suggests that it is difficult to arrive at an opinion backed by evidence about that earlier event which could be thought to challenge the supremacy of the Peloponnesian war, *i.e.* the Trojan war, and the still more ancient things (I 1.2): he makes us wonder whether anything can be known regarding the most ancient things. Yet since the development from that antiquity of which we have some direct knowledge to the present is, on the whole, a progress in security, power, and wealth, it becomes sufficiently clear that at

---

[15] I 1.2; cf. II 41.4.
[16] Cf. Plato, *Republic* 368e7–8.

the beginning there was unlimited insecurity, weakness, and poverty. The reason for this was the unlimited rule in the beginning of
unrest, of motion. Very slowly and sporadically man found some
rest. During the periods of rest and security—periods which lasted
much longer than the periods of motion alternating with them—
power and wealth were built up. Power and wealth were built up
not in and through motion but in and through rest (I 2, 7, 8.3, 12,
13.1). Rest, not motion, peace, not war, is good. The process
reached its peak in Sparta and Athens at the outbreak of the Peloponnesian war. The Peloponnesian war, the greatest motion, follows
on the greatest rest, embodies the greatest rest. Only for this reason
can it be the greatest motion. Therefore the understanding of the
Peloponnesian war which makes manifest the nature of war makes
manifest also the nature of peace: Thucydides' work enables one to
understand not only all past and future wars but the past and future
things simply (I 1.3 end, 22.4).

The rise from original and universal insecurity, weakness, and
poverty to security, power, and wealth became in certain places the
rise from original and universal barbarism to what one may call
Greekness, the union of freedom and love of beauty. The very name
"Greeks" is recent. So is the Greek way of life. Originally the Greeks
lived like barbarians. Originally the Greeks were barbarians. In the
most ancient antiquity there were no Greeks (I 3, 6). In the initial
universal unrest or motion all men were barbarians. Rest, long
periods of rest, were the conditions for the emergence of Greekness.
Greekness is late and rare; it is the exception. Just as humanity
divides itself into Greeks and barbarians, Greekness in its turn has
two poles, Sparta and Athens. The fundamental opposition of motion and rest returns on the level of Greekness; Sparta cherishes
rest whereas Athens cherishes motion. The peak of Sparta and
Athens was reached at the outbreak of the Peloponnesian war. In
that greatest motion, power, wealth, and Greekness, built up during
a long rest, are used and used up. Greeks and barbarians, the elements and the gods, seem to have conspired to do the utmost
damage to Greekness (I 23.1–3). The decline begins. The greatest
rest is that in which Greekness reaches its peak; it finds its culmina-
tion, its end in the greatest motion. The greatest motion weakens,
endangers, nay destroys, not only power and wealth but Greekness
as well. It leads soon to that unrest within the city, the *stasis*, which
is re-barbarization. The most savage and murderous barbarism,

which was slowly overcome by the building up of Greekness, re-appears in the midst of Greece: Thracian mercenaries in the pay of Athens murder the children attending a Greek school. Thucydides envisages the ruin of Sparta and Athens: just as his contemporaries have looked at the remains of barbarians on Apollo's island, he has seen with his mind's eye the ruins of Sparta and Athens (I 8.1, 10.1–2). He was familiar with the thought that "by nature all things will eventually also decline," for he makes his Pericles express that thought (II 64.3). It is not in vain that he reports about the new powers in the north, the great Odrysian empire and, above all, the amazing progress of Macedon under king Archelaus (II 97.5–6, 100.2).

The Peloponnesian war, a singular event, is distinguished from all other singular events by the fact that it is the climactic Greek war. In studying that war, one sees the Greeks at their peak in motion; one sees the beginning of the descent. The peak of Greekness is the peak of humanity. The Peloponnesian war and what it implies exhausts the possibilities of man. Just as one cannot understand that greatest motion without understanding the greatest rest, one cannot understand Greekness without understanding barbarism. All human life moves between the poles of war and peace and between the poles of barbarism and Greekness. By studying the Peloponnesian war Thucydides grasps the limits of all human things. By studying this singular event against the background of the ancient things he grasps the nature of all human things. It is for this reason that his work is a possession for all times.

Thucydides was compelled to prove the supremacy of the Peloponnesian war by bringing to light the weakness of the ancients because men believed in the supremacy of the Trojan war. The Trojan war owed its renown to Homer. By questioning the supremacy of the Trojan war Thucydides questions the authority of Homer. By proving the weakness of the ancients he proves that the account given by the ancients was not true in the decisive respect: he proves the weakness of the ancients, and in particular of Homer, in regard to wisdom. By proving that the Greeks who fought the Peloponnesian war were at their peak, he proves that his wisdom is superior to Homer's wisdom. But for Thucydides' inquiry, the glamor of antiquity—a glamor made immortal by Homer—would always outshine the solid superiority of Thucydides' time. Thucydides confronts us with the choice between Homeric and Thucydidean

wisdom. He engages in a contest with Homer. Homer lived long
after the Trojan war; this alone makes him a questionable witness
to the Trojan war. Above all, Homer is a poet. Poets magnify and
adorn and they tell fabulous stories; they thus conceal the truth
about human beings and human nature. Homeric wisdom reveals
the character of human life by presenting deeds and speeches which
are magnified and adorned. Thucydidean wisdom reveals the character of human life by presenting deeds and speeches which are not
magnified and adorned. The Greek princes followed Agamemnon
to Troy not, as the poets suggest, out of graciousness but out of fear
or compulsion. The strange course of the Trojan war is to be explained prosaically by the Greeks' lack of money.[17] Thucydides'
prosaic treatment of the Trojan war (to say nothing of his treatment
of the Peloponnesian war) foreshadows Cervantes' treatment of
knight errantry.

The new wisdom is then superior to the old wisdom as wisdom.
Yet it is precisely by trusting Homer that Thucydides succeeds in
bringing to light the truth about the Trojan war (I 10.1-3). Above
all, Homer was admired because he revealed the truth which he
knew in a way that is most pleasing. Thucydides does not seem to
deny that his wisdom too will be pleasing: "The non-fabulous character of my account will perhaps appear to be less pleasing to the
ear." It will not appear less pleasing than Homer's poetry to those
whose ears have been properly trained.[18] Thucydides' severe and
austere wisdom too is music: inspired by a Muse, if by a higher and
therefore severer and more austere Muse than Homer's. In a word,
it is perhaps more enlightening to see Thucydides as engaged in a
contest with Homer than as a scientific historian: human wisdom
rather than anything else is the core of Greekness.

Thucydides deals in the Introduction to his work first with the
superiority of the Peloponnesian war to all earlier wars (I 1-19)
and then with the superiority of his kind of account to all earlier
accounts (I 20-22). Thucydides is concerned not only with the war
but also with his *logos*. The progress in wisdom achieved by him is
akin to the progress of which he speaks most comprehensively in his
"archeology." His age could boast of a progress beyond the whole
past in experience, craft, and knowledge, especially in Athens (I

---

[17] I 3.3; 9.1, 3; 10.3; 11.1, 3; 21.1; 22.4.
[18] Cf. Cicero, *Orator* 39.

49.1–3, 70.2, 71.2–3). His archeology is in perfect agreement with what his Pericles says in the Funeral Speech about the achievements of his generation as compared with those of the preceding generations (II 36.1–3) and about the questionable character of Homeric wisdom (II 41.4). However highly Thucydides may have thought of Sparta, moderation, and the divine law, his thought belongs altogether to innovating Athens rather than to old-fashioned Sparta. The conventional opening of his work ("Thucydides the Athenian") carries a non-conventional message.

Thucydides makes one wonder whether anything can be known about the most ancient things. Yet the oldest things include the things which are at all times, and it is with things of this kind that the possession for all times is concerned. Thucydides sees human nature as the stable ground of all its effects—of war and peace, barbarism and Greekness, civic concord and discord, sea-power and land-power, the few and the many. The nature of man cannot be understood without some understanding of nature as a whole. War being a kind of motion and peace being a kind of rest, they are only particular forms of the universal, all-pervasive interplay of motion and rest. Accordingly Thucydides is concerned with things other than human as well as with human things, and not only with such non-human things as directly affected the Peloponnesian war, as the plague and earthquakes. He speaks of land making inroads on the sea and of the sea making inroads on the land and suggests natural causes of these happenings (II 102.3–4, III 89). He suggests a natural explanation of Odysseus' Charybdis (IV 24.5). What his wily Demosthenes seems to have called "the nature of the place," he calls "the place itself" (IV 3.2, 4.3). Most striking is his account of the plague—a mighty change, hence motion—which surpassed all remembered earlier destructions of human beings anywhere as much as the Peloponnesian war surpassed all earlier wars (II 47.3, 48.3, 53.2). Instead of speculating on whether the opposition of sea and land (and hence of sea-power and land-power and therefore in particular of Athens and Sparta) must be understood ultimately in the light of the opposition of motion and rest, we reconsider the relation of motion and rest to progress and decline on the one hand, to Sparta and Athens on the other. However much progress may owe to rest, progress itself is motion. Besides, not only rest but also motion, in particular war, leads to power and wealth (I 15.1–2, 18.2–3, 19). Finally, as some of Thucydides' characters contend, rest is ruinous to craft and knowledge, whereas the opposite is true of motion (I 71.3, VI 18.6). Yet it is also true that the statesman who has acquired knowledge, like Pericles, as opposed to the fickle multitude, represents superhuman rest in the midst of human motion —rest confronting, understanding, and mastering motion (I 140.1, II 61.2, 65.4). Thucydides' work could be written because he found rest in the midst of the greatest motion (V 26.5). The highest things which we find in Athens are akin to rest or are the highest form of rest. For it is not so much motion as a certain kind of interplay of motion and rest which is responsible for the ancient poverty, weakness, and barbarism, and it is not rest but another kind of interplay of motion and rest which is responsible for present wealth, power, and Greekness. However much all things may always be in motion, the highest at which human thought arrives—motion and rest—is stable. The highest form of rest is not, like the form represented by Sparta, opposed to daring but presupposes the utmost daring: in the olden times men had no daring (I 17). The highest form of rest can therefore not be coordinated with moderation.

If motion and rest are the most ancient things, they will transcend or comprise the gods. From Homer's Shield of Achilles we might learn that the gods are more visible in war than in peace. In the war which was more war than any other war, in the greatest war, of which Thucydides studied the most minute details, he found no trace of the gods: are they likely to have been more effective in smaller wars and in particular in the Trojan war? Or is not precisely this the core of Homer's magnifying and adorning, that he traces the Trojan war and many of its incidents to the gods? Will our insight into the barbarism and the weakness of the ancients, and in particular their weakness regarding wisdom, not affect our view about the gods and the divine things which are decidedly ancient?[19] Two men stand out in Thucydides' account of antiquity, Minos and Agamemnon. He says nothing of Minos' ancestry and he speaks only in a somewhat garbled fashion of Agamemnon's ancestry.[20] His archeology leaves one wondering whether the gods could have been anything for him but immensely magnified barbarians of the remote past. If this should prove to be correct, the divine law to which he

---

[19] Cf. Euripides, *Helen* 13–14.

[20] I 4 and 9.1–2. Cf. the first mention of a god in I 13.6 (cf. I 8.1) with I 126.3–5. Consider II 68.3–5 and 102.5–6.

refers so powerfully cannot be a law laid down by any god; its origin and hence its essence becomes altogether obscure. If however the divine law properly understood is the interplay of motion and rest, one must study his work in the light of the question of how that divine law is related to the divine law in the ordinary understanding.

Thucydides belongs in a sense to Periclean Athens—to the Athens in which Anaxagoras and Protagoras taught and were persecuted on the ground of impiety.[21] The Funeral Speech in which his Pericles sets forth what his Athens stands for is silent about the divine law. His Pericles speaks only of the unwritten laws or, more precisely, of such unwritten laws as have been laid down for the benefit of the human beings who suffer injustice; transgression of these laws leads to disgrace at Athens—nothing is said to the effect that it is followed by divine retribution. He is silent about the gods or the strictly superhuman. He does mention sacrifices: when speaking of the relaxations from toil which are provided by the city (II 37.3, 38.1; cf. Aristotle, *Eth. Nic.* 1160a19–25). In the sole reference to the superhuman which occurs in any of his three speeches, he says that one must bear the superhuman (like the plague) "of necessity" whereas one must bear what the enemy inflicts "bravely"; he never says that one must revere the superhuman (II 64.2). The only Periclean reference to a god—a reference to the monetary value of the image of the goddess (Athena)—occurs characteristically in the center of a Thucydidean summary of a Periclean speech (II 13.5). Thucydides' argument in favor of Sparta, of moderation, of the divine law—important as it is—is only a part of his teaching. The praise of Sparta—the highest praise occurring within the archeology—thought through to its conclusion would lead to the highest praise of the most ancient antiquity.[22] This whole line of thought is contradicted by the explicit and opening thesis of the archeology as a whole—the thesis asserting the supremacy of the Peloponnesian war—and all that that thesis implies. The contradiction corresponds to the opposition between old-fashioned Sparta and innovating Athens, between admiration for antiquity and admiration for the present as the peak. Only the former—the equation of the good with the old or ancestral—seems to be in

---

[21] Plutarch, *Nicias* 23.2–3.
[22] Cf. the *ek palaitatou* in I 18.1 with I 1.2.

agreement with the view of the city as city. Yet the city thinks differently at different times. We learn from Thucydides that the admiration for antiquity, just as the admiration for moderation, is at home in peace whereas men tend to regard every war in which they are engaged, every present war, as the greatest (I 21.2), perhaps because during war the present calls for the supreme effort. Thucydides' bald assertion regarding the supremacy of the Peloponnesian war is then in accordance with a natural prejudice and therefore not offensive. But it so happens that what in many cases is merely a prejudice is in the case of the Peloponnesian war a demonstrable truth which when demonstrated eradicates forever the much more powerful prejudice in favor of antiquity, the prejudice which is at home in peace, when men live securely and protectedly. The view which belongs to war, the admiration for the present and all this implies, so far from being simply wrong, is truer than the opposite view.[23] War is a "violent teacher": it teaches men not only to act violently but also about violence and therewith about the truth. War is a violent teacher not only of everyone except Thucydides but also of Thucydides himself. Taught by that teacher Thucydides presents the war as it unfolds. Generally speaking, he lets us see the war at each point as it could be seen at the time; he shows us the war from different viewpoints. In doing this he could not help presenting his own conversion from the peace time view to the war time view or his most advanced education. The result of this innermost process animating his work is the classic political history. In his work we observe the genesis of political history, political history in statu nascendi, still visibly connected with its origin. Thucydides is concerned above everything else with war, more generally with foreign policy; the overriding concern with domestic politics, with the good order within the city, he leaves to the moderate citizens (cf. IV 28.5).

By the process animating Thucydides' work we do not mean then a change of his thought of which he was not necessarily aware and which has left traces in his work of which he was not necessarily aware. We rather have in mind that deliberate movement of his thought between two different points of view which expresses itself in the deliberate dual treatment of the same subject from different points of view, for instance of the Athenian tyrannicides.

---

[23] Consider VI 70.1.

He devotes the highest praise to the justice and goodness of that noble Spartan Brasidas (IV 81) and then asserts that Brasidas was decidedly opposed to peace between Sparta and Athens because of the honor which he derived from his victories (V 16.1). The first judgment is that of a man who surveys the whole war; the second judgment brings out how Brasidas appeared at the time to the peace parties, especially to the peace party in Sparta.[24] Not unlike his teacher, Thucydides is as flexible as he is austere. His seeing and showing things from a variety of points of view which he does not explicitly identify leads us naturally to the speeches of his characters through which he shows things as they appear to a named individual or city at a given time. The writing of those speeches thus appears to be only a special case of Thucydides' general procedure. Every speech is a part—a part of a peculiar kind—of Thucydides' speech.

## 4. *The Speeches of the Actors and the Speech of Thucydides*

We must try to find out what particular kind of Thucydides' speech is constituted by the speeches of his characters. After having completed his proof of the superiority of the Peloponnesian war to all earlier wars or rather of the present to antiquity, he comes to speak of the difficulty attending the discovery of the truth concerning antiquity.[25] That truth is concealed by time. But distance in time is not the only reason why men are mistaken; local distance is also of some importance. "Human beings" or "the many"[26] are not deterred by these difficulties from having firmly held thoughts about the past and about foreign things. These thoughts became known to Thucydides through men's speeches. The truth brought to light by him about antiquity or, which is the same thing, about the superiority of the Peloponnesian war to all earlier wars, will be seen to be the truth by those who look at things by starting from the deeds

---

[24] Cf. V 14 (the reason why both Athens and Sparta favored peace) with 15 (the reason for the Spartans' taking the initiative toward peace).

[25] I 20 beginning. The passage makes clear that the whole preceding discussion deals with the ancient things, either directly or indirectly; it deals with them indirectly by showing the superiority in strength of recent times to antiquity.

[26] I 20.1, 3; cf. I 140.1.

(facts) themselves, *i.e.* not from what people say or the speeches (cf. also I 11 end). Immediately after having spoken of his treatment of the ancient things, he turns to his treatment of the Peloponnesian war; what he says about the bulk of his work is shorter than what he says about his archeology. The Peloponnesian war is not difficult of access because of temporal distance and not altogether difficult of access because of local distance; hence in this case the speeches, *i.e.* the reports about the deeds, would seem to be no obstacle to the discovery of the truth. It is in this delicate manner that Thucydides opens our minds to the thought that "human beings" may be as profoundly mistaken about what is going on before their eyes as about happenings in the remotest past in the remotest countries. The first difficulty concerns the speeches delivered before the outbreak of the Peloponnesian war and during that war. Some of the speeches Thucydides himself had heard; but it was difficult for him to remember the exact wording; the difficulty of knowing the exact wording was, to say the least, no less in the case of those speeches for the knowledge of which he had to rely on reports by others. He decided therefore to write the speeches himself, keeping as close as possible to the gist of what the speakers had said—writing in each case how the speaking man or body of men "seemed" to him to have said to the highest degree what was appropriate in the circumstances about the subject at hand. (This implies, I believe, that he abstracted from the defects of diction from which a given speaker might have suffered but did not endow any speaker with qualities of understanding and choosing which he lacked.) As for the deeds done in the war, the "how it seemed" to him did not enter at all in his narrative.[27] What Thucydides says about the speeches is surrounded on both sides by references to "deeds."[28]

The only thing which seems to emerge with sufficient clarity from Thucydides' statement about the speeches is that what "seemed" to Thucydides is more present in the speeches than in his account of the deeds. He does not make clear why he wrote the speeches at all; he merely makes clear how, after having decided to write the speeches, he brought them as close to the truth as possible. It goes

---

[27] This must be taken with a grain of salt; cf. II 17.2, III 89.5, VI 55.3, VII 87.5, VIII 56.3, 64.5, 87.4 (cf. *ibid.* 3 beginning); cf. also I 1.3; 9.1, 3; 10.4.

[28] Cf. also I 21 end with I 23 beginning.

without saying that the question of why he wrote the speeches cannot be answered by reference to Homer's practice. Some points may be learned through consideration of the immediate context of Thucydides' statement. However great the value of the speeches may be, the deeds are more trustworthy than the speeches. Yet the deeds became known to Thucydides partly through speeches, *i.e.* through the reports of eyewitnesses; these reports were vitiated to some extent by the bad memory and the partiality of the reporters (I 22.3). It is reasonable to assume that not all speakers of the speeches recorded within the work were free from these failings and that Thucydides appropriately preserved this characteristic when he wrote the speeches which he ascribed to those speakers. He divides the subject matter of his work into the speeches delivered both prior to the war and during the war and the deeds done during the war. Since he devotes considerable space to the deeds done prior to the war, he thus draws our attention to the fact that in an important respect the speeches simply precede the deeds. The speeches which simply precede the deeds concern the causes of the deeds, men's plans and intentions: only speeches can make manifest the immanifest (III 42.2). They concern above all the causes of the war, the causes openly "spoken," as distinguished from the truest cause which remains unspoken or unavowed (I 23.4): the speeches may be deceptive not only because of the bad memory and the partiality of the speakers; they may also be meant to deceive. Of the speeches Thucydides says that it was difficult to remember the exact wording and hence he did not remember it, whereas of the deeds he says that he found out the truth about them with toil. When he denies that his book is necessarily unpleasing, he may have thought of the speeches in the first place.

What do the speeches achieve that the most perfect report about the speeches could not have achieved? Such a report would have revealed to us the intention of the speech, the arguments used by the speaker to support that intention as well as those used to refute the opponents, the order of the arguments as well as the weight which the speaker assigned to each argument; it would have included a description of the abilities, the manners and the present disposition of the speaker as well as of the disposition of the audience; it would have told us whether or to what extent the speech of the speaker agreed with his deeds if the latter did not become known to us through the narrative. What we would still miss is the presence of the speaker: we would not see him by hearing him; we would not be exposed to him, affected by him, perhaps bewitched by him. The most perfect Thucydidean reports about the speeches would be parts of Thucydides' speech like all its other parts; we would not see Thucydides' speech in its peculiarity; and we would be exposed only to Thucydides. For what distinguishes Thucydides' speech from the speeches of his characters? The speeches are partial in a double sense. They deal with a particular situation or difficulty, and they are spoken from the point of view of one or the other side of the warring cities or contending parties. Thucydides' narrative corrects this partiality: Thucydides' speech is impartial in the double sense. It is not partisan and it is comprehensive since it deals, to say the least, with the whole war. By integrating the political speeches into the true and comprehensive speech, he makes visible the fundamental difference between the political speech and the true speech. No political speech ever serves the purpose of revealing the truth as such; every political speech serves a particular political purpose, and it attempts to achieve it by exhorting or dehorting, by accusing or exculpating, by praising or blaming, by imploring or refusing. The speeches abound therefore with praise and blame, whereas Thucydides' speech is reserved. The speakers answer questions—and not merely questions of the moment but the most fundamental and permanent questions concerning human action—which Thucydides does not answer, and they do so in a most persuasive manner. Thus the reader is almost irresistibly tempted to agree with the speaker and to believe that Thucydides, who after all wrote the speech, must have used the speaker as his mouthpiece. Thucydides helps us indeed in judging of the wisdom of the speeches, not only by his account of the deeds but also by giving us his judgment of the wisdom, not indeed of the speeches but of the speakers, yet he does not do this in all cases and, above all, in no case is his explicit judgment, be it of men or of policies, complete. In fact, precisely the speeches more than anything else convey to us his judgment of the speakers and not only of the speakers.

The Corcyreans in addressing the Athenians seem to commit an "unconscious contradiction": "Corcyra will have it both ways—'the war is anyhow coming' and 'this action will not involve a *casus belli.*'"[29] Yet an action desirable or necessary with a view to an

---

[29] Gomme, *loc. cit.* 169.

expected war, even if the action is regarded as provocative by the prospective enemy, does not necessarily constitute a breach of the treaty with that power, and the Corcyreans consider no other *casus belli* than the breach of such a treaty. It is more important however to take cognizance of the fact that a contradiction committed unconsciously by Thucydides' speakers is not necessarily committed unconsciously by Thucydides: it reveals the predicament of the speaker and is meant to reveal it. The speech may also reveal how the speaker overcomes the predicament in which he finds himself. The Spartans claim to wage the war for the freedom of all cities against the tyrant city Athens. The cities subject to Athens or allied with her were however bound to her by treaties; to switch from the Athenian alliance to the Spartan alliance, especially at a time when the Athenians were hard-pressed, was thought to be not only unjust but also dishonorable (III 9). Accordingly, when the Spartan Brasidas attempts to induce the Acanthians to forsake their alliance with Athens, he does not even allude to the fact of that alliance; he tacitly conveys the view that a city cannot be allied to Athens except under duress. He cannot entirely dispense with threats of what he will do to the Acanthians if they do not comply with his request, but he threatens them with no more than that he will force them to be free; this use of force will be perfectly just because the Acanthians' lack of freedom endangers the freedom of all other cities or the good common to all cities. Still, the Acanthians might fear that after having liberated the cities at present enslaved by Athens, the Spartans will enslave them in turn. Brasidas refutes this fear by assuring the Acanthians that he has bound the Spartan government by the greatest oaths that it will not attempt anything of this kind (IV 85–87). Just as Brasidas' speech solves in a masterly manner by speech the whole problem of Greek politics, Hermocrates' speech to the all-Sicilian assembly in Gela (IV 59–64) is a masterpiece of statesmanly foresight. Foreseeing many years before the event the Athenian attempt to conquer Sicily, he tries to put a stop to all intra-Sicilian frictions in order to unite the Sicilians against the common enemy, their enemy "by nature." Sicily is indeed divided "by nature" into Dorians and Ionians, and the Athenians are Ionians; but the Athenian invasion will be prompted, not by racial hatred, but by desire for the wealth of all Sicily. What enables Hermocrates to see the danger from afar, and to suggest a remedy in time, is his understanding of human nature; he does not blame the Athenians for their aggression since in his view the desire for aggrandizement is natural to man as man regardless of what conventions or words ("names") may make one believe. Yet, as he is forced to admit, what unites the Sicilians is "name" rather than "nature" (race),[30] and, as he is not forced to admit in the present circumstances, if the desire for aggrandizement is natural to man as man or at any rate to the city as city, powerful and nearby Syracuse is as much to be feared by her weaker neighbors as more powerful but far away Athens. The difficulty which Brasidas overcomes by claiming to trust in the greatest oaths of the highest Spartan authority cannot be overcome by Hermocrates who is compelled to appeal to nature. Continuing to disregard entirely the disposition of the audience while however assuming its being composed of tolerably decent men, we may find that the greatest difficulty had to be faced by Alcibiades in his speech in Sparta. Having been accused by the Athenians of a capital crime connected with shocking acts of impiety and having fled to Sparta, he wishes to revenge himself on Athens by showing the Spartans how they can bring down their and his enemy. He has to overcome two powerful prejudices against himself. In the first place, as an Athenian politician he had been notorious as an enemy of Sparta. Above all, he had just betrayed or was about to betray his own city to its greatest enemies. He disposes of the two objections by one and the same answer: he was against the Spartans because they had wronged him; he turns now against the Athenians because they have wronged him (VI 89–92). Being conscious of his unique ability as well as of his renown for it, and not being bound to any particular city because of his infinite versatility, he is not compelled to avoid self-contradiction by having recourse to oaths. He does contradict himself regarding his and his family's posture toward democracy: the Athenian regime which they managed is not truly democratic, and it is democratic but they could not change it because of the war (VI 89.4–6); but both answers serve his purpose equally well.

Thucydides gives an indirect characterization of the Athenian democracy through the speech of the Syracusan demagogue Athenagoras (VI 36–40). Reports had reached Syracuse from many sides to the effect that the Athenian invasion fleet was approaching, but it took a long time before the reports were believed even by a

---

[30] Cf. also VI 77.1 end, 79.2, 80.3.

minority of the Syracusans. After Hermocrates, who was of course sure of the truth of the reports, had addressed the Syracusan assembly, Athenagoras opposed him, dismissing the reports as an inept move made by the Syracusan oligarchs to frighten the multitude and thus to make themselves masters of the city. In Athenagoras' view the Athenians are much too clever to embark on such a foolhardy and hopeless enterprise as the conquest of Sicily. The only thing that will put an end to the subversive activities of the Syracusan oligarchic youth is democratic terror. This terror is justified because there is no sound or respectable reason for opposing democracy—the regime which is both fair and wise: it gives a more than equal share in the common good to the deserving men among the rich, and the multitude is the best judge of the wisdom of the speakers. Thucydides has entrusted to Athenagoras the clearest and most comprehensive exposition of the democratic view which occurs in his work, for the ringing sentences of the Funeral Speech describe not democracy as such, but the Athenian regime.[31] This fact alone must make his speech an object of the greatest interest to us. As is shown by the deeds, the Syracusan democrat was mistaken at least to the extent that he did not know and understand the Athenian democracy: the Athenian invading force did come with the full approval of the Athenian multitude and it would have succeeded in its mission if Athenagoras' counterparts in Athens had not recalled Alcibiades from the invading force for reasons not dissimilar to those of Athenagoras, with the full approval of the Athenian multitude. Athenagoras did not know the Athenian multitude because he was unable to look beyond the party strife within Syracuse; he lacked the understanding and even the information that Hermocrates possessed. The Athenian democracy was a special kind of democracy, an imperial democracy exercising quasi-tyrannical rule over her so-called allies. Even Cleon and precisely Cleon speaks of the difficulty—he can afford to call it impossibility —of combining empire with democracy. Cleon could preserve this combination to some extent because he was able to imitate, or to ape, Pericles.[32] Observations like these do not go to the root of the matter; they do not touch what Aristotle would call the matter of Athenian democracy, the nature of the Athenian people (cf. I

---

[31] Cf. especially II 37.1 with II 65.9.
[32] III 37.1–2; 38 beginning (cf. II 61.2).

70.9). At the end of the address to the troops before a naval battle, the Peloponnesian commanders tell them that none of them will have an excuse for acting as a coward and if anyone tries to act cowardly he will be properly punished, while the brave ones will be honored properly. The parallel to this conclusion in the address of the Athenian commander Phormio is his statement that the troops are about to engage in a great contest: they will either make an end to the Peloponnesians' hope for naval victory or else bring the fear regarding the sea nearer home to the Athenians.[33] The Peloponnesians appeal to the self-interest of the individual; the Athenian appeals only to what is at stake for the city. There were no doubt additional reasons—reasons connected with the particular situation —for this difference between the two speeches; yet this does not do away with the fact that Thucydides' Phormio, if contrasted with his Peloponnesian antagonists, *i.e.* unconsciously, confirms the view explicitly stated by the Corinthians that the Athenians were singularly public-spirited: the Athenian uses his body as if it were the most external, the most foreign thing to him in order to sacrifice it for his city, and he uses his innermost thought, most peculiar to him, in order to do something for his city (I 70.6).

Thucydides has presented the nameless Athenian perhaps most powerfully but surely most gracefully through the speech of the Athenians at Sparta (I 72–78). Those Athenians happened to be in Sparta on business of their city when the Corinthians and other Spartan allies attempted to incite Sparta to war against Athens by complaining to the Spartan assembly about Athenian encroachments. Having heard of this anti-Athenian action they requested and received permission of the Spartans to address the Spartan assembly in order to counteract the effects of the Corinthian charges. The speech constitutes an action on behalf of their city which they undertook without having been commissioned to do it by their city. This is the only speech of this kind in Thucydides' work. The speech is unique for still another reason which concerns Thucydides' speeches in general. It is the only speech preceded by a summary, given by Thucydides in his own name, of the gist of the speech—a summary which to some extent agrees literally with what the speakers themselves say at the beginning of their speech about the

---

[33] II 87.9, 89.10. Cf. VI 69.3. Phormio addresses the Athenians alone, not any allies: II 88.3.

purport of their speech.[34] The most important difference between
Thucydides' summary and the opening remark of the speech itself
is this: Thucydides says that the Athenians wished to show how
great their city was in regard to power; the Athenians say that they
wish to make manifest that their city is worthy of mention, or is
important. How then do they reveal the power of Athens? No part
of their speech is devoted to this subject. The main subjects of the
speech are these: (1) Athens has well deserved of Greece in the
Persian war (73.2–74); (2) Athens cannot be blamed for either the
acquisition of her empire or for the way in which she manages it
(75–77). Since the Athenian action in the Persian war laid the
foundation for the empire, the speech can be said to be devoted
to the justification of the Athenian empire in contradistinction to the
exhibition of Athenian power. It is true that by barely mentioning
the Athenian empire they would point to Athenian power, but since
everyone present knew the existence of the Athenian empire, even
their worst enemy could not say that they showed how great the
power of their city was, let alone that they boasted of their power.
Their worst enemy, a Spartan ephor, does say that they praised
themselves but he finds that praise rightly in what they said about
Athens' merit in the Persian war.[35] It is indeed in the part of their
speech devoted to the Persian war that they come closest to speaking explicitly of Athens' power. The Athenians, they say, saved
Greece by contributing the largest number of ships, a most intelligent commander (Themistocles), and the most daring zeal. But
what made Athens worthy of empire is not the large navy but the
zeal and intelligence shown at Salamis (74.1–2, 75.1). These qualities—the superior intelligence of their leaders and the daring zeal of
the people—, they intimate, and not the navy, are the core of Athens'
power. Thucydides himself tells us that at the time of Salamis,
Sparta was much more powerful than Athens (I 18.2) in all respects other than these qualities. Or, as his Pericles puts it, at the
time of Salamis when they had abandoned their city, the Athenians
had so to speak nothing but their intelligence and daring, those
virile qualities which created Athenian power rather than that
Athenian power had created these qualities (I 143.5, 144.4). By

---

[34] The speech which comes closest to the Athenians' speech in this respect
is that by Phormio (II 88–89).

[35] I 86.1; cf. I 73.2–3.

speaking, *i.e.* acting, as they do, the Athenians in Sparta show forth the mainstay of Athens' present power. To this extent they silently confirm what the Corinthians had said to the Spartan assembly about the profound difference between the Athenians and all others. But the Corinthians had inferred from this difference that the Athenians are therefore a menace to all others and especially to the Spartans. The Athenians must deny the soundness of this inference. They do this in an extraordinary manner. They trace their threatening power to compulsion: they were compelled to build their empire by fear, by honor, and by interest; in ceding to that compulsion they did what the Spartans, nay what all other men would have done in their place: they ceded to human nature. What distinguishes their exercise of imperial power from that of all others is the singular fairness in their dealings with their subjects. It is above all by the amazing frankness with which they defend the Athenian acquisition of empire that they reveal Athenian power, for only the most powerful can afford to utter the principles which they utter. The charge that Athens threatens Sparta is treated by them with contempt: the Athenians just as the Spartans have never committed the mistake of starting a war with a power equal to their own; all differences between Athens on the one hand and Sparta and her allies on the other can and should be settled peacefully, according to treaty. One has spoken of the provocative irony of the Athenians while asserting that "quite clearly Thucydides did not think that it was the Athenian aim to be provocative, but the contrary."[36] The speech is better described as both fastidious and frank. Thucydides knew as well as Socrates that it is easy to praise Athens before an Athenian audience.[37] What the Athenians did in Sparta was not easy. Thucydides is at least as fastidious as these Athenians. One cannot say of him however that he did not have his reticences.

In order to appreciate fully the sole speech of the Athenians in Sparta, one must also contrast it with the sole speech of the Spartans in Athens (IV 17–20).[38] Under Demosthenes' inspiring leadership

---

[36] Gomme, *loc. cit.* 254.

[37] Plato, *Menexenus* 235d.

[38] The other counterpart of the sole speech of the Spartans in Athens which was delivered when the Spartans apprehended the loss of three hundred men, is a possible second speech of the Athenians in Sparta after the disastrous plague (II 59.2). The Spartans would have made peace if the Athenians had listened to their request; Pericles would have prevented a peace even if the Spartans had listened to the Athenian ambassadors' request.

the Athenians had succeeded in defeating the Spartans at Pylos and in cutting off a considerable Spartan detachment on the island of Sphacteria. The Spartan authorities, despairing of relieving that detachment and anxious to avoid at all costs its capture or destruction, send an embassy to Athens to start negotiations for peace. The ambassadors cannot help referring in their speech to their present predicament or the Athenians' great success. They do it by speaking of the Athenians' good luck: if you act wisely you will gain honor and glory in addition to the good luck; they slyly suggest that the Athenians' victory did not bring them honor and glory. They warn them not to trust that luck will always be on their side, for in war luck is of utmost importance; if the Athenians do not make peace now, and fail in their enterprises afterward, they will be thought to owe their present success to luck and not to their strength and intelligence (17.4–18.5). In this underhanded and grudging manner they do admit the fact, which they denied in the preceding sentences, that the Athenians owe their present success to their virtue. Their lack of frankness and of pride is not redeemed by graciousness. Their king Archidamus had claimed that they alone because of their moderation do not become insolent in success and that they cede less than others to adversity. Whatever may be true of their moderation in success, in deed they ceded to adversity after Pylos infinitely more than the Athenians did after their disaster on Sicily.[39]

It is safe to conclude that at least in some cases the speakers did not intend to convey the impression of themselves which their

---

[39] I 84.2, VIII 1.3. Lacking frankness from different motives explains the second speech of the Corinthians in Sparta (I 120–124). By pointing out the dangerous power of Athens in their preceding speech, they had contributed to the Spartans' decision to wage war against Athens. After the decision was made they feared, not without cause (I 125.2), that the Spartans (and the other allies) would not wage the war with sufficient vigor and speed to save besieged Potidaea: "what a man plans in his confident belief in the future is very unlike what he carries out in practice [for when it comes to practice, fear intervenes]." The paraphrase is Gomme's who characteristically omits the thought which we put in brackets. The Corinthians trace the anticipated lack of vigor and speed of their allies to the latter's overconfidence in victory because they do not wish to speak of the lukewarmness of their allies' concern with Potidaea, i.e. of the difference of interest between Corinth and her allies (cf. 120.2) and because they do not wish to speak unduly of their allies' fear of Athenian power; their fear of that fear explains why they speak as hopefully of the prospects of the war as they do.

speeches in fact convey. More generally, the speeches written by
Thucydides convey thoughts which belong, not to the speakers, but
to Thucydides. This is perfectly compatible with the possibility that
Thucydides, being a historian, has kept as closely as possible to
what the speakers actually said or that no opinion expressed in any
speech can be assumed to be Thucydides' opinion. The wording of
the speeches surely is Thucydides' own work. No one would go so
far as to say that the actual speakers began with identically the
same words with which their speeches, edited by Thucydides,
begin. For instance, the first speech occurring in the work opens
with "Just (Right)" and the second speech, which is a reply to the
first, opens with "Necessary (Compulsory)." The thought indicated
by these two opening words taken together, the question of the
relation of right and necessity,[40] of the difference, tension, perhaps
opposition between right and compulsion—a thought which is not
the theme of either speech—is Thucydides' thought. This thought
so unobtrusively and so subtly indicated illumines everything which
preceded the two speeches and everything which follows them.
These two opening words indicate the point of view from which
Thucydides looks at the Peloponnesian war.

## 5. *Dike*

How does the Peloponnesian war come to sight in the light of the
distinction between right and compulsion? In Thucydides' view the
Athenians compelled the Spartans to wage war against them; this
compulsion is the truest cause of the war, although the least mentioned one, as distinguished from the openly avowed causes. The
latter were the dissensions between Athens and Corinth concerning
Corcyra and Potidaea (I 23.6). Thucydides speaks first of the facts
constituting the avowed causes and then of the fact constituting
the unavowed cause, thus inverting the temporal order of the
events: the avowed causes are "first with regard to us" whereas the
true cause is hidden and kept hidden. But when one studies his
account of these avowed causes, one observes that they are as "true"
as the truest cause and in fact a part, even the decisive part, of the
latter. The truest cause of the war was that the Athenians, by
becoming great and thus putting the Spartans to fear, compelled

---

[40] Cf. Parmenides (*Vorsokratiker*, 7th ed.) fr. 8 lines 14 and 35.

them to wage war. Yet the Athenians' actions, at any rate in regard to Corcyra, made them still greater or at least promised to make them still greater than they were before those actions. The avowed cause of the war which is inferior in truth to the unavowed cause is different from the compulsion exercised by Athens' growing power, regardless of whether that compulsion was exercised before the Corcyrean affair or not. It is the breach of the thirty-year treaty between Sparta and her allies and Athens and her allies, *i.e.* an unjust action, an action against right. "Compulsion" differs from "right."

In the same context in which Thucydides contrasts the truest and least avowed cause with the openly avowed and less true causes he says that the Athenians and the Peloponnesians broke the treaty (I 23.4, 6). Just as he failed to make clear that the alternative to "compulsion" is "right," yet did make clear that the compulsion was exercised by Athens, he fails to make clear who it was who violated right, *i.e.* broke the treaty. No such violation to speak of had occurred prior to the Athenian alliance with Corcyra. Both in concluding and in performing their treaty with Corcyra the Athenians were anxious not to break their treaty with the Peloponnesians (I 44.1, 45.3, 49.4; cf. 35.1–4, 36.1). The Corinthians deny the contention of the Corcyreans and the Athenians that the Corcyrean-Athenian alliance is compatible with the thirty-year treaty (I 40.1–41.4; cf. 53.2, 4; 55.2). Thucydides, the best judge for whom one could wish, does not decide the controversy. He says in effect that the Athenian treaty with Corcyra, which was at war with Corinth (Sparta's ally), "compelled" the Athenians and the Corinthians to come to blows (49.7). If it is impossible to decide whether the later treaty conflicted with the stipulations of the earlier treaty, the earlier treaty might have been broken without either side having been guilty of breach of treaty (cf. 52.3). The action of the Athenians in regard to Potidaea surely did not constitute a breach of the treaty, which fact did not prevent the Corinthians from claiming that it did (66–67; 71.5). The Athenian ambassadors in Sparta as well as the Spartan king deny that Athens had broken the treaty (78.4, 81.5, 85.2) whereas the Spartan ephor denies that the Athenians had in any way refuted the charges against Athens and contends that Athens had done wrong to Sparta's allies. The Spartan assembly agreed with the ephor (86–88). Thucydides makes clear that the Spartans' decision was caused less by the consideration of right than by compulsion, in other words, that the consideration of right was not simply lacking in truth or irrelevant. The Spartans assert as definitely that the Athenians had broken the treaty or had acted against right (118.3) as Pericles denies it (140.2, 141.1, 144.2, 145). In Thucydides' view there was at this time a "confusion" of the treaty (146), *i.e.* obscurity as to whether the treaty had been violated or not but no breach of the treaty for which one side was clearly responsible. On the other hand what happened in Plataeae in the following spring was clearly a breach of the treaty, but the rights and wrongs of the case are not entirely clear, for whereas the Thebans (Sparta's ally) had invaded Plataeae (Athens' ally) while the treaty was still in force, yet there was already "confusion" of the treaty, they had been called in by a respectable part of the Plataean citizenry (II 5.5, 7, 7.1, III 65–66, V 17.2). With the actions in Plataeae the war had surely started, unless the Spartans were willing to abandon their badly needed Theban ally to Athenian revenge which they could not in reason be expected to do, and the Spartan invasion of Attica which followed almost immediately thus could appear to be in perfect accordance with right.

Six years after the outbreak of the war, after Pylos, the Spartan envoys addressing the Athenian assembly say that it is unclear which side started the war (IV 20.2). One could say that this statement does not necessarily express the Spartans' conviction but was inevitable for them in the circumstances or in agreement with the sly and humble character of their speech as a whole. But it is also possible that after they had so conspicuously failed to bring down the tyrant city, they were more willing than at the beginning of the war to admit that the wrong was not entirely on the side of the Athenians. In his account of the tenth year of the war (his whole account covers twenty-one years), Thucydides states unambiguously in his own name that the war began with the Spartan invasion of Attica (V 20.1), thus implying that it was Sparta which had broken the treaty. At the same time he reproduces or imitates the previous confusion by intimating, through what he says in the same passage on the precise date of the beginning of the war, that it was Thebes which broke the treaty by her attack on Plataeae. He seems to suggest in the same breath that Sparta started the war (broke the treaty) and that Thebes started the war (broke the treaty). The crucial obscurity would seem to be removed by the fact that the Spartans themselves, and apparently no one else, were handicapped in the first part of the war (431–421) by their awareness of having started the war unlawfully, for the Thebans had attacked Plataeae while the treaty was still in force and they themselves had failed to act according to the treaty in another manner; even if Sparta had not broken the treaty by her own actions, she would have broken it by not disassociating herself from the action of Thebes. The situation was entirely different during the second part of the war, for then there was not the slightest doubt that the treaty had been broken by Athens (VII 18.2–3). In the first part of the war, right was on the side of Athens while in the second part right was on the side of Sparta. By coincidence, in the first part of the war Thucydides was on the side of Athens while in the second part he was to some extent even literally on the side of the Peloponnesians (V 26.5).

If we survey the fate of the issue of right in Thucydides' work, we arrive at the result that he discloses the truth about this issue least ambiguously near the center of his narrative. For the same reason for which his initial remark (I 23.6) failed to make clear that the alternative to "compulsion" is "right," *i.e.* the keeping or breaking of the treaty, and still less who it was who violated right, he conceals as long as possible the fact that it was Sparta which violated right. In saying, in his initial remark, that the Athenians compelled the Spartans to wage war, he may be said to intimate that the Spartans started the war; but he surely conceals entirely the fact that Sparta broke the treaty. The strange character of his treatment of Spartan guilt in the first part of the war becomes still more visible when one contrasts it with his treatment of Athenian guilt in the second part; in the latter case he has no hesitation whatever in stating his own judgment without any ambiguity whatever (VI 105.1–2; cf. V 18.4). The treaties were solemnly sworn; their breach was a violation of divine law. Thus the question of who started the war is linked to the question concerning the divine law.[41] When the Spartans were about to break the treaty and asked the god in Delphi whether they should wage war, he encouraged them, "as is said," to wage it with all their might (I 118.3) without warning them in any way against breaking the treaty. On the con-

---

[41] Cf. the references to the gods by whom the oaths had been sworn in I 71.5, 78.4, 86.5. The importance of oaths in the relations among cities appears most clearly from II 5.6 and context.

trary by urging them to go to war the god seems to have expressed his belief that in starting the war they would not break the treaty; according to all ordinary criteria the gods seem to help the Spartans in the first five years of the war (I 123.2, II 54.4–5). But when the war lasted longer than the Spartans encouraged by the god may have expected and especially after their misfortune at Pylos, they became doubtful of whether Apollo's oracle gave a sufficient guarantee of the lawfulness of their war or perhaps whether the oracle was not the work of the Delphian priestess rather than of Apollo (cf. V 16.2; I 112.5). They began to believe that their misfortunes had befallen them fittingly because of their violation of right. Still later, contrasting their misfortunes in the first part of the war with their excellent prospects regarding the second half, as well as their injustice in the former with their clear justice in the latter, they reasonably[42] believed that they had failed in the former because of their injustice rather than their ineptitude and that they would be victorious in the latter because of their justice.[43] There is no question that the Spartans remained victorious in the second part of the war and therefore in the war as a whole, and to this extent not only Apollo's initial oracle but perhaps even the gods' concern with oaths may be said to have been vindicated (cf. V 26.4). But for Thucydides it was apparently a question whether the connection between injustice and defeat on the one hand and justice and victory on the other was more than coincidence. As he puts it on a different occasion, it was not the transgression of a superhuman command which brought about a certain misfortune but it was the misfortune which brought about the transgression (II 17.1–2; cf. II 53.3–4).

All this does not mean that the Spartans were wrong in regarding themselves as guilty of the breach of the treaty and still less that Thucydides regarded the question of right as irrelevant. Neither rest and Greekness nor even war is possible without treaties among cities, and the treaties would not be worth keeping in mind if the partners could not be presumed to keep them; this presumption must at least partly be based on past performance, *i.e.* on the justice of the parties. To that extent fidelity to covenants may be said to be

---

[42] Cf. the similarly inspired remark of the Spartan Clearchus in Xenophon's *Anabasis* II 2.3.

[43] Cf. VII 18.1–2. Cf. the Spartan parallels in I 128.1 and V 16.2–3, and the Athenian parallel in V 32.1.

by nature right. But since this bond is for obvious reasons not sufficient, men have recourse to divine sanctions. Both oaths and treaties are a kind of speeches which must be judged, as all other speeches must be judged, in the light of the deeds. Treaties form a part of Thucydides' work just as do the speeches of the actors. The treaties differ from the speeches in two ways: they are quoted verbatim whereas the speeches are not, and whereas the speeches are delivered from one side of the conflict, the treaties represent an agreement among the conflicting parties. The treaties may thus be said to reflect on the political plane Thucydides' own impartial speech.

To repeat, Thucydides distinguishes the truest and least avowed cause of the war from the openly avowed and less true causes. The truest cause was the Athenians' compelling the Spartans to wage war against them and the most avowed cause was the Athenians' alleged breach of the treaty. One sees again how much Thucydides' primary point of view is Spartan. The truest cause not being easily avowable by the Spartans[44] and the most avowed cause being rather weak, the Spartans had to think of strengthening the latter in order to have a cause which would be very strong (I 126.1). For this purpose they used two arguments or sets of arguments, the first taken from sacral law and the second being merely political. Justified by the Spartan procedure, Thucydides treats the two in complete separation from one another. He sets forth and explains the Spartan argument taken from sacral law and the Athenian rejoinder which is taken from the same field at much greater length than the Spartan political argument and the Athenian reply.[45] This is all the more remarkable since one of the political arguments—that which dealt with the Athenian decree regarding Megara—appears to have been of much greater importance than any other cause except the truest.[46] Yet in contradistinction to the political argument in question, the arguments dealing with sacral things had a clear basis in law. The Spartans demanded of the Athenians that they cleanse themselves from a pollution which they had contracted while quenching Cylon's attempt, apparently backed by Apollo, to make

---

[44] Cf. I 86.5.

[45] As appears from I 139 beginning, I 126–138 (about 325 lines) are devoted to the arguments taken from sacral law; if one insists on calling the passage dealing with Themistocles (135.3–138 end) an excursus, one may deduct 97 lines; the political arguments and Pericles' reply to them (139.1–4, 140.3–4, 144.2) take at most 36 lines.

[46] I 139.1, 140.4.

himself tyrant of Athens: the demand had the subsidiary advantage of casting aspersion on the ritual purity of Pericles, Sparta's most determined opponent (126–127; cf. I 13.6). The Athenians, acting probably on Pericles' own advice, replied with the demand that the Spartans cleanse themselves from the two pollutions they had contracted, the first in an action against some Helots and the second while punishing their king Pausanias for his attempt to betray the Greeks to the Persian king. The Spartan demand, especially if it is considered in the light of the excellent Athenian reply (not one but two pollutions and both more recent than the Athenian pollution), is no doubt ridiculous in the eyes of Thucydides; "here the lion laughed," says an old commentator. But apart from the fact that this story will prove to be not the only one bringing to light ridiculous features of Sparta, the ridiculous character of the Spartan demand does not entitle one to find it strange that Thucydides attaches so much greater weight to it than, say, to the Megarian decree, nor that "a special embassy should have been sent with this idle demand, however superstitious the Spartans may have been."[47] To draw a line between superstition and religion in a universally valid manner is not an easy task, especially after natural theology has ceased to be the generally accepted basis of discussion; nor is it easy to draw a line between genuine religious concern and the hypocritical use of religion in Spartans or in others; to say nothing of the fact that taking enlightenment for granted is tantamount to transforming enlightenment into superstition.

One must consider the Cylon story also as part of its broad context, *i.e.* of Thucydides' whole account, given in the first book, of the causes of the Peloponnesian war. The first book consists of the following parts:

I. Introduction (ch. 1–23): from the most ancient times till 431.

II. The openly avowed causes (ch. 24–88): from 439 till the first half of 432.

III. The truest cause (ch. 89–118): from 479 till 439.

IV. Continuation of II (ch. 119–125): second half of 432.

V. The causes meant to strengthen the openly avowed causes and continuation of IV (ch. 126–146): from ca. 630 till the end of 432.

[47] Gomme, *loc. cit.* 447.

The transitions from I to II, from II to III, and from IV to V are returns from later events to earlier ones. In particular Thucydides turns from the openly avowed causes which are later in time and less true to the truest and least avowed cause which is first in time. From this fact taken by itself we are led to expect that the archeology which begins at the beginning is meant to bring to light the simply first cause or causes (as distinguished from the first cause of the Peloponnesian war) which as such are the simply true and simply "unspoken" or immanifest causes. This expectation is confirmed by the study of the archeology. Thucydides could not have written the archeology if he had not "returned" from the present to the beginnings in a number of stages; his order of presentation imitates in a manner his order of finding. The central part of the first book consists of two sections: (1) the Athenian hegemony (ch. 89–96) and (2) the Athenian empire (ch. 97–118); the Athenian empire rather than the Athenian hegemony is the truest cause of the Peloponnesian war. Thucydides indicates the importance of the second section by introducing it with a preface (97.2). In that preface he is completely silent about the fact (which would have borne being restated) that he is about to lay bare the truest cause of the Peloponnesian war. Instead he presents that second section (which deals with events that occurred between ca. 476 and 440) in the first place as a kind of supplement to available accounts of the preceding epochs, if not as an improved version of Hellanicus' chronicle, and only secondarily as an exhibition of how the Athenian empire was established. If we turn from what one may call Thucydides' second preface to his first preface—his statement on the character of his whole work (I 20–22)—we observe to our surprise that there too he is completely silent about the subject of "cause." He presents there his "quest for the truth" as quest for what was truly done and truly said, i.e. for the true facts, and not for the true causes.[48] It also deserves mention that while Herodotus mentions "cause" in the opening of his work, the "scientific historian"

---

[48] As for the distinction between "fact" and "cause" cf. I 23.4–5. Perhaps the most important difference between the remark on the Athenian tyrannicide in I 20.2 and the repetition of that subject in VI 54–59 is precisely the fact that only in the latter is the cause of the tyrannicide made clear (cf. 54.1, 57.3, 59.1). Contrast V 53 (the central event of the thirteenth year) about a "cause" which was merely a "pretense" with I 23.6.

Thucydides does not.[49] In these manners he indicates the gravity of the question regarding the true causes—of a question which otherwise could seem to be (as it is for the scientific historian) a matter of course.

## 6. *Ananke*

From what has been said, it follows that the question of the true cause must be understood in the light of the distinction between Right and Compulsion. The Spartans believed that their injustice had caused their adversity in the first part of the war. Thucydides will only believe that that Spartan belief might have had an adverse effect on their conduct of the war. This does not mean that right belongs as it were to the sphere of mere seeming and only compulsion to the sphere of being, or that right and compulsion are simply opposites. Sparta indeed broke the treaty, but she was compelled to do so because she saw that a large part of Greece was already subject to the Athenians, hence feared that they would become still stronger and hence was forced to stop them before it was too late.[50] Compulsion excuses; it justifies an act which in itself would be unjust (cf. IV 92.5). The Athenians on the other hand, it seems, acted unjustly; they were not compelled to increase their power

---

* In I 1.3 Thucydides seems to say that no clear and certain knowledge of what happened prior to the Peloponnesian war is available (cf. also I 20 beginning) yet he cannot possibly mean this, for he gives a clear account at least of what happened in the decades immediately preceding that war; above all, his very attempt to prove the superiority of the Peloponnesian war to the earlier wars requires clear and certain knowledge of the earlier wars; likewise his quest for the causes of the Peloponnesian war, *i.e.* for things preceding that war, would not make sense if his remark in I 1.3 were taken literally. But Thucydides was not illiterate. One must then consider the import of the literally understood passage. If there is no clear and certain knowledge of what happened prior to the Peloponnesian war, there cannot be clear and certain knowledge of the supremacy of the Peloponnesian war; the belief in that supremacy is only a prejudice just like the belief in the supremacy of any other war on the part of the contemporaries of that war (I 21.2). If there is no clear and certain knowledge of what happened prior to the Peloponnesian war, there cannot be clear and certain knowledge of its causes, let alone of its truest cause; those causes are veiled in mystery; it is at least as reasonable to give an account of them in Homeric terms as in Thucydidean terms.

[50] I 23.6, 86.5, 88, II 8.5.

ever more (for instance, by allying themselves with the Corcyreans or by embarking on the Sicilian expedition); they were prompted not by compulsion but by *hybris* (cf. IV 98.5–6). This would not necessarily mean that they lost the war on that account. Yet partly the Athenians themselves and partly Thucydides through his narrative show that Athens was herself compelled to increase her power or was prompted by fear of the Persians and of the Spartans to found her empire and to enlarge it; she was compelled to become the tyrant city; she was compelled to compel Sparta to wage war against her. In their speech in Sparta the Athenians go considerably further. They claim that they were compelled to found their empire and to bring it to its present form above all by fear, then also by honor, and later also by interest (I 75.3). If being induced by honor or glory and especially by interest is regarded as compulsory and participating in the exculpation conferred by the compulsory, it is hard to see how any war or how any acquisition and exercise of tyrannical rule by one city over others can ever be unjust.[51] Accordingly when they repeat the three motives which compel cities to become imperial, the Athenians change the order by speaking of "honor, fear and interest." They go so far as to say that Athens has merely followed what was always established, namely, that the stronger keep down the weaker, *i.e.* that recourse to fear is not needed at all in order to justify empire; the innovation lies not with the Athenians but with the Spartans who now suddenly have recourse to "the just speech" which has not hitherto deterred anyone strong enough from aggrandizing himself (I 76.2). The Spartans do not contest the Athenian thesis. To discuss generalities of this kind would be in their eyes to exhibit excessive cleverness in useless matters (cf. I 84.3). On the proper occasion Pericles himself will state the Athenian thesis in Athens herself (II 63.2). But the Athenians are not the only ones who state it (cf. IV 61.5). On the other hand, the Athenian Euphemus, speaking in Camarina—perhaps reduced to euphemism because the situation of the Athenians in Sicily was not as simple as their situation before the outbreak of the war or on Melos—while not avoiding the comparison of the imperial city to a tyrant, justifies both the Athenians' empire and their

---

[51] With a view to IV 98.5 one would have to say that on the basis of what the Athenian ambassadors in Sparta assert, the very possibility of *hybris* and hence of divine law does not exist.

Sicilian expedition by their concern with their salvation or security alone, by their fear alone.[52]

Even if according to the instruction silently conveyed by Thucydides' narrative all cities which have the required power act in accordance with the Athenians' thesis regarding the compulsory power of interest, it would perhaps not necessarily follow that they are in fact compelled to act in this manner. The issue is decided in the dialogue between the Athenians and the Melians. During the peace between the two parts of the Peloponnesian war, the Athenians resolved to make themselves masters of the island of Melos, a Spartan colony but neutral in the war because of Athens' naval power. Before beginning the assault, the Athenians make an attempt to persuade the Melians to come over to their side. Just as, immediately before the outbreak of the war, Pericles did not permit the Spartan ambassadors to address the Athenian people (II 12.2; cf. IV 22) because he feared that they might deceive it, the Melian government takes the same precaution against the same danger. In order not to deceive even the Melian government, the Athenian ambassadors propose that they not make a long speech to which the Melians would reply with a long speech, but that their exchange should have the character of a dialogue.[53] The Athenian ambassadors talk as if they had been listening to Socrates' censure of Protagoras or Gorgias. Through their proposal Thucydides surely throws new light on the speeches with which his work abounds and at the same time stresses the unique importance of the dialogue which occurred on Melos. The dialogue takes place behind closed doors. Yet in the Melians' view it is a dialogue which, owing to the presence of the Athenian army, cannot lead to agreement but only to either war or their surrender into slavery; they have no hope that they might persuade the Athenians to go back to where they belong. According to the Athenians it is indeed the present facts which the Melians can see with their eyes, namely, the Athenian forces, which must be the starting point of the dialogue about how the Melians can be saved from present danger. The Melians cannot

---

[52] VI 83.2, 4; 85.1; 87.2. Cf. the limited meaning of compulsion according to which it excludes interest and the like in VII 57.

[53] We consider here only the speeches not the butchery; what Thucydides thought about that deed may be inferred from his judgment on the intention to butcher the Mytileneans (III 36.4, 6 and 49.4).

but admit this. The Athenians next determine the principle of the deliberation. The issue is not what is just but what is feasible—what the Athenians can do to the Melians and the Melians can do to the Athenians; questions of right arise only when the power to compel is more or less equal on both sides; if there is so great inequality as between Athens and Melos, the stronger does what he can and the weaker yields. The Athenians have no doubt that the Melians with whom they converse, *i.e.* the leading men as distinguished from the people, know the truth of the principle which they stated, yet they prove to be mistaken. The Melians are however compelled to argue on the basis of interest as distinguished from right. Arguing on this basis they remind the Athenians of the fact that there is an interest common to Melos and Athens: he who is today the stronger may be the weaker at some future time and then his former victims or their friends will take a terrible revenge on him for what he has done to the weaker in the heyday of his strength. The Athenians are not frightened by that prospect, for the power which will defeat them in the future will think of its interest rather than of vindictive justice and the Athenians will be as prudent to cede to their victor's interest as, they hope, the Melians will be at the present time; an imperial power must think not of its situation under its future victor but of its present subjects who indeed, in case of successful rebellion, will think of nothing but revenge; it is precisely in order to deprive their island subjects of all hope of resistance to Athens' naval power that the Athenians must become masters of Melos; precisely Melos' peacefully becoming an ally of Athens is that common interest to which the Melians appeal: the preservation of Melos as an ally of Athens is profitable to both Melos and Athens. The Melians are reduced to speechlessness, for their question whether the Athenians will not be satisfied with the Melians being their friends instead of their enemies and at the same time unallied with either Athens or Sparta is absurd; even assuming that friendship and neutrality in the same respect are not mutually exclusive, the Melians surely also wish to be friends of Sparta, Athens' enemy. The Athenians cannot make this point at this time in the debate because they are not at war with Sparta. But the Melians understand the situation sufficiently so as to limit themselves to offer continued neutrality rather than friendship: can the Athenians not tolerate neutrals? After all, there is a difference between the Athenians subjugating cities which are their colonies or otherwise have become their dependencies and then rebelled, and their subjugating a city which never belonged to them. They thus surreptitiously bring in the consideration of right as distinguished from interest. The Athenians counter this argument by denying that there is a difference between these two kinds of cities as far as right is concerned; surely the cities subject to Athens believe that their subjection is due to Athens' superior power; the important distinction is to be made from the point of view of Athenian interest as distinguished from right; accordingly one must distinguish not between legitimate subjects of Athens and neutrals, but between mainland cities and island cities; the mere fact that there are island cities not subject to Athens is taken as a sign of Athens' deficient naval power and is hence detrimental to Athens; the Athenians do not fear, as the Melians advise them to do, that as a consequence of their action against Melos all hitherto neutral cities will ally themselves with Athens' enemies, for the mainland cities know that they are not threatened by Athens whereas all island cities are a threat to Athens. When speaking of the mainland cities the Athenians had mentioned, somewhat inadvertently, the "freedom" of these cities as distinguished from the actual or potential condition of the islanders. The Melians take this as an admission that if they yield they will be enslaved. They are set to defend their freedom at all costs. By taking up the issue "freedom-slavery," they do not in violation of the rule of the dialogue introduce the issue of right; they remain within the sphere of interest in so far as it is obviously to a man's or a city's interest to be free, yet they enlarge that sphere in so far as freedom is also something noble; they feel that they would be base cowards by not risking everything for their freedom. The Athenians deny that yielding to much greater power is disgraceful; not to yield would show a lack of good sense or of moderation—of that virtue of which men of Spartan blood must be proud. The Melians tacitly admit that yielding to much greater power is not disgraceful but they question that the Athenians' power is much greater than theirs. Surely, the Athenians are more numerous than they but the outcome of a war does not depend merely on number; so they have hope. The Athenians and Melians thus agree that the issue is not whether one should act nobly or basely but whether there is ground of hope for the Melians. The Melians are hopeful. The Athenians warn them against hoping; not their small number but their total weakness, which is quite manifest, makes it hopeless for them to risk everything for the sake of their independence; they can still be saved by human means; the sensible rulers of Melos will not commit the mistake of the many who, when the manifest hopes fail, have recourse to the immanifest ones supplied by soothsayers and oracles which are surely ruinous. Thereupon the Melians reveal the grounds of their hope and thus the whole extent of their disagreement with the Athenians. Two things, they say, decide the issue of wars, power and chance; as for chance it depends (to some extent or altogether) on the divine, and the divine favors the just; as for the deficient power of the Melians, it will be strengthened by the alliance with the Spartans, who will come to the rescue of Melos if only for sheer shame. The question of whether the Melians act nobly by resisting the Athenians has been reduced to the question of whether they act wisely in doing so; one cannot act nobly by acting foolishly. Whether they act foolishly or not is now seen to depend entirely on how well grounded is their hope in the divine on the one hand and in the Spartans on the other. The Melians had not mentioned the divine when speaking of power. To the Melians' hope for divine help to the just, the Athenians oppose the following view of the divine and of justice. Both the divine and the human are compelled by their natures without any qualification each to rule over whatever is weaker than it; this law has not been laid down by the Athenians nor were they the first to act in accordance with it, but they found it in being and they will leave it in being for the future, forever, in the certainty that the Melians and all others would act on it if they had the same power as the Athenians. (One could say that according to the Athenians this law is the true divine law, the law of the interplay of motion and rest, of compulsion and right, compulsion obtaining among unequals and right obtaining among cities of more or less equal power.) That this law obtains among men, the Athenians claim to know evidently, whereas its being in force in regard to the divine is for them only a matter of opinion. This does not mean that they are not quite certain whether the Melians' belief in just gods may not have some foundation, but rather that they are not quite certain whether the divine exists or that they do not wish to deny its existence. Differently stated, the Athenians deny that they act impiously for in acting as they do they imitate the divine; in addition, the divine could not have forbidden the stronger to rule over the weaker because the stronger is compelled by natural necessity to rule over the weaker. What is true of divine help is true also of Spartan help. The Melians must be inexperienced and foolish indeed if they believe that the Spartans will help them for sheer shame. The Spartans are decent enough among themselves in that, in their relations with one another, they comply with the customs of their country; but in their relations with other men they, more obviously than other men, regard as noble what is pleasant, and as just what is expedient. (The Spartans behave habitually toward non-Spartans as the Athenians behaved among themselves during the worst times of the plague—II 53.3.) The Melians question the Athenians' view of Sparta (as distinguished from the Athenians' view of the gods) at least to the extent that they assert that precisely self-interest, as distinguished from the noble and the just, will induce the Spartans to come to their help. The Melians and Athenians have now reached agreement as to the necessity of disregarding completely what we would call all religious and moral considerations. The Athenians rejoin that self-interest induces men to act in the manner in which the Melians hope that the Spartans will act only when it is safe to do so; the Spartans are therefore the least likely to gamble; and to come to the rescue of Melos is obviously a very great gamble. The Melians cannot deny the notorious fact that the Spartans are very cautious men. From here on they can speak only in the optative mood. The Athenians are justified in saying that the Melians have not said a single word which would give support to their confidence; their strongest arguments are mere hopes. The Athenians conclude with a sober warning: it is sheer folly to call the Melians' becoming a tribute-paying ally of Athens a disgraceful act; the Melians will be truly disgraced if, by foolishly compelling the Athenians to fight and defeat them, they will bring it about that they all will be killed and their women and children be sold into slavery. After having deliberated among themselves, the Melian rulers repeat their rejection of the Athenian proposal; they repeat that they trust in chance, which depends on the divine, and in the Spartans. The Athenians leave them with the remark that they are the only ones who regard the future things as more evident than things seen, and who behold the unevident by virtue of wishing it as already occurring; their ruin will be proportionate to their trust in Sparta and in chance and in hopes. As appears from the sequel, the Athenian prediction comes true.

The Melians are defeated in speech before they are defeated in deed. One must blush to say so, but one is compelled to admit to oneself that in Thucydides' view the Melians' resistance to the Athenians' demand was a foolish act and the fate of the Melians is therefore not tragic. The last doubt which may remain is removed by what he says about the Chians' failure in their revolt against Athens. The Chians were much more powerful and wealthy than the Melians, but, being sober or moderate, they were as concerned with safety as the Spartans. By revolting against the Athenians they may seem to have disregarded their safety or to have acted irrationally, but this is not the case. They took that risk when according to all ordinary considerations it was wise to take it: at the time of the revolt they had many good allies on whose help they could count and, as the Athenians themselves had to admit, Athens' cause was almost hopeless as a consequence of the Sicilian disaster; no one could be blamed for not having foreseen Athens' extraordinary resilience.[54] One can explain Thucydides' implicit judgment on the action of the Melians in two ways which are not mutually exclusive. The city may and must demand self-sacrifice from its citizens; the city itself however cannot sacrifice itself; a city may without disgrace accept even under compulsion the overlordship of another city which is much more powerful; this is not to deny of course that death or extinction is to be preferred to enslavement proper. There is a certain similarity between the city and the individual; just as the individual, the city cannot act nobly or virtuously if it lacks the necessary equipment, i.e. power, or, in other words, virtue is useless without sufficient armament.[55] If the action of the Melians was foolish, one must wonder whether this fact throws any light on the most striking reason of their action, i.e. their view that the gods help the just or harm the unjust. This view is the Spartan view (cf. VII 18.2). It is opposed to the Athenian view as stated most clearly in the dialogue with the Melians. The Melian dialogue leaves one wondering whether on the basis of the common belief one would not have to state Thucydides' view by saying that trust in help from the gods is like trust in help from

---

[54] VIII 24.4–5. Cf. with this passage III 40.1: Cleon judges the "mistake" of the Mytileneans from the point of view of justice; Thucydides judges the "mistake" of the Chians from the point of view of safety or prudence. Cf. IV 108.3–4. Cf. also the case of the Orchomenians (V 61.5).

[55] Aristotle, *Eth. Nic.* 1178a23–33; Xenophon, *Anabasis* II 1.12.

the Spartans or that the gods are as little concerned with justice in their dealings with human beings as the Spartans are in their dealings with foreigners; the fact that the gods' existence is not explicitly discussed between the Athenians and the Melians does not prove that it was of no concern to Thucydides. Taking the question of right entirely by itself, *i.e.* disregarding the gods altogether, one may say that there is a kinship between injustice and motion and between justice and rest,[56] but that just as rest presupposes motion and issues in motion, justice presupposes injustice and issues in injustice. It is precisely for this reason that human beings seek support for right in the gods or that the question of right cannot be considered entirely apart from the question concerning the gods. In the Melian dialogue the Athenians remain victorious. There is no debate in Thucydides' work in which the Spartan or Melian view defeats the Athenian view. After their surrender to the Spartans, the Plataeans are permitted to defend themselves against the capital charge of not having helped the Spartans in the war; they appeal to right and to the gods. Their worst enemies, the Thebans, acting as their accusers, answer them on the ground of right without referring to the gods. The issue of necessity or expediency, as distinguished from that of right, and in particular the issue whether it is expedient for the Spartans and their allies to kill the Plataeans, is not raised. The Plataeans are killed, the Spartans having identified, according to the Plataeans' contention, the just with what is immediately profitable to them (III 56.3), for it was profitable to them to give in to the Thebans' savage hatred for the Plataeans; the Spartans act in accordance with what the Athenians told the Melians to be the Spartan way of acting (cf. III 68.4). Quite different were the proceedings in Athens regarding the fate of the Mytileneans who had failed in their revolt against their Athenian ally. Whereas in the Peloponnesian camp there was no one to oppose the killing of the helpless Plataeans, in Athens there was a debate as to what should be done to the helpless Mytileneans. Cleon, who favors the butchery, is the one who appeals to right: the Mytileneans acted most unjustly, they preferred force to justice, they were prompted by *hybris,* and the execution of all of them is nothing but their just punishment (III 39.3–6); in addition, in this case at any rate the just perfectly agrees with what is profitable

---

[56] Cf. Aristotle, *Eth. Nic.* 1104b24–25 and Isaiah 30.15–16. Cf. Pindar, *Pyth.* VIII beg.

in the long run for Athens. Diodotus, who opposes the killing of the Mytileneans, argues entirely on the ground of what is profitable for Athens to do to the Mytileneans; he does not question her right to kill them all (III 44, 47.5–6). Similarly it is the harsh Spartan ephor who was responsible for Sparta's breaking the treaty and not the nice king Archidamus who appeals above all to right (I 86); and the Athenians, who entered the first part of the war with justice on their side, never mention their justice and still less boast of it. It seems that the case for right or the appeal to right is made only by those Thucydidean speakers who are either completely helpless or else unjust.[57] This does not mean, to repeat, that the principle stated most forcefully by the Athenians on Melos is incompatible with justice in the sense of fidelity to covenants; it is perfectly compatible with such fidelity; it is only incompatible with covenants which would limit a city's aspirations for all future times; but such were not the covenants with which Thucydides had to be seriously concerned.

The Athenians' assertion of what one may call the natural right of the stronger as a right which the stronger exercises by natural necessity is not a doctrine of Athenian imperialism; it is a universal doctrine; it applies to Sparta for instance as well as to Athens. It is not refuted by the facts of the Spartans' moderation, of their satisfaction with what they possess, or of their unwillingness to go to war. In other words, the natural right of the stronger does not lead in all cases to expansionism. There are limits beyond which expansion is no longer safe. There are powers which are "saturated." The Spartans were as "imperialist" as the Athenians; only their empire was so to speak invisible because their empire had been established much earlier than the Athenian empire and had reached its natural limit; it was therefore no longer an object of surprise and offense. By overlooking this fact, one moves in the direction of the supreme folly committed during World War II when men in high places acted on the assumption that there was a British Empire and British imperialism but no Russian Empire and Russian imperialism because they held that an empire consists of a number of countries separated by salt water. Chios which was second only to Sparta in moderation, was second only to Sparta regarding the number of her slaves. Sparta was moderate because she had grave troubles with

---

[57] For the second case cf. *Republic* 366c3–d1.

her Helots; the Helots made her moderate.[58] Thucydides just as his Athenians on Melos did not know of a strong city which failed to rule a weak city when it was to the former's interest to do so, merely for reasons of moderation, *i.e.* independently of calculation.

## 7. *The Dialogue on Melos and the Disaster in Sicily*

Yet is not precisely according to Thucydides' presentation the Athenian dialogue with the Melians followed by the Athenian disaster in Sicily? Is that disaster, which included the killing by the sword or by hunger of thousands and thousands of Athenian prisoners, not the punishment for the Athenians' speech and deed on Melos? Is it not its consequence whether mediated by the gods or not? This thought is perhaps the best example of what Thucydides meant by stories delightful for the ear, for he makes it quite clear that however unjust, daring, or immoderate the attempt to conquer Sicily may have been, its failure was not due to its injustice or daring; despite their deed and speech on Melos, the Athenians' Sicilian expedition could well have succeeded. Nor can one say that the Melian dialogue, revealing the abandonment of Pericles' political principle by the Athenians, prepared the abandonment by them of Pericles' cautious war policy. While Pericles might never have said what the Athenians said on Melos and while he might not have regarded the Athenians' action against Melos as expedient, his political principle did not differ from that of those Athenians (II 62.2, 63.2). The Sicilian expedition ran counter to Pericles' view of how the war should be conducted but Thucydides never says that Pericles' views were always sound. On the contrary, to repeat, he regarded the Sicilian expedition as perfectly feasible (I 144.1; II 65.7, 11; cf. also VI 11.1). According to him, the Sicilian expedition failed because of the fundamental defect of post-Periclean, as distinguished from Periclean, domestic politics; after Pericles there was no longer among the leading men that perfect harmony between private interest and public interest that was characteristic of Pericles; the concern with private honor and private gain prevailed. Thanks to his manifest superiority Pericles became as it were naturally the first man, whereas none of his successors possessed that superiority, but each had to fight for his place in the sun and therefore was compelled to make concessions to the *demos* which were

---

[58] VIII 40.2 and 24.4. Cf. I 101.2, 118.2, IV 41.3, 80.3–4, V 14.3.

detrimental to the city. It was the overriding concern with private interest which ruined the Sicilian expedition and ultimately caused the loss of the war (II 65.7–12). Post-Periclean Athens lacked that singular public-spiritedness which was the honor of Athens from the time of the Persian war until the age of Pericles (I 70.6, 8; 74.1–2). As Pericles makes clear in the beautiful sentences of his Funeral Speech, Athens more than any other city gave free rein to the individual's development toward graceful manysidedness or self-sufficiency or permitted him to be a genuine individual: so that he could be infinitely superior as a citizen to the citizens of any other city. In what is in Thucydides' work his farewell speech, Pericles reminds his fellow citizens of the necessity to be devoted wholeheartedly to their city. In this respect there appears to be complete agreement between the statesman and the historian. Thucydides is concerned above everything else with the cities (the Athenians, the Spartans and so on) as distinguished from the individuals, therefore with the warlike or peaceful relations of the city with other cities rather than with their inner structure; therefore he deals with the lives and deaths of the individuals only from the point of view of the cities to which they belong.

Those who contend that there is a connection between the Melian dialogue and the Sicilian disaster must have in mind a connection between the two events which Thucydides intimates rather than sets forth explicitly by speaking of the emancipation of private interest in post-Periclean Athens. The Melian dialogue shows nothing of such an emancipation. But it contains the most unabashed denial occurring in Thucydides' work of a divine law which must be respected by the city or which moderates the city's desire for "having more." The Athenians on Melos, in contradistinction to Callicles or Thrasymachus, limit themselves indeed to asserting the natural right of the stronger with regard to the cities; but are Callicles and Thrasymachus not more consistent than they? Can one encourage, as even Pericles and precisely Pericles does, the city's desire for "having more" than other cities without in the long run encouraging the individual's desire for "having more" than his fellow citizens?[59] Pericles was indeed dedicated wholeheartedly to the

---

[59] The intermediate stage between the city and the individuals is the politically most relevant groups within the city, the powerful or rich and the multitude. Their antagonism culminating in civil war is between the antagonism culminating in war among the cities and the antagonism culminating in treason and the like among individuals.

common good of the city but to its common good unjustly understood. He did not realize that the unjust understanding of the common good is bound to undermine dedication to the common good
however understood. He had not given sufficient thought to the
precarious character of the harmony between private interest and
public interest; he had taken that harmony too much for granted.

Thucydides looks at the deaths of men from the point of view
of the cities to which they belong. He notes carefully what was
done to the dead after the battles; their seemly burial is the final
act of their city's care for its sons; by their death they do not cease,
and yet they cease, to belong to their city: Hades is not divided
into cities. The customary practice becomes the theme in Pericles'
Funeral Speech, since it was an ancient law in Athens to bring the
bodies of the fallen soldiers home for public and common burial
and to have the fallen soldiers praised immediately after the burial
by an outstanding citizen (II 34.1, 35.3). Pericles does not approve
of the law which instituted these funeral speeches because of the
difficulty in satisfying the listeners: for some of them no praise is
sufficient and others regard the praise as exaggerated. One cannot
praise highly enough those who brought the supreme sacrifice and
yet the praise must remain credible. In addition, not all fallen
soldiers led equally praiseworthy lives—some were even good-for-
nothings (II 42.3), and died an equally praiseworthy death. Pericles
overcomes the difficulty by praising above all the city, or the cause
for which all of them died equally. It is the praise of the city of
Athens and of what it stands for on which the fame of Pericles'
Funeral Speech is founded. Not so much the city as city as a city of
the stature of Athens can demand the supreme sacrifice. Yet all
cities demand it equally and in many cases are obeyed with no less
dedication than the city of Athens: the noble death for the fatherland is not the Athenians' nor even the Greeks' preserve. And even
the Athenian's death for his fatherland which is of unique glory is
not exhausted by its being a death for Athens. Thucydides draws
our attention to this difficulty by making his Pericles avoid the
words "death," "dying," or "dead bodies": only once does his Pericles
speak in the Funeral Speech of death, and then only in the expression "unfelt death" (II 43.6).[60] Accordingly, in the allusion to the

---

[60] This was imitated by Plato in his *Menexenus;* Plato goes even further
than Thucydides' Pericles. Contrast with this not only the Gettysburg Address
but even the *Epitaphioi* of Demosthenes, Hyperides, and Lysias.

climactic event of dying that Pericles makes, he causes it to last only a very brief moment.[61] The glory of the city of Athens is to make the individuals, the survivors, both the soldiers and the mourners, oblivious of the agonies of their comrades and their beloved. But Pericles is not a Spartan addressing Spartans, as he had made abundantly clear through the bulk of his speech. He cannot altogether avoid at least mentioning the grief of the individuals who lost their sons, brothers or husbands. The callousness with which he speaks of, or rather alludes to, the grief especially of the aged parents who lost their only son, cannot easily be surpassed. He is punished appropriately. To the widows he can say no more than to address to them this statesmanlike admonition: they should be as good as women can be, and that wife is best who is least mentioned for good or for ill in male society. His wife was the famous Aspasia. The statesman who looked at life and death only from the point of view of the city forgets his private life. It is most fitting that in Thucydides' narrative the praise of Pericles should precede Pericles' death by thirty months (II 65.6). It is no less fitting that the Funeral Speech is followed immediately by Thucydides' account of the plague—an account which abounds with mentions of death, dead, dying, and corpses and which deals with an event that brought home to everyone the limitations of the city. Thucydides does not mention the fact that Pericles lost two of his sons and the largest part of his kin and friends through the plague and died as a consequence of the plague. His last speech, delivered under the impact of the plague, takes up the subject of "private calamities" with greater force than the two earlier speeches. That speech is immediately followed by Thucydides' praise of Pericles the guiding theme of which is the conflict between the private and the public. Thucydides praises especially Pericles' foresight in regard to the war: his foresight was limited to the war; he could not have foreseen the plague but he did not foresee or consider sufficiently the things which were brought home to his fellow citizens and even to him by the plague (II 65.6; cf. 64.1–2).

To return to the question concerning the connection between the Melian dialogue and the Sicilian disaster, that connection is established by the fact that it is in the long run impossible to en-

---

[61] II 42.4. Cf. also 43.2 beginning where he seems to deny that death is each one's own while asserting that "the ageless [not "immortal"] praise" is each one's own.

courage the city's desire for "having more" at the expense of other
cities without encouraging the desire of the individual for "having
more" at the expense of his fellow citizens. This reasoning seems
to support the "Spartan" praise of moderation and of the divine law.
Yet we have seen that this praise is not accepted by Thucydides in
the last analysis. If Thucydides was consistent, he must have accepted the view set forth by Callicles and Thrasymachus while
avoiding, as a matter of course, its crudities and superficialities. The
test will be his teaching on tyranny. In different ways both the
Spartans and the Athenians were opposed to tyranny. Sparta was
never ruled by a tyrant; Athens threw off the yoke of her tyrants
with the help of the Spartans; the admiration for the Athenian tyrannicides Harmodius and Aristogeiton was an important part of
the manner in which the Athenian democracy understood itself.
After having indicated in his Introduction that the view held by the
Athenian multitude about the Athenian tyrannicides includes a
grave factual error, he gives on the proper occasion, in the sixth
book, a detailed account of Athenian tyranny and its end. Thucydides was compelled to explain the fear of tyrants which gripped the
Athenian *demos* so eager to be itself a tyrant. The celebrated deed
of the Athenian tyrannicides was caused, we learn, not by public-
spirited love of liberty but by erotic jealousy. Aristogeiton, a mature
man, was in love with the youth Harmodius to whom Hipparchus,
the brother of the tyrant Hippias, made unsuccessful advances; hurt
in his erotic feelings and fearing that the powerful Hipparchus
might succeed in his attempts by the use of force, Aristogeiton resolved on putting down the tyranny. Yet Hipparchus did not dream
of using force; he committed however the folly of hurting Harmodius out of spite by insulting the latter's sister. By some accident the
two lovers failed to kill the tyrant yet did kill his brother whom
later legend promoted to the rank of tyrant for the greater glory
of the killers. The celebrated deed was an irrational act as regards
its first as well as its immediate cause and, above all, as regards its
effect. For only after the slaying of Hippias' brother did the tyranny
become harsh and bloody since the tyrant became frightened. Prior
to that act, the tyranny was popular; the Athenian tyrants were
men of "virtue and intelligence";[62] while not imposing heavy taxes

---

*I.e.* they had the same qualities as Brasidas (IV 81.2). VI 54.6–7 shows
that there is no conflict between tyranny and piety; cf. also I 126.3–4 and
Aristotle, *Politics* 1314b38ff.

they adorned the city, managed the wars and brought the sacrifices in the temples; they left the laws of the city as they found them; they only arranged that there was always one of themselves in the ruling offices. This state of things which, it would seem, was in no way shocking and degrading, came to an end by the irrational act of the tyrannicides which started a chain of actions as the result of which Hippias was expelled from Athens. He went to the king of Persia, whence he came many years later, as an old man, with the Persian army to Marathon. Thucydides was enabled to destroy the popular and populist legend partly because he had access to an oral tradition which was not accessible to every Athenian. Perhaps one will find that Thucydides' truthful account of Athenian tyranny is not a vindication of tyranny as such, for he says that owing to the fact that the tyrants were concerned only with their own safety and the advancement of their own houses, they hardly did any deed worth mentioning and surely did not embark on large-scale expansion of their cities' power.[63] But we do not yet know whether Thucydides regarded empire as the highest good, for to say that under certain conditions empire is possible and necessary is not the same as to be an "imperialist." After all, under certain conditions civil wars too and tyrannies become possible or necessary.

The conflict between public and private interest to which Thucydides traces the Sicilian disaster has another side to it of which he does not speak, for good reasons, in his eulogy of Pericles, but which becomes apparent from his narrative. We shall not forget the case of Alcibiades to which above all he points when contrasting post-Periclean Athenian politics with the situation under Pericles. We shall first consider two other cases. Demosthenes, the most lovable of Thucydides' characters, having committed a grave blunder in Aetolia owing to which a considerable number of better Athenians than those praised by Pericles in his Funeral Speech had perished, did not return to Athens because he was afraid of what the Athenians would do to him on account of his failure. He was suffi-

---

[63] I 17, 18.1–2, 20.2, VI 53.3–59.4. Just as Thucydides knew "privately" of what truly happened at the time of the so-called tyrannicide, he must also have known privately the correspondence between the Greek traitors Themistocles and Pausanias and the Persian king which he quotes verbatim (I 128.7, 129.3, 137.4). The tyrant Hippias also ended as a traitor of the Greeks to the Persian king. The phenomena "tyranny" and "treason," rooted in the opposition of self-interest and public interest, belong together. As for the possibility of an Athenian tyrant at the time of the Peloponnesian war, cf. especially VIII 66.

ciently versatile to compensate the city for his defeat by a splendid victory in the next campaign in the same region, after which victory it was safe for him to return (III 98.4–5, 114.1). We catch here a glimpse of the most serious conflict between private and public interest in Athens: public-spirited men must fear for their safety if they commit serious mistakes or what the *demos* regards as serious mistakes. In cases like this it is not love of private gain or prestige but a man's more legitimate concern for his safety and honor which comes into conflict with public service.[64] During the Sicilian expedition Demosthenes was sent to Sicily with a strong army in order to assist Nicias who was not sufficiently strong to reduce Syracuse. He wished to avoid Nicias' great mistake which consisted in postponing his assault on Syracuse too long; he therefore launched an attack as soon as possible; he suffered a severe defeat. The situation was in every aspect much graver than after his defeat in Aetolia. Hence he did not think for one moment of his own safety and proposed immediate return of the whole armament to Athens. Nicias still had hope of success at Syracuse. But the reason which he gave openly in a council of war for rejecting Demosthenes' proposal was that the Athenians would take a dim view of the withdrawal of the armament from Syracuse unless they had voted for it in advance; if the men in command in Sicily take it upon themselves to return to Athens, the Athenian vote on the commanders in Sicily will be swayed by clever calumniators; the very servicemen who are now most in favor of an immediate return to Athens will assert after their return that the Athenian commanders had committed treason, having been bribed by the enemy; knowing the natures of the Athenians, he prefers to stay in Sicily and to die at the hands of the enemies as an individual ("privately") rather than to perish through the Athenians ["publicly"] on a degrading charge and unjustly (VII 47–48). Nicias regarded this reasoning as publicly defensible: no one could deny that his and Demosthenes' safety and honor were at the mercy of unscrupulous demagogues and of the easily excitable and ignorant *demos;* he preferred for himself an honorable death in battle. But by choosing "privately" his death in Sicily, he chose "publicly" the destruction of the Athenian armament in Sicily and therewith, as far as in him lay, the ruin of Athens; out of justi-

---

[64] Cf. Machiavelli, *Discorsi* I 28–31.

fied fear of the Athenian *demos* he acted like a traitor. If men of the integrity of Demosthenes and Nicias could, if to different degrees, be swayed by fear for their safety to take such questionable courses, the conduct of Alcibiades appears in a different light than it otherwise would. When the Athenians recalled him from Sicily to defend himself against a capital charge, while suspecting him in addition of being involved in a plot to establish a tyranny in Athens (VI 53, 60–61), he did not return to Athens, justly fearing that he would be killed as a matter of course without receiving a fair hearing; he had practically no choice but to escape to Sparta, to become a traitor to his fatherland, and, regardless of whether he had ever desired to become a tyrant, to embark on a policy of amazing versatility—playing the Spartans against the Athenians, the Persian king against both the Spartans and the Athenians, the Athenian oligarchs against the Athenian *demos*, and the Athenian *demos* against the Athenian oligarchs—which for some time made him the arbiter of all powers and which might have made him the monarch of Athens and not only of Athens.

Let us reconsider at this point the diagnosis of the Sicilian expedition which Thucydides indicates in his very eulogy of Pericles. The Sicilian expedition could have succeeded but for the fact that Pericles' successors were concerned more with their private good than with the common good: Alcibiades was driven to prefer his private good to the common good because the Athenian *demos* compelled him to become a traitor to Athens and to attempt to become her tyrant; the Sicilian expedition would have succeeded if the Athenian *demos* had trusted Alcibiades (VI 15.4). The earlier tyrannies (like that of Pisistratus and his sons) were indeed incompatible with empire; empire—at any rate the empire studied by Thucydides, the Athenian empire—is not possible without the full participation of the *demos* in political life; the *demos* is enthusiastically in favor of the grandest imperial enterprise ever undertaken by any Greek city but it ruins that enterprise by its folly; it brings about a situation in which it looks as if only Alcibiades, whom it distrusts and hates and whom it had driven to actions which in the case of any other man would be called desperate, could save the city by in effect becoming a tyrant. The Sicilian expedition would not have succeeded, it would not even have been attempted in the circumstances, under Pericles. To attempt such an enterprise and to succeed in it, Athens needed a leader of greater stature, of a better *physis* than Pericles.[65] The Melian dialogue is connected with the Sicilian disaster by the same thought which connects the Funeral Speech with the plague: by the question regarding the precarious harmony between the public and the private.

The connection between the Melian dialogue and the Sicilian disaster is closer than that between the tyrant city and the tyrannical individual. The Athenians on Melos had but scorn for the Melians' hope for divine help to the just, for any hope for any divine help. They spoke indeed behind closed doors but to hear them one would believe that all Athenians shared their views. In fact however they spoke only for a part of Athens—for modern, innovating, daring Athens whose memory barely extends beyond Salamis and Themistocles. But precisely when the new Athens was put to its test through the Peloponnesian war, and therefore the rural population of Attica had to be uprooted, all Athenians were reminded most forcefully of their being rooted in remote antiquity, in an epoch when the belief in the ancestral gods was in its greatest vigor. The very Funeral Speech reminds one of the singular glory of Marathon as distinguished from Salamis.[66] The older stratum of Athens asserted itself—if in a "sophisticated" manner[67]—during the Peloponnesian war as narrated by Thucydides through Nicias who brought about the peace with Sparta called after him and who opposed the Sicilian expedition. Nicias can be said to be that leading and patriotic Athenian who came closest to holding the "Spartan" or "Melian" view as previously described. To see this one must follow his fate as it unfolds in Thucydides' pages. By doing so we shall arrive at a somewhat clearer understanding of Thucydides' manner of writing.

The first action of Nicias was an attack on an island close to Athens; the action was undertaken in the interest of Athens' safety against attacks from the sea; part of the action consisted in "liberating" the entrance for Athenian ships between the island and the mainland (III 51; cf. II 94.1). The Spartans had begun the war out of concern with their safety; they claimed to wage the war for the

---

[65] The praise of Antiphon's virtue (VIII 68.1) must be understood as part of the "Alcibiadean" context: Antiphon is not praised, as Brasidas and the Athenian tyrants are (IV 81.2, VI 54.5), for the fact that he possessed both virtue and (political) intelligence.

[66] I 73.2–74.4, II 14–16, 34.5, 36.1–3; cf. Plato, *Laws* 707b4–c6.

[67] Plato, *Laches* 197d.

"liberation" of the Greek cities from Athenian domination. We next
find Nicias in charge of an unsuccessful attempt to reduce the island
of Melos (III 91.1-3); Athenians of a different stamp succeed where
Nicias failed. On the next occasion on which we hear of him, his
enemy Cleon had made him responsible in the Athenian assembly
for the fact that the Spartans cut off on the island of Sphacteria had
not yet been reduced; in order to beat off the attack, Nicias, taking
up a suggestion made by others, proposes that Cleon should go to
Sphacteria and resigns his military command in favor of Cleon; he
hoped as all other moderate men did that Cleon's expedition would
be the end of the abominable demagogue (IV 27.5-28.5). Nicias
hoped in vain; his apparently shrewd move merely led to Cleon's
greatest triumph and therewith to the gravest defeat of the moderate
Athenians; his move against Cleon foreshadows his move against
Alcibiades in the debate about the Sicilian expedition: a move
meant to be conducive to the cause of moderation assured the
defeat of that cause. Nicias' fourth action is a campaign against
Corinth which ended in a victory of no consequence; two facts are
remarkable: the victory was due to the Athenian knights, and Nicias
religiously took care that two Athenian corpses in the hands of the
enemy were surrendered to the Athenians under a truce (IV 42-44).
There are amazing parallels to both facts in the Athenian defeat in
Sicily. It must suffice here to say that the inferiority of the Athenians
in cavalry may have been the decisive reason for their Sicilian defeat—more important than the more startling blunders underlined
by Thucydides. This military mistake was due equally to Nicias
and to Alcibiades (VI 71.2; cf. 20.4, 21.2, 22, 25.2, 31.2 as well as the
later references to cavalry in the account of the Sicilian expedition).
It surely is in perfect harmony with the spirit of Thucydides' silent
instruction not to mention that military blunder but merely to enable the reader to see it. And it is surely in perfect agreement with
the spirit of Thucydides' quest for causes that he might find the
decisive fault of the Sicilian defeat in an unspectacular blunder of
the kind indicated—a blunder not unconnected indeed, as a moment's reflection shows, with the spectacular ones. In the year following Nicias was in charge of the conquest of an island inhabited by
Spartan subjects; there was a battle but the resistance of the enemy
was not strong; the vanquished were treated very mildly, not at all
as the Melians were treated after their defeat; the conquest was
easy thanks to Nicias' secret negotiations with some of the islanders
(IV 53-54). The action foreshadows Nicias' policy with regard to

the Syracusans. Nicias' sixth action was undertaken against Brasidas; Nicias was at least partly responsible for the fact that the inhabitants of a city which had turned from the Athenian alliance to the Spartans were not butchered by the angry soldiery after its subjugation (IV 129–130). The last and most famous action of Nicias prior to the Sicilian expedition was the peace with Sparta which separates the two parts of the Peloponnesian war. This action was rendered possible by the deaths of Brasidas and Cleon. Through Cleon's death Nicias had become what he was eager to become, the leading man in Athens. He was eager for peace because he wished to give rest both to himself and to the city from the toils of war for the present and because for the future he did not wish to expose his hitherto untarnished good fortune to fortune's whims (V 16.1): there seems to be perfect harmony between his private interest and the public interest. But the peace proved very soon to be unstable, and Nicias was attacked as responsible for a peace which was allegedly not in the interest of Athens (V 46): leaders, to say nothing of others, are exposed to fortune's whims not only in war. Only after having shown us Nicias in such a large number of deeds of so great a variety does Thucydides let us hear a speech by Nicias. No other character is introduced by Thucydides in this manner; the unique introduction corresponds to Nicias' unique importance.[68]

In his first speech (VI 9–14) Nicias attempts to dissuade the

---

[68] Cf. the report about a speech by Nicias in V 46.1. As for Brasidas, cf. II 86.6 (or 85.1) with the only preceding mention of him in II 25.2. The deeds of Alcibiades preceding his first speech are no less in number than Nicias' but they are less varied. The unique significance of Nicias consists in the fact that he is the representative *par excellence* of moderation in the city of daring. As the pious gentleman warrior who is concerned with his military renown and with omens, he represents also the class of readers primarily addressed by Thucydides whose work deals above all with war and with omens (cf. I 23.2–3); that work is best understood if one reads it as primarily addressed to the Niciases of the future generations, potential pillars of their cities who will be attracted as a matter of course by the account of the greatest war which was so great because of the large number of battles as well as of omens. Among those primary addressees there will be some who can learn to raise their sights beyond Nicias or who can ascend. That ascent will be guided in the first place by Thucydides' explicit praise of men other than Nicias: of Themistocles, Pericles, Brasidas, Pisistratus, Archelaus, Hermocrates, and Antiphon (cf. note 71 below). But it will also eventually be guided by Thucydides' praise, only silently conveyed, of Demosthenes and Diodotus.

Athenians from the Sicilian expedition. He makes that attempt a
few days after they had already decided on the expedition and
elected him against his will as one of the three commanders. There
had been no change in popular sentiment between the two meetings
of the assembly (cf. III 35.4): Nicias' success depends entirely on
his power of persuasion. He begins his attempt to persuade the
Athenians by suggesting that his self-interest would induce him to
favor the expedition: he would derive honor from it since he would
be a commander and he is less afraid than others to die; he opposes
the expedition, then, because he is concerned exclusively with the
common good. Yet, one might well say, how can he derive honor
from being a commander of the expedition if the expedition cannot
be crowned with success? Why then does he oppose it? In fact, he
opposes it from self-interest—from a self-interest which in his view
is as much in harmony with the common good in the case of the
Sicilian expedition as it was in the case of the Peace of Nicias. He
admits this in a way by adding at once that a good citizen ought
to be concerned with his body and his property since precisely this
concern makes him concerned with the well-being of the city. If
he has any hope of success, he will try to persuade the city to preserve what it possesses and not to risk it for the sake of immanifest
and future things; he will wish, that is, that the Athenians will act
as he himself—the wealthy and famous Nicias who is completely
satisfied with the wealth and the fame which he possesses—is
prompted to act or that they will act in the Spartan manner (cf. I
70.2–3, VI 31.6). The enemy to be feared, he asserts, is Sparta, anti-
democratic Sparta, and not Syracuse; the Spartans may use the
opportunity supplied by the Athenians' entanglement in Sicily for
no longer remaining at rest: the Athenians ought to remain at rest.
He tries to make his hearers oblivious of the fact that the Spartans
tend to remain at rest and that more than the Athenians' going to
Sicily would be needed to stir them into action. Without foreseeing
and willing it, he provides in a manner for this additional incentive.
He can only hope that he will dissuade the Athenians from the
expedition; to say the least, he must reckon with the possibility
that, in accordance with the formal decision made in the preceding
meeting of the assembly, he and Alcibiades will be in joint command of the expedition. Yet in order to dissuade the Athenians from
the expedition, he discredits his fellow commander: Alcibiades is
concerned only with his private good; he cannot be trusted. No one

can say whether or to what extent this attack on Alcibiades' character, which proved to be wholly ineffectual at the moment, contributed under other circumstances to the Athenians' recalling Alcibiades from Sicily and hence to the stirring of the Spartans into action against Athens; but no one can deny that Nicias' calumny of Alcibiades is in harmony with the manner in which the Athenians treated Alcibiades a short time later in manifest disregard of the interest of their city. Thucydides' judgment on Alcibiades from the point of view of civic virtue agrees with Nicias' judgment but, having reflected more deeply even than Pericles on the complex relation between private interest and the interest of the city, he is less sure than Nicias that Alcibiades' concern with his own aggrandizement is simply opposed to the interest of Athens, and he is quite sure that the success of the Sicilian expedition depended decisively on Alcibiades' participation in it on the side of the Athenians (VI 15). At any rate Alcibiades, who calls on the Athenians to act in the Athenian, not in the Spartan, manner convinces them that by entrusting the command of the expedition to him and Nicias jointly, they will make sure that his defects (if they are defects) are compensated not only by his outstanding virtues but by Nicias' virtue as well. In his second speech (VI 20–23) Nicias makes a last effort to dissuade the Athenians from the expedition by making clear to them the magnitude of the effort required to guarantee the success of the enterprise; he does not realize that in doing so he merely gives the Athenians what appears to them to be the most competent expert advice as to how they can achieve the end which they most passionately desire or that he proves the wisdom of Alcibiades according to whom the cooperation of Alcibiades' nature and Nicias' experience is needed for the success of the expedition. Nicias is obviously not fit to be the sole or even the chief commander of the expedition (cf. VII 38.2–3, 40.2). While the Athenians are engaged in preparing the expedition, they receive the first inkling of the impending disaster: a gross act of impiety is committed in Athens and this appeared to be a bad omen for the expedition in the eyes of the Athenians, the large majority of whom lacked the lights which distinguished the Athenian speakers on Melos; the popular fear of the gods is used against Alcibiades by those who compete with him for popular favor; but for certain calculations they would have impeached him for impiety at once; they will bring about his criminal prosecution within a very short time; while one has no right to assume that Nicias was involved in these follies, one cannot deny that both the distrust of Alcibiades and the popular fear are in harmony with Nicias' way of thinking. For the time being, the preparations for the expedition are continued and completed; the expeditionary force sails. The Sicilian expedition surpasses everything undertaken by Pericles; whereas Pericles stood for love of the beautiful qualified by thrift, the Sicilian expedition, being in the style of Alcibiades whose fellow commander was the exceedingly rich Nicias, was inspired by love of the beautiful on the level of lavishness;[69] it reminded of Xerxes' expedition against Greece; yet after Alcibiades' recall, the man at the head of this proud enterprise will be the man less tainted by *hybris* than any of his Greek contemporaries. One must wonder whether Alcibiades' *hybris* would not have been more conducive to Athens' success than Nicias' lack of it. Despite Alcibiades' recall, the Athenians in Sicily were quite successful at first: Nicias was a competent general. In addition the third of the three commanders in charge of the expedition, Lamachus, was still alive, and no one can say to what extent the early successes of the Athenians against Syracuse were due to this man whom we had almost forgotten to mention and who was more given to daring than Nicias. But Alcibiades had stirred the Spartans into action and a Peloponnesian force was on its way for the relief of hard-pressed Syracuse. In addition, Lamachus had died fighting and Nicias had fallen sick. Yet Nicias, being now the sole commander and again underestimating the power of the abominable traitor Alcibiades, was more hopeful than ever before (VI 103–104). His hope is disappointed: the Peloponnesian force arrives and the situation of the Athenians in Sicily deteriorates rapidly. Yet Nicias is now in his element: no daring action is possible any more; the only way of salvation is inactivity and caution; but caution will lead to salvation only if the Athenians at home act quickly either by calling back the armament from Sicily very soon or by sending strong reinforcements very soon (VII 8, 11.3); apart from being cautious Nicias can only hope. Acting with utmost caution toward his own fellow citizens because he knows their natures (14.2, 4), he does not dare to tell them that the only safe course of action is the immediate recall of the armament from Sicily; he can only hope that they will draw this inference from his report about the situation in Sicily. This hope too is disappointed. The Athenians send strong reinforcements under Demosthenes who intends to avoid

---

[*] Cf. VI 31 with 12.2 and V 40.1; cf. also VII 28.1, 3, 4.

Nicias' mistake which consisted in lack of daring, but who fails in his daring effort because the enemy forces are already too strong. The only way of salvation is immediate return to Athens. Nicias opposes this course partly from fear of the Athenians, partly from hope that the Syracusans might still give in because of the enormity of the expense which they were incurring on account of the war. When the situation deteriorates still further, Nicias changes his mind; but just as the Athenians are about to withdraw, an eclipse of the moon occurs whereupon "the majority of the Athenians," with whom the excessively pious Nicias entirely agrees, at the advice of the soothsayers refuse to move until "three times nine" days have passed (50.3–4). As a consequence, the situation of the Athenians deteriorates still further. The wholly unexpected happens. Their navy is defeated by the Syracusan navy; the spirit of initiative, daring, and inventiveness by which the Athenians hitherto excelled has left them and now animates their enemies; the Athenians have become Spartans and the Athenians' enemies have become Athenians; the Syracusans see before them the prospect of a naval victory of the grandeur of Salamis; the Athenians are utterly discouraged. They attempt to escape by sea from the region of Syracuse where they had become besieged instead of the besiegers; the Syracusans are resolved to prevent their escape. Nicias attempts to encourage his utterly discouraged troops by a speech which, if read in the light of the deeds, conveys a single thought: the salvation of every one of you and of the city as a whole depends on your acting on the view the truth of which is known to you from experience, namely, that chance may for once be on our side. The ensuing naval battle in the harbor of Syracuse is watched with the utmost concern by the part of the land forces which had not embarked, especially by the Athenians whose feelings change from one extreme to the other as the naval battle, as far as they can observe it, changes from success of their compatriots to their failure. When the spectators see their side prevailing, they again become confident and turn to calling on the gods that they should not deprive them of salvation; only while they have hope based on the apparent strength of their human friends do they pray (71.3, 72.1; cf. II 53.4). Eventually the Syracusans prevail. The Athenian defeat was however not as disastrous as was thought by the bulk of the Athenians, who were now still more dejected than ever before. It was still possible for them to save themselves by retreating on land during the night, especially since the Syracusans were preoccupied with a holy day—a day of sacrifice to Heracles—but a ruse of the statesmanly Hermocrates, which compensated for his fellow citizens' ill-timed piety, deceived the trusting Nicias into delaying the retreat until daybreak, *i.e.* until it was too late. Only two days after the naval battle do the Athenians begin their retreat, leaving their sick and wounded behind in a state of utmost misery; no one listens to the prayers of the latter although all their departing comrades are in tears despite the fact that they have suffered things, and are in fear of suffering things, terrible beyond tears (75.4). They had left Athens with high hopes and solemn prayers to the gods; now they express their despair in cursing the gods (75.7; cf. VI 32.1–2). Nicias however has not changed: he still has hope, he encourages the army to go on hoping and not to blame themselves overmuch. He presents himself as a model to them: he who was thought to be a favorite of chance is now in the same danger as the meanest of them and in addition very sick although he has spent his life in acting in many ways toward the gods according to custom and law and toward men justly and without arousing the envy of men or gods. He is hopeful for the future because he has led a virtuous life although he cannot deny that the present misery, which does not at all correspond to his merit, frightens him. Could it be true that there is no correspondence between piety and good fortune? Or is this misfortune only a part of the Athenians' misfortune, and are the Athenians not as guiltless as he himself? Surely not every Athenian present can look back at his life with the same satisfaction as Nicias; in particular most of those present had passionately desired the Sicilian expedition which Nicias had opposed; perhaps that expedition which reminded us of Xerxes' expedition against Greece, having been undertaken from *hybris* due to prosperity, has aroused the envy of some god; but surely by now we have been sufficiently punished. If the expedition was an unjust act, it was a human failing, and human failings are not punished excessively. We are now worthier of the gods' pity than of their envy. Nicias does not fail to add the remark that they are still strong enough to resist the enemy provided they keep order and discipline (77). Yet neither his piety and justice nor his generalship (cf. 81.3) can save the Athenians nor himself. When everything is lost he surrenders to the Spartan commander Gylippus, who is anxious to save him, one reason being that the Spartans were obliged to Nicias for his kindness toward the Spartans after Sphacteria and for the peace called after him; but Gylippus has to give in to Corinthian and

Syracusan pressures just as his countrymen had to give in to the Thebans' demand for the butchery of the Plataeans. "Nicias deserved least of the Greeks of my time to arrive at such a degree of misfortune because of his full devotion to the pursuit of virtue as understood by old established custom" (86.5). Thucydides' judgment on Nicias is precise, as precise as his judgment on the Spartans according to which the Spartans above all others succeeded in being moderate while prospering: both judgments are made from the point of view of those on whom he passes judgment. They are precise by being incomplete. His judgment on the Spartans does not reveal the cause of Spartan moderation and hence its true character. His judgment on Nicias does not reveal the true character of the connection between the fate of men and their morality. Nicias like the Spartans believed that the fate of men or cities corresponds to their justice and piety[70] (cf. VII 18.2), to the

---

[70] Cf. VII 18.2. Cf. the Athenian parallel in V 32.1 (*i.e.* near the center of Thucydides' account of the central year of the war as narrated by him); the Athenian reflection on the connection between injustice and adversity belongs to the time of Nicias' ascendancy. The difference between the Athenian ambassadors on Melos and the Athenian people is illustrated also by the negotiations between the Athenians and the Boeotians after the Athenian defeat at Delium. The Athenians had occupied and fortified a temple of Apollo. The Boeotian commander in his address to the troops before the battle points out the sacrilegious character of the Athenians' action and draws the conclusion that the gods will help the Boeotians (IV 92.7). The Athenians lose the battle. The Boeotians refuse to permit the Athenians to gather their dead on the ground that the Athenians had desecrated the temple at Delium; the Athenians attempt to show that the ground is specious (97–99). Thucydides' account of this controversy is considerably more extensive than his account of the battle. In his commentary on the passage Gomme remarks that "Thucydides is curiously interested in this sophistical stuff" and that "his insistence on this argument of words was due to his feeling that the Boeotian refusal to allow the Athenians to collect their dead was another evil result of the war—an abandonment of one of the recognized, and humane, usages of Greece." The "humane" usage was based on a specific piety, *i.e.* a specific understanding of the divine, and its status was therefore not fundamentally different from that of the prohibition against the pollution of temples; from the point of view of the Athenian ambassadors to Melos—or of Socrates—the fate of the corpses would be a matter of utter indifference. Thucydides' "curious interest" in the casuistry regarding sacral matters is a necessary consequence of his interest in the fundamental issue of Right and Compulsion to which the Athenians explicitly refer in their reply to the Boeotians (98.5–6). We see here again that Thucydides is more open-minded or takes less for granted than "the scientific historian."

practice of virtue as understood by old established custom. But this correspondence rests entirely on hope, on unfounded or vain hope.[71] The view set forth by the Athenians on Melos is true. Nicias, and the Athenians in Sicily with him, perished in the last analysis for the same reason that the Melians perished. This then is the connection between the Melian dialogue and the Sicilian disaster, the unique dialogue and the uniquely narrated deed: not indeed the gods, but the human concern with the gods without which there cannot be a free city, took terrible revenge on the Athenians. Just as the Athenians on Melos mistakenly assumed that the leading Melians, as distinguished from the Melian populace, would as a matter of course agree with their view of the divine (V 103.2–104) and hence of right, so they mistakenly assumed that the Athenian *demos* would never need a leader like the Melian leaders. Pericles, who would never have said what the Athenians on Melos say, would for the same reason never have undertaken the Sicilian expedition in the circumstances in which it was undertaken. Alcibiades, who might have said what the Athenians on Melos say, might have brought the Sicilian expedition to a happy issue. But Alcibiades' proved or presumed impiety made it necessary for the Athenian *demos* to entrust the expedition to a man of Melian beliefs whom they could perfectly trust because he surpassed every one of them in piety.

## 8. *The Spartan Manner and the Athenian Manner*

This much is clear: the theme "Sparta-Athens" is not only not exhausted but is barely touched by the question as to which of the two cities broke the treaty or compelled its antagonist to break the treaty, for unless it is kept back by weakness of one kind or another, every city is itself compelled to expand. This reason however justifies Athenian imperialism in the same way in which it justifies the imperialism of Persia or of Sparta. By implication it justifies the dominion of the rich over the poor or vice versa as well as tyranny. In other words this reason does not do justice to the truth intended by the "Spartan" praise of moderation and the divine law.

---

[71] Therefore Nicias' virtue is not unqualified; it is law-bred, in contradistinction to the virtue of Brasidas (IV 81.2), the Athenian tyrants (VI 54.5), and Antiphon (VIII 68.1).

Besides, the meaning of "compulsion" is not quite clear: the Melians were not compelled to submit to the Athenians. But one might say that if the alternative to submission is extinction, submission is compulsory or necessary for sensible men. The Athenians at the time of Salamis were not compelled to submit to the Persians because they had a considerable navy, the most intelligent leader Themistocles and the most daring zeal (I 74.1–2); does this mean that given these conditions they were compelled to fight? Surely once they had fought and won and then wished to prevent the recurrence of the extreme danger from which they had saved themselves, they were compelled to embark on their imperial policy. The very least one would have to say is that there are different kinds of compulsion.

The statements of the Athenians on Melos are so shocking because they justify their empire and hence their action against Melos ultimately by nothing except the natural necessity by virtue of which the strong—anyone who is strong—rules the weak and thus treat every consideration of right—such as the higher right of Athenian imperialism as contrasted with the imperialism of any barbaric power—with utmost disdain. Only toward the end of the dialogue do they mention in passing as a matter too obvious for emphasis that their demand on the Melians keeps within reasonable limits. Yet even these Athenians cannot help indicating that Athenians are men of a different character than Spartans. The Spartans, they say, in their dealings with foreigners, more patently than all other men they know regard the pleasant as noble and the expedient as just; since expediency, to say nothing of pleasure, calls for safety and only the just and the noble induce one to seek dangers, the Spartans generally speaking are least inclined to take dangerous courses (V 105.4, 107). The Athenians in other words do not patently or simply identify in their dealings with non-Athenians the pleasant with the noble and the expedient with the just; they are somehow concerned with the noble or beautiful in every respect; in the words of Pericles, they love the beautiful; the daring for which they are famous is not bestial or savage or mad but is inspired by generous sentiments. This suggestion is more shocking than everything else which the Athenians on Melos say or suggest because it is so flagrantly contradicted by the ensuing butchery of the Melians, although it must be admitted that that disgraceful action does not necessarily follow from the principles stated by the ambassadors and that, as far as we know, the ambassadors were not responsible for that action. What the Athenians on Melos say about the peculiarity of the Spartans and hence indirectly about the Athenians compels us to say that the atrocity committed afterward is so shocking precisely because it was committed by Athenians and not by Spartans; one must demand more from Athenians than from Spartans because the Athenians are men superior to the Spartans. Even the Athenians on Melos are witnesses to this superiority for more than one reason. The Athenians in Sparta are less ambiguous witnesses to the same fact. The latter are indeed compelled to justify the Athenian empire. They must show "what kind of city" Athens is and that she is worthy of imperial rule: she was compelled to acquire the empire and she is compelled to preserve it, but what compelled and compels her to do so is not merely fear and profit but also something noble, honor; accordingly she exercises her imperial rule in a juster, more restrained, less greedy manner than her power would permit her to do and the same power will lead others in her place in fact to do. What the Athenians in Sparta stated in order to prevent the outbreak of the war is completed on the grandest scale in Athens by Pericles in his Funeral Speech for the purpose of showing that Athens more than any other city is worth dying for. Athens differs from all other cities—the cities which resemble her merely imitate her—in such a way that she above all others deserves to rule an empire. The qualities which distinguish her are those which Sparta above all others lacks: generosity without pettiness or calculation, freedom, generous gaiety and ease, courage in war which stems not from compulsion, dictation, and harsh discipline but from generosity, in brief, a well-tempered love of the noble and the beautiful. In other words, the ultimate justification of the Athenian empire is less compulsion, fear, or profit than everlasting glory—a goal to the pursuit of which the Athenians are not compelled, or with which they are not obsessed, but to which they have freely and fully dedicated themselves.[72]

But let us turn from the speeches to the more trustworthy deeds or facts. The first outstanding fact—first certainly in time—which Thucydides presents and which is most obviously relevant to the issue now under consideration is the contrast between the Spartan

---

[72] By the last sentence I have tried to bring out Pericles' implicit reply to what the Corinthians say in I 70.8–9.

king Pausanias and the Athenian Themistocles. They were the most famous men among the Greeks of their time, in the forefront of the fight against Persia, and both ended ignominiously after having betrayed Greece to Persia. Thucydides does not pass judgment on their acts of treason. Themistocles became the founder of the Athenian empire through his superior intelligence, versatility, and guile; Pausanias involuntarily and against Sparta's interest drove the other Greeks who needed protection from Persia into the arms of Athens by his stupid violence and tyrant-like injustice. Pausanias wrote to the Persian king because he was trying to become the ruler of Greece with the help of the Persian king; Themistocles had been ostracized by the Athenians and wrote to the Persian king only when he was compelled to do so by persecution on the part of Sparta and Athens. When Pausanias' un-Spartan conduct came to the notice of the authorities in Sparta, they called him home and he returned: he was nothing without Sparta, without his hereditary position in Sparta; the Spartans had very strong grounds—grounds which had the force of proofs—for suspecting him of high treason. But in accordance with the supreme fairness which they customarily practice among themselves, they did not start criminal proceedings against him until they had proof beyond a shadow even of unreasonable doubt. No such consideration was given to the leading Athenians in Athens. Thanks to her regime, Sparta was less threatened by outstanding individuals or potential tyrants than Athens was or believed to be. Themistocles may have been dangerous to Athens; Pausanias was never a danger to Sparta. Nor was Themistocles compelled to return to Athens; he was something without Athens; for he owed most of his power to his nature as distinguished not only from *nomos* but from any other kind of imparted knowledge; his superior nature (his "genius") would assert itself everywhere, in Persia as well as in Greece; Pausanias, on the other hand, while in no way outstanding by his nature—Thucydides has nothing to say about his nature—owed all his power to law, and any virtue he possessed to the strict discipline of Sparta which was wholly ineffective when he was away from Sparta. Sparta may have been a better city than Athens; Athens surpassed her by far by natural gifts, by her individuals.[73]

Thucydides presents to us a galaxy of outstanding Athenians—

---

[73] I 90.3–91, 93.3–4, 95–96.1, 128–138. Cf. Plato, *Laws* 642c6–d1.

outstanding by intelligence or sheer cleverness and efficiency, by nobility of character or *hybris*—and only a single outstanding Spartan, Brasidas. Sparta was less threatened by outstanding men than Athens because she had so few of them; the Spartans were members of a herd rather than individuals; Sparta did not, like Athens, bring forth lions.[74] How petty and how poor does the Spartan traitor Pausanias look in contrast with the Athenian traitors Themistocles and Alcibiades. It goes without saying that there is no Spartan whom one could for one moment dream of comparing to Pericles, who appears to be unrivalled even among the Athenians of his time as Thucydides indicates in the following manner: Pericles' speeches are the only speeches delivered in Athens by an Athenian which do not form part of pairs of speeches (cf. I 139.4). As for Brasidas, the exception to the rule, he confirms the rule; he is the Athenian among the Spartans; he is the only Thucydidean character who ever makes a dedication to Athena and apparently sacrifices to her (IV 116.2, V 10.2; cf. II 13.5). He surpasses the other Spartans not only by his intelligence, initiative, ability to speak, and justice but also by his mildness (IV 81, 108.2–3, 114.3–5). He is the only Thucydidean character praised by the author for his mildness. This praise must be rightly understood. Men like Nicias and Demosthenes were no less mild than Brasidas. Brasidas' mildness deserved praise not only in contrast with the violence of his Athenian antagonist, Cleon, but above all because mildness was so rare among Spartans as distinguished from Athenians. Cleon is the counterpart of Brasidas because just as Brasidas is the Athenian among the Spartans, Cleon is in a sense the Spartan among the Athenians. As we observed earlier, in another sense Nicias is the Spartan among the Athenians. Thucydides respects Nicias or at any rate is friendly towards him whereas he loathes Cleon. Cleon betrays the soul of Athens. His version of imperialism is not ennobled by any thought of everlasting glory. In his view imperialism is irreconcilable with any thought of generous compassion or any pleasure deriving from speeches. His imperialism is guided solely by considerations of the profitable or expedient. He does appeal to justice but only to punitive justice to be inflicted by Athens on her faithless allies—a kind of justice which in his view coincides with Athens' interest. He has only contempt for the love of glory and generosity and the love of

---

[74] Plato, *Laws* 666e1–7; Aristophanes, *Frogs* 1431–1432.

speeches for which Pericles had praised Athens by speaking of her "love of beauty and love of wisdom" as distinguishing her specially from Sparta. Owing to his great credit with the *demos* Cleon can openly call democracy in question in an assembly of the Athenian *demos*, something that Alcibiades can do only in a Spartan assembly. Like a Spartan he condemns the generous desire of the Athenians to spare the lives of the Mytileneans by appealing to the moderation which shows itself in unquestioning submission to the wisdom of the law, *i.e.* to unchangeable laws of questionable goodness. The gist of his only speech may be said to be that the proposal to spare the Mytileneans is so manifestly absurd that the proposers cannot have had any other motive except to exhibit their cleverness by defending a manifest absurdity and that those who might vote for the proposal cannot have had any other motive except to express their admiration for that cleverness.[75] He is severely punished for his contempt of speeches. Before the battle of Amphipolis, Cleon, who had condemned the Athenians for being enamored of being "lookers-at" of speeches and of sophists, turned to "look at" the place and its environs, whereas Brasidas made a speech to his troops and won the battle (V 7.3–4, 10.2–5; III 38.4, 7). Yet however irrational Cleon may have been on this and other occasions he is reasonableness itself compared with the Spartan Alcidas whom the Spartans trusted more than they did Brasidas. Following the Spartan practice, he killed the Athenian allies whom he had taken prisoner; he stopped the slaughter immediately when some friends of Sparta drew his attention to the fact that he did not promote the liberation of the Greeks from Athenian domination by killing men who had never lifted their hands against the liberating Peloponnesians and were Athenian allies only under duress; if he did not stop his practice he would convert many who were at present friends of Sparta into her enemies (III 32; cf. II 67.4). Alcidas was not cruel; he did not kill because he enjoyed killing; he killed because Spartans always killed in such circumstances, as a matter of custom and of course. We see him gaping when the friends of Sparta suggest to him their simple thought; he is intelligent enough to grasp its truth. What is meant to amaze us is the fact that this simple thought had never occurred to him or to any other Spartan with the exception of Brasidas, who

---

[75] III 37–38; 40.2, 4. Cf. I 71.3 and 84.3.

was at that time still entirely powerless.[76] Alcidas is as much below Cleon as Cleon is below Demosthenes and Nicias. Thucydides does not pass judgment on Alcidas' callousness, whereas he does pass judgment on Cleon's violence: he knows what he can expect from Spartans on the one hand and from Athenians on the other.

These observations receive powerful support from the contrast between the Spartans' dealings with the conquered Plataeans and the Athenians' dealings with the conquered Mytileneans (III 52–68). Both actions are judicial. The crime of which the Spartans judge is Plataeae's loyalty to Athens, *i.e.* a line of conduct which is criminal only on the basis of the assumption, questioned soon after by the Spartans themselves, that the cause of Sparta is identical with the cause of justice; the crime of which the Athenians judge is Mytilene's admitted breach of her treaty with Athens. The Plataeans are condemned and executed without a single voice except their own being raised in their favor before the Spartan tribunal; the Mytileneans are first condemned but then when the Athenians regret their cruel decision, the case for the Mytileneans is as powerfully stated by an Athenian as was the case against them, with the result that they have a hairbreadth escape. The issue debated before the Spartan tribunal is exclusively whether the Plataeans were just or unjust, guilty or innocent; both the Plataeans and their accusers, the Thebans, defend themselves against the charge of injustice and accuse the other party of injustice (III 60, 61.1, 63 beginning); the issue debated in the Athenian assembly is not exclusively or even chiefly whether the Mytileneans were guilty or innocent but whether it is expedient for Athens to kill all of them indiscriminately: the Athenians in contradistinction to the Spartans assume that killing must serve a purpose other than the satisfaction of the desire for revenge. There is a certain resemblance between the position taken by the Thebans who demand the killing of the Plataeans and Cleon who demands the killing of the Mytileneans—both the Thebans and Cleon do not like "fine speeches" (III 67.6–7 and

---

[76] III 79.3 (cf. 69.1 and 76; cf. III 93 end with 92.5 end [Alcidas is in the center]). Cf. also II 86.6 (the Spartan commanders call the soldiers together and then, seeing the mood of the soldiers, decide to address them) and 88.3 (Phormio sees the mood of the soldiers and then calls them together in order to address them). Cf. the reference to "seeing" in Phormio's speech (89.1, 8) and the silence about it in the Spartans' speech. The theme "seeing" is not dropped in the narrative of the battle which follows on these speeches.

37–38); nevertheless Cleon's Athenian opponent, Diodotus, has something important in common with Cleon which distinguishes both Athenians from the Spartans and their allies: both demand that not only the fact of the crime but also the wisdom of punishing it capitally be considered. It goes without saying that the Spartans do not execute the Plataeans out of blind obedience to a divine law or the demands of justice but from concern with their immediate self-interest; they give in to the Thebans' hatred of the Plataeans because they regard the Thebans as useful to them for the war (III 68.4) or, as the Plataeans put it and as the Athenian ambassadors on Melos will repeat, the Spartans define justice as their present convenience (III 56.3, V 105.4). However shocking the Athenians' later action against the Melians may be, the Athenians surely did not act hypocritically as the Spartans did toward the Plataeans. The Spartans, one is tempted to say, are petty calculators even when they act justly whereas the Athenians are of generous frankness in their very crimes since they do not even attempt to disguise their crimes as acts of justice. The Athenians, who ally themselves with the Messenians, do not claim, as they might have done, to wage the war in order to liberate the Messenians from Spartan tyranny; the Athenians' enemies, who claim to wage a war of liberation against the tyrant city of Athens in the same spirit in which they do not tolerate tyrants within cities, restore as a matter of course a tyrant whom the Athenians had deposed (II 30.1, 33.1–2; cf. I 122.3). Thucydides expresses his judgment on Sparta's claim to wage a war of liberation against Athens in the following manner. He states the case for that claim, *i.e.* for the Spartans' claim that they are waging a just war, most forcefully immediately after his account of the Thebans' peacetime attack on Plataeae and immediately before his account of the first Spartan invasion of Attica, *i.e.* between his accounts of the "Peloponnesians'" decisive breaches of the treaty (II 8.4–5).[77] The only Spartan who through his whole conduct gives some weight to the

---

[77] He follows a similar procedure in his first two statements about Pericles' unique position in Athens (I 127.3 and 139.4); in the first statement he does not praise Pericles whereas he does in the second; between the two statements he gives his account of Cylon and of Pausanias-Themistocles; the account in the center indicates the reason for Pericles' outstanding qualities; the center illuminates what precedes it and what follows it. In the example discussed in the text the center is illuminated by what precedes it and what follows it.

Spartan claim is Brasidas. Compared with the Spartan claim which was an attempt to lift the Peloponnesian war to the heights of the Persian war, the Athenian (Periclean) conception of the war is sobriety itself: the war serves no other purpose than to preserve the empire; the conception appeals to the intelligence rather than to desire, fear, or other passions. Thucydides' description of the Peloponnesian war as the greatest war because of the greatness of the sufferings which it brought agrees more with the Periclean than with the Spartan conception: the splendor of this war is to be found in the speeches rather than in the deeds. It would be a gross exaggeration to say that the Spartans' concern with justice or piety was merely hypocritical; they feared the gods genuinely; that fear induced them sometimes to spare the lives of their helpless enemies or to be mild as in the case of the Helots of Ithome (I 103.2–3) who appeared to be protected by an oracle. The Plataeans, as distinguished from those Helots, were not protected by an oracle but at most only by ancient oaths. The Athenians did not need oaths or oracles in order to save the Mytileneans; their mildness or generosity came from their manner or their souls.

One may try to strengthen the case for Sparta by pointing to such Athenian atrocities as their complicity in the treacherous slaughter of the upper-class Corcyreans (IV 46–48) who were surely inimical to Athens—an atrocity of which one may nevertheless say that it does not rival the Spartans' treacherous slaughter of the finest men among the Helots who had distinguished themselves in fighting Sparta's war (IV 80.2–5). Yet there is surely a kind of Athenian atrocity which has no parallel in Sparta: the Athenians' savage rage against each other after the mutilation of the Hermae and the profanation of the mysteries (VI 53.1–2, 60). In this case at any rate the fear of the gods which restrained the Spartans from savagery drove the Athenians into savagery. Especially if one considers this action in the context of the Athenians' treatment of their leading citizens in general, one becomes again inclined to say that Sparta was a better city than Athens. From this point it is only one step to saying that, in spite or because of their radical antagonism of manners, Sparta and Athens were worthy antagonists not only because they were the most powerful Greek cities but because each was in its own way of outstanding nobility. One may find a confirmation for this view in the following story. Contrary to the Greek notion of Spartan manliness according to which a Spartan would rather die than give up his arms, the Spartan survivors of the fighting on Sphacteria surrendered to the Athenians and their allies; the captors could not believe that their captives were of the same kind as the Spartans who had fallen; one of the Athenian allies therefore asked one of the captives out of spite if the slain were perfect gentlemen; the Spartan replied that a spindle (meaning an arrow), *i.e.* a woman's tool, would be worth much if it could distinguish between true men and others, thus indicating that it was a matter of chance who had been hit by a missile and who had not (IV 40). It is gratifying to see that the mean question which called forth the laconic reply was not raised by an Athenian.

This is the place for two general remarks. As has often been said, Thucydides is concerned with "causes"—with those of the Peloponnesian war as well as those of all particular incidents of that war. The statement is correct provided one means that the most important causes are for him such things as the character of Sparta on the one hand and of Athens on the other, and that this kind of cause is understood by him less as the product of conditions (climatic, economic, etc.) than as the specification of the most comprehensive "causes," *i.e.* motion and rest. Causes in Thucydides' sense are not merely "material" and "efficient." For Thucydides the course of the war is the self-revelation of Sparta and Athens rather than the outcome of a strategy. Secondly, for the understanding of the superiority of the Athenian manner to the Spartan manner one cannot rely on the Funeral Speech, which expresses Thucydides' view only through the deflecting medium of Pericles' turn of mind. In Pericles' view Athens does not need a Homer or whoever by his poems gives delight for the moment, not because like Thucydides he disdains boasting or chanting Athens' praises but because he himself regards himself as superior to Homer and the other poets in magnifying and adorning. Thucydides too exaggerates, especially when he says that the Peloponnesian war affected "so to speak the greatest part of mankind," but how far does he remain behind Pericles who says that "all (kinds of) things from every land" are imported into Athens and that the Athenians have opened for themselves "every sea and land" and have left "everywhere" everlasting memorials of bad things and good.[78] Pericles' speech is a public, political, popular utterance whereas Thucydides' speech is "politic"

---

[78] I 1.2, 21.1, 22.4, II 38.2, 41.4, 42.1–2, 62.1.

in Hobbes's sense. The Funeral Speech is the greatest document of the harmony between Pericles and the city of Athens and especially its *demos*, which trusts him as much as it is capable; his superior intelligence is manifest to the *demos* because it is intelligible to the *demos*; he is, so to speak, an open book for the *demos*; when they disagree with him they see very soon that the disagreement was due entirely to their weakness or confusion;[79] his superiority is obvious, unambiguous, not like the ambiguous superiority of Themistocles and Alcibiades. Pericles justly occupies the center of the triptych the outer figures of which (Themistocles and Alcibiades) are superior to him only by nature but not by law. The extremes end in disaster; Pericles' end is inconspicuous—as "normal" as his life. As for his Funeral Speech, one must not in reading it forget for one moment the fundamental harmony between Pericles and the Athenian *demos* or between Pericles' private good and the common good of Athens as he and most Athenians understood it. When reading, for instance, the unforgettable sentences about the Athenians' love of beauty or nobility and their love of wisdom, or about the whole city of Athens being the school of Greece, one ought not to think of Sophocles and Anaxagoras but of what the average Athenian was likely to think when he heard these sentences or, which is the same, of the things to which Pericles explicitly refers in the very context. It is no small part of Thucydides' art that the reader is almost irresistibly tempted not to take this precaution.

The treatment of the Plataeans and of the Mytileneans shows us the contrast between Sparta and Athens as judges; Pylos and Sicily show us the contrast between Sparta and Athens in adversity. The opening part of the account of the Athenian action at Pylos (IV 3–6) is surrounded by accounts of Athenian failures in Sicily and in Chalcidice: Pylos was the right place for reaching a favorable decision of the war. Pylos had been chosen by the daring and versatile Demosthenes who could learn from his mistakes and who at the time when he brought about the seizure of Pylos had no official position. Thanks to this thoroughly un-Spartan man, the Athenians succeeded in beating the Spartans at their own game; they defended

---

[79] In his eulogy of Pericles Thucydides says (II 65.9) that when Pericles saw the Athenians "out of season insolently bold, he would with his orations put them into a fear"; Thucydides characteristically gives no example of a Periclean speech of this description. Cf. pages 152–53 above.

the Spartan territory which they had occupied by fighting as land soldiers against a Spartan naval attack (12.3; cf. 14.3) with the result that more than 300 Spartans were cut off on the island of Sphacteria. The apprehended disaster—the apprehension of the capture or killing of the cut-off Spartan force—sufficed to induce the Spartans to sue for peace without having had the benefit of Apollo's advice, *i.e.* to do something which the Athenians had been induced to do against the advice of Pericles by an actual disaster of an entirely different order of magnitude, namely, the plague. The true parallel to the Spartan action after their defeat at Pylos is however the Athenian action after their defeat in Sicily. The Sicilian disaster, of which everyone thought that it had brought down Athens, only called forth a still greater Athenian war effort. Under the influence of Cleon the Athenians decline the Spartan request for peace. Thucydides does not pass judgment on the Athenian response nor on the Spartan request, for no judgment is implied in his recording the fact that the strongest opponent of peace with Sparta was Cleon. Cleon was indeed, as Thucydides says in a different context, the most violent Athenian citizen and Thucydides strongly disapproved of his posture toward the Mytileneans (III 36.4, 6; 49.4); but this does not prove that in his opinion Cleon was always wrong and in particular that he was wrong in not acceding to the Spartan request for peace after Pylos. After all, Cleon's leading opponent on this occasion was Nicias, a man distinguished by decency rather than by wisdom or daring. Nor does Thucydides call into question Cleon's judgment regarding the Spartan peace offer by showing him somewhat later in a most laughable posture, for apart from the fact that Cleon, and not his laughing opponents, had the last laugh, the question in the latter scene concerns, not Cleon's political judgment but his strategic judgment which, to the extent to which it was guided by Demosthenes' judgment, proved to be excellent. To this one must add that it is, to say the least, doubtful whether Demosthenes' sound advice would have been of any avail but for Cleon's laughable, even mad (IV 39.3), but firm action in the Athenian assembly.[80] Thucydides might seem to pass unfavorable judgment on the Athenian response to the Spartan peace offer by saying that the response was due to the Athenians' "desire for

---

[80] IV 28–30. For the action on Sphacteria Demosthenes' experience in Aetolia was important; cf. not only IV 30.1 but also III 97.2–98.5, IV 28.4 and 32–34.

more," to a desire mentioned disapprovingly by the Spartan ambassadors to Athens in their speech (21.2, 17.4) and disapproved
for the duration of the Peloponnesian war by Pericles himself (I
144.1, II 65.7). Yet, as we have seen, Thucydides distinguished between wisdom and its opposite not simply in accordance with
Spartan notions of moderation or the Periclean notion of what could
safely be done during the Peloponnesian war. It is undoubtedly
significant that Thucydides uses in this context an expression used
in the same context first by the Spartans: he is doing his best to
look at the Pylos affair from the Spartan point of view. This is the
reason why he apparently minimizes the Spartan breaches of the
local armistice at Pylos (23.1) and above all why he seems to treat
Demosthenes' brilliant success as a gift of chance. The Spartans
treat that success in this manner however not merely in order to
detract from their enemy's glory but above all because they believe
in the connection between chance or luck and the gods and in
particular between bad luck and divine punishment: it is precisely
in their speech at Athens that they express for the first time some
doubt as to who began the war, *i.e.* broke the sworn treaty (IV
20.2), and it is precisely their adversity at Pylos more than anything
else which made them believe that their bad luck was a deserved
punishment for their breach of the treaty (VII 18.2). Thucydides
makes clear in his account of the fighting at Pylos that he does not
share the view of chance presupposed by the Spartan view; he there
characterizes as a reversal of chance what he explains to have been
no more than an action by the Spartans and Athenians that was in
contradiction to the opinion about the two cities which prevailed
at the time (IV 12.2). Or, as his Pericles puts it, "we are accustomed to hold chance responsible whenever something happens
against calculation."[81] To return to the present subject, however
laughable Cleon's conduct in the Athenian assembly might have
been, his conduct on Sphacteria was not. More seriously laughable
than anything Cleon did was the unconditional surrender of the
survivors of the 300 Spartans on Sphacteria if it is compared with
the noble conduct of the Spartans at Thermopylae and with the
Spartans' claim regarding themselves as that claim was generally
understood (IV 36.3, 40.1). Thucydides alludes to this disproportion
in the following manner: whereas he and everyone else always

---

[81] I 140.1. Cf. II 91.3–4 with the reference to chance in the Peloponnesians'
speech (87.2) and the silence about it in Phormio's speech. Cf. *Wasps* 62.

called the Spartans on Sphacteria "men" (*hoi andres*), he calls them "human beings" (*anthropoi*) when he shows their helplessness as they are at the mercy of light-armed soldiers who are never more than mere "human beings."[82] This allusion differs from the mean taunt directed by an Athenian ally against the Spartans captured at Sphacteria by the fact that it is in no way directed against the Spartans who fought so well on Sphacteria but against the city of Sparta. Perhaps the harshest indictment of the Spartans is supplied by the fact that but for the defeat at Pylos (and the Athenian conquest of Cythera—IV 55), they would never have deviated from their customary practice to the extent of permitting a man of Brasidas' qualities to make his campaign in the north and hence would never have waged the war in the spirit of a war of liberation: a great panic, caused by a (relatively) petty defeat, not alleviated by Athenian willingness to forget who started the war and who abetted the butchery of the Plataeans, compelled the Spartans to tolerate for a short while, as long as was absolutely necessary, a generous policy. By his successes and his death Brasidas removed that compulsion and rendered possible the Peace of Nicias and therewith the return to Sparta of the prisoners taken on Sphacteria. Yet Brasidas' success was not Sparta's success. How little the Greeks believed that Sparta had been cleansed from the disgrace of Pylos by Brasidas' success is shown by the fact that in their view Sparta was rehabilitated only by her victory at Mantinea: only in the light of the victory at Mantinea did the Spartans' failure at Pylos appear to the other Greeks as having been caused by ill-luck and not by decay (V 75.3).

The battle of Mantinea took place in the central year of the Peloponnesian war, which lasted for twenty-seven years. The Spartans were at war with Argos while the Athenians were allied with both Sparta and Argos but in fact fighting on the side of Argos. There had almost been a battle between the Spartans and the Argives earlier in the year, but at the last moment the Spartan king Agis and two Argive generals had concluded on their own a four-month armistice. Agis' action was strongly resented by the Spartans with the result that they made an entirely new law according to which the king's power of making decisions was subject to control

---

[82] IV 34.2; cf. 33.2 and 38.3–4. Cf. also II 5.4–6.4 and III 97.2–98.4. Cf. note 26 above.

by ten councilors elected by the city and accompanying him on the campaigns (V 63). The new law of course did not affect the law concerning the order of battle. Owing to the suddenness with which the enemy appeared on the battlefield of Mantinea, if not to the further fact that the Spartans were more frightened than ever before in their memory, every one of them eagerly took his place, well known to him in the traditional order of the army which Thucydides describes in the center of his account of the fourteenth year of the war.[83] He was able to describe the order in which the

---

[83] At the end of III Thucydides mentions the eruption of Mt. Aetna which took place in the spring before he mentions the end of the winter. "The reason for this superficially illogical writing is clear: Thucydides did not want to begin a new 'book' with the mention of an incident, the eruption of Etna, which, worth recording for its own sake, had nothing to do with the war; it was best to tuck it away at the end of a 'book', even if that meant, strictly, putting it in its wrong year . . ." Gomme II 704. Assuming that Gomme means by a "book" the account of one year of the war, one must say that Thucydides begins his account of the eighth year of the war with the mention of an eclipse of the sun and of an earthquake—of natural phenomena which also occurred in the spring and which also had apparently nothing to do with the war. The end of III is the end of the account of the sixth year, of the only year the account of which both almost begins (III 89) and literally ends with the mention of natural phenomena; the account of the fifth year almost ends with the mention of a natural phenomenon (III 88.3). The transition from the fifth to the sixth year is the center of the first part of the war (cf. V 20). (The distinction between the natural and that which is not natural, *i.e.* above all the conventional, would seem to be the key to Thucydides' "philosophy of history," to a teaching silently conveyed through a narrative which affects to come as close as possible to a mere chronicle. The distinction mentioned is reflected in Thucydides' following the "natural" calendar ["according to summers and winters" —V 20.2–3, 26.1] which is the same for Spartans and Athenians, for Greeks and Persians, as distinguished from any "conventional" and hence necessarily local calendar. An oracle had predicted that the war would last thrice nine years [26.4]. Thucydides opens his narrative of the tenth year [and only of that year] with the account of an act of piety [V 1] on the part of the Athenians—of an act apparently connected with their sense of guilt [cf. V 32]. In that account he refers back to an earlier event by using the phrase "as I have made clear before," a phrase which occurs otherwise only in VI 94.1, *i.e.* the beginning of the account of the eighteenth year of the war; near the end of that account Thucydides speaks of the Spartan sense of guilt regarding the war [VII 18.2, 4]. [For the connection between V 1 and VI 94.1, cf. also I 13.6.] Cf. also note 70 above. Another hint is conveyed by the fact that Thucydides ends his account of each year sometimes with the phrase "this is the end of the *n*th year of the war" and sometimes with the phrase "this is the end of the *n*th year of the war which Thucydides has described.")

two opposed armies were arranged but not to state the number of fighters on each side: the number of the Spartans was unknown because of the secretiveness that was due to their regime, and the number of the others was concealed by their boasting. Yet since the Spartan order never changes, Thucydides can figure out, or enable his reader to figure out, the exact number of the Spartans who took part in the battle.[84] The Spartans do not seem to have been aware of the tension between secrecy and an unchangeable order or of the fact that such a disorderly thing as unregulated boasting can be more conducive to concealing the truth than any regulations. Or, to take a less ridiculous example, while the Spartans succeeded in concealing the manner in which they made 2,000 brave Helots vanish from sight, they did not succeed in concealing the fact that they had destroyed them (IV 80.4), since human beings who are alive are likely to come to sight from time to time. It is no accident that the two sole examples which Thucydides adduces in order to show the ignorance of Greeks regarding contemporary things are Spartan (I 20.3): Spartan secretiveness leads to ignorance regarding things Spartan, and given this ignorance one does not, for obvious reasons, run a great risk in praising the Spartans. Let us also remember here the Spartans' ridiculous concern with the ritual impurity of Pericles. To return to the battle of Mantinea, whereas Sparta's enemies advanced with passion, the Spartans advanced slowly in accordance with their law.[85] Agis, observing a danger which arises in every battle, tries to avert it by giving novel orders without being interfered with by any of the ten new councilors (cf. V 65.2). Two Spartan officers refuse to obey (from cowardice, as their accusers successfully claimed afterward). As a consequence of their complete lack of experience (for the commands were completely new and the new guardians of the old were not effective), the Spartans would have lost the battle but for the courage which they displayed at the critical moment (70–72.2). We note in passing that Sparta lost the fruit of the splendid victory in the year following (82–83). Thucydides does not claim that his description of the battle of Mantinea is quite exact; the truth of the description is comparable to the truth of the speeches;

---

[84] V 66–68. Cf. V 74 end and II 39.1.
[85] Cf. IV 108.6.

this may be one reason why he gives only summaries of the speeches with which the commanders addressed their troops before the battle (69, 74.1). At any rate the section of his work which shows the complete restoration of Sparta's renown and exhibits the beauty of her order of battle, *i.e.* which is most in accordance with the praise of Sparta near the beginning and near the end of his work, reveals at the same time most clearly and specifically Spartan ineptness, the Spartan comedy.

The battle of Mantinea is succeeded by the dialogue between the Athenians and the Melians which in its turn is succeeded by the Sicilian expedition. The dialogue on Melos separates the Spartan comedy from the Athenian tragedy. Thucydides as it were bids us compare "Sicily" with "Pylos" (VII 71.7) on the one hand and with "Mycalessus" (VII 29–30) on the other. Compared with the fate of the Athenians in Sicily, the fate of the Spartans on Sphacteria is indeed laughable. The fate of Mycalessus on the other hand is no less worthy of compassion than that of the Athenians in Sicily. Yet the latter is more deeply moving than the former. The reason would seem to be that the Mycalessians in no way deserved their unfathomable misfortune by any act of *hybris* whereas the Athenian disaster was the consequence of grave mistakes, of guilt: Sicily follows immediately on Melos. No one can read Thucydides' account of the Sicilian disaster with the feeling that the Athenians got what they deserved; to say the least, the disaster was not proportionate to the fault; this feeling is expressed by Nicias in accordance with his way of thinking (VII 77.1, 3–4). Of Nicias Thucydides says that he deserved his misfortune least of all the Greeks of his time (VII 86.5). He suggests a similar judgment regarding the Athenians. Yet the case of the Athenians is radically different from that of Nicias. Nicias did not deserve his misfortune because of his full dedication to law-bred virtue. Athens' nobility was of an entirely different kind, of a nobler kind. The Sicilian expedition, undertaken against the will of Nicias, originated in the nobility of her daring— of her willingness to risk everything for the sake of everlasting glory, of her love of the beauty of everlasting glory which Pericles had praised (II 64.3–6). Just as the Funeral Speech is followed by the plague, the Melian dialogue is followed by the Sicilian expedition. The Sicilian expedition, or rather its cause, not only the *stasis*, is a kind of grave sickness but a noble sickness. Thucydides speaks of the *eros* of the Athenians for the Sicilian expedition.[86] Pericles had called upon the Athenians to become lovers (*erastai*) of their city (II 43.1). It was the community of lovers of their city who desired to adorn their beloved with the jewel Sicily. One could say that "Athens in Sicily" is greater than Pericles' Athens according to Pericles himself: it surpasses all other "everlasting memorials of evils" (II 41.4) which Athens has left anywhere. The *eros* of the Athenian for Sicily is the peak of his *eros* for his city, and that *eros* is his full dedication to his city, the willingness to sacrifice, to forget everything private for the sake of the city, a willingness which finds an appropriate and hence not unambiguous expression in what Pericles says in his Funeral Speech about the aged parents, the widows, and the orphans of the fallen soldiers. Or, as Alcibiades indicates, only glory after death brings about the perfect harmony between the private and the public (VI 16.5). If the highest *eros* is that for the city and if the city reaches its peak in an *eros* like that of Athens for Sicily, *eros* is of necessity tragic or, as Plato seems to suggest, the city is the tragedy *par excellence*.[87] In accordance with all this, Athens' defeat is her triumph: her enemies have to become in a manner Athenians in order to defeat her;[88] she is defeated because she has succeeded in becoming the teacher of Hellas. As for Sparta, her victory, whether due to Apollo or not, is of interest only as the reverse side of Athens' defeat.

## 9. *The Questionable Universalism of the City*

The reasoning which culminates in the opposition of the Spartan comedy and the Athenian tragedy starts from the "Athenian" assumption that precisely regarding the city the noble cannot be reduced to the pleasant and is superior to it. That assumption will also lead one to question the seemingly inhuman judgment on the choice made by the Melians to which we were led by starting from the assumption common to the Athenians and Thucydides which

---

[86] VI 24.3. This is the only time that Thucydides himself uses the noun *eros*. Only one of his characters uses that noun: Diodotus (III 45.5). When speaking against the Sicilian expedition Nicias blames the *dyserotes tōn apontōn* (VI 13.1).

[87] *Laws* 817b.

[88] Cf. I 71.3 with VII 21.3–4; 36.2, 4; 37.1; 40.2; 55.

finds its clearest expression in what the Athenians say against the Melians' resolve. We must therefore take a further step. That necessity derives also from these considerations: according to Thucydides the Sicilian expedition was not doomed to failure or its failure cannot be explained by Athenian *hybris* however noble; the account of the Sicilian expedition is not the end of Thucydides' work; the agreement between Thucydides and Pericles is less complete than the argument of the preceding section assumed. In a word, that argument is too "poetic" in Thucydides' sense to be in ultimate agreement with his thought.[89]

According to Pericles, the present splendor of Athens gives rise

---

[89] If Thucydides has left his work unfinished, it does not follow that he did not intend to end it in the manner in which, and with the sentence or word with which, the version as we have it ends: an earlier version may cover the whole ground which the final version is intended to cover; the earlier version would differ from the final version only in lacking the final polish. It is, then, necessary to wonder whether the eighth book may not have been intended to be the last book. The core of the work is the two sequels "Funeral Speech–Plague" and "Melian Dialogue–Sicilian Disaster." These sequels suggest in the first place the "Spartan" notion of "moderation and the divine law." At closer inspection one sees "the Spartan comedy and the Athenian tragedy." The eighth book shows that this second thought too is "a beautiful falsehood": Athens does not go down; Athens' defeat in the Peloponnesian war is not the consequence of her failure in Sicily; she still could have won the war in the manner in which Pericles had planned to win it. The core of the Spartan comedy is "Pylos–Mantinea"; but "Mantinea" is also the non-comical restoration of Sparta's renown after Pylos. There is a corresponding non-tragic restoration of Athens' renown after Sicily: Kynossema (cf. VIII 106.2, 5 with V 75.3). To state the case in a formula—Pylos : Mantinea = Sicily : Kynossema. Athens' restoration after Sicily is, to say the least, not unconnected with the change from the democracy to the polity of 411 (VIII 97) which change in its turn is, to say the least, not unconnected with the return of Alcibiades from Sparta to Athens (86.4–8): the impious Alcibiades (53.2) restores moderation in Athens (cf. also 45.2, 4–5). The absence of speeches from VIII—with the exception, which is not negligible, of the excerpt from Pisander's speech in 53.3, a speech making clear the decisive importance for Athens' hope of the recall of Alcibiades and the modification of the democracy—together with the absence of speeches from V 10–84—helps to bring out the unity and the lustre of "the Melian Dialogue and the Sicilian Disaster." (As for the meaningful character of the end of VIII, consider also the reference to the Athenians' purification of Delos in 108.4.) Xenophon's account of the end of the Peloponnesian war, *i.e.* his implicit account of why Athens lost the war, is in full agreement with Thucydides; see especially *Hellenica* II 1.25–26 and context.

THE CITY AND MAN

to the universal renown which she enjoys at present, and the splendor and the renown together vouch for her everlasting and universal fame in the future. She possesses universal control of the sea. She was or is present in every land. Her empire extends over more Greeks than any other Greek empire ever did, and if she wishes, it is susceptible of still further expansion. During the Peloponnesian war the conquest of Sicily, Carthage, and the whole mainland of Greece is already envisaged.[90] The longing for sempiternal and universal fame points towards universal rule; the concern with sempiternal and universal fame calls for boundless striving for ever more; it is wholly incompatible with moderation. The universalism of Athens, the universalism of the city (as distinguished from the desire for a limited goal like the rule over Sicily) is doomed to failure. It points therefore to a universalism of a different kind. Pericles says that the Athenians have left everywhere sempiternal memorials of evil things (which they inflicted on others or suffered themselves) and of good ones (of victories they gained and of benefits they bestowed). Thucydides on the other hand calls his work a sempiternal possession which is useful (I 22.4, II 41.4). Memorials are only to be looked at; possessions are owned. Memorials are very visible or obvious and they are not useful; a possession need not be obvious in order to be useful. Memorials are ambiguous and for show; a useful possession is of unambiguous solidity. The difference between the sempiternal memorials of evil things and of good ones and the sempiternal possession which is useful points to the difference between the brilliant and sham universalism of the city and the genuine universalism of understanding. For Thucydides bases his claim on behalf of his work on the fact that it brings to light the sempiternal and universal nature of man as the ground of the deeds, the speeches, and the thoughts which it records.

In the light of the full difference between the universalism of thought and the universalism of the city we understand Thucydides' agreement, not with Sparta, but with that moderation and piety by which Sparta claimed to be guided and which reveals itself less ambiguously in Nicias than in Sparta. It is hard but not altogether misleading to say that for Thucydides the pious understanding or judgment is true if for the wrong reasons; not the gods but nature

---

[90] II 41.4; 62.2, 4; 64.3, 5; VI 15.2, 34.2, 90.2–3, VII 66.2.

sets limits to what the city can reasonably attempt. Moderation is conduct in accordance with the nature of human things. The agreement between Thucydides and "Sparta" is reflected in the agreement between the men of noble simplicity and the men of Odyssean versatility who both become the victims of ruthless men with second-rate minds in times of civil discord (III 83). But the agreement between Thucydides and the Spartans, or the Melians, or Nicias, must not blind us to the fact that there is an equally important agreement among all political men, the Athenians included, by virtue of which they all differ from Thucydides. There is indeed a primary opposition between those (the Spartans, Nicias, the Melians) who merely wish to preserve the present or available things and those (the Athenians) who are haunted by the hope for immanifest future things. But on closer inspection the former too prove to depend on such hope.[91] In a language which is not that of Thucydides, there is something reminding of religion in Athenian imperialism.[92]

We must not forget however the kinship between the universalism of thought (Thucydides) and the universalism of the city (Athens)—a kinship which Thucydides has indicated most clearly by establishing some agreement between his archeology and the Funeral Speech. There is indeed a profound kinship between Thucydides' thought and the daring which is characteristic of Athens. However ambiguous that daring, that *mania*, which transcends the limits of moderation, may be on the political plane, it comes into its own, or is in accordance with nature, on the plane of thought, of the thinking individual. It comes into its own, not in Periclean (or post-Periclean) Athens as such but in the thought or the work of Thucydides. Not Periclean Athens but the understanding which is possible on the basis of Periclean Athens is the peak. Not Periclean Athens but the work of Thucydides is the peak. Thucydides redeems

---

[91] Cf. I 70.2, 7, V 87, 103.2, 113, VI 31.6, 93.

[92] The opposition and the agreement in the decisive respect between Pericles and Nicias may be illustrated by the following facts. Pericles avoids speaking of death and the dead in his Funeral Speech; the Funeral Speech is followed by the plague with its abundance of dead. Nicias in a way abandoned the fruit of his victory over the Corinthians by asking them for permission to collect two corpses which the Athenians had left behind (IV 44.5–6); at the end of his career, in Sicily, he was unable to arrange for the burial of the unnumbered Athenian corpses which were not in the hands of the enemy (VII 72.2, 75.3, 87.2).

Periclean Athens. And only by redeeming it does he preserve it "for ever." As little as there would be an Achilles or an Odysseus for us without Homer, as little would there be a Pericles for us without Thucydides: the everlasting glory for which Pericles longed is achieved not by Pericles but by Thucydides. The political daring and the virtues and vices which go with it make possible the highest daring. Understanding the universal and sempiternal things, seeing through the delusions by which the healthy city stands or falls, is possible only for thinkers who ride a tiger. One must go beyond this. In Athens the two heterogeneous universalisms become in a way fused: the fantastic political universalism becomes tinged, colored, suffused, transfigured by the true universalism, by the love of beauty and of wisdom as Thucydides understands beauty and wisdom, and it thus acquires its tragic character; it thus becomes able to foster a manly gentleness. The "synthesis" of the two universalisms is indeed impossible. It is of the utmost importance that this impossibility be understood. Only by understanding it can one understand the grandeur of the attempt to overcome it and sensibly admire it.

If the city cannot be understood except in the light of the universalism peculiar to it toward which it tends, and if that universalism in its turn by its essential defect points to the universalism of thought, we understand why Thucydides could present his whole wisdom in the form of a narrative interspersed with speeches which is severely limited to things political, which is severely political—which is silent about what is at present called Athenian culture. For many of our contemporaries that silence is not qualified, as it should be, by what he says and indicates about his work, his *logos*, for they understand the remarks in question as "methodological." Yet he does not only speak, however laconically, about his work and thought; as we have tried to show, he presents his thought, even his education, and therewith "Athenian culture." Through his work he makes us, in the light of the interplay of motion and rest, understand war and peace, barbarism and Greekness, Sparta and Athens; he enables us to understand, as far as in him lies, the nature of human life or to become wise. But one cannot become wise through understanding Thucydides' thought without realizing at the same time that it is through understanding Thucydides' thought that one is becoming wise, for wisdom is inseparable from self-knowledge. We know from Thucydides himself that he was an

Athenian. Through understanding him we see that his wisdom was made possible by "the sun" and by Athens—by her power and wealth, by her defective polity, by her spirit of daring innovation, by her active doubt of the divine law. By understanding his work one sees with one's own eyes that Athens was in a sense the home of wisdom. Only through becoming wise oneself can one recognize wisdom in others. Wisdom cannot be presented as a spectacle, in the way in which battles and the like can be presented. Wisdom cannot be "said." It can only be "done." Only through understanding Thucydides' work can one see that Athens was in a sense the school of Hellas; from Pericles' mouth we merely hear it asserted. Wisdom cannot be presented by being spoken about. An indirect proof of this is the insipid and at best shallow character of the chapters on the intellectual life of this period or that which form part of otherwise good modern histories.

One is led toward the deepest stratum in Thucydides' thought when one considers the tension between his explicit praise of Sparta—of Spartan moderation—which is not matched by a praise of Athens on the one hand, and on the other, the thesis of the archeology as a whole regarding the weakness of the ancients—a thesis which implies the certainty of progress and therewith the praise of innovating Athens. Thucydides does not unqualifiedly identify himself with "Athens." We must therefore reconsider the thesis of the archeology. The archeology sketches the emergence of Greekness, power, and wealth out of original barbarism, weakness, and poverty; it thus creates the impression that barbarism belongs together with weakness and poverty or that non-Greeks are pre-political savages (I 6.1, 5–6). It barely hints at the fact that there were powerful and wealthy non-Greek societies before there were any such Greek societies (I 9.2, 11.1–2, 13 end). Yet by admitting that some non-Greeks were civilized before Greeks one does not question the belief in progress. This belief is questioned not by Thucydides himself but by Diodotus. Still, Diodotus' speech reveals more of Thucydides himself than does any other speech. That speech contrasted with Cleon's speech which it opposes as well as with the Thebans' speech accusing the Plataeans reveals itself as a characteristically Athenian act—as no less characteristic of Athens than the Sicilian expedition but differing from the Sicilian expedition because it is inspired by moderation and mildness. It ought not to be surprising that the only action recorded by Thucydides which properly reflects his thought on the political plane is an act of humanity which is compatible with the survival of Athens and even of her empire.

In order to prevent the killing of the Mytileneans which was favored by Cleon, Diodotus must first combat Cleon's denigration of his opponents and especially his calumniation of them as prompted by discreditable, selfish interest. Cleon's manner of proceeding is harmful to the city; it causes suspicion and fear and thus deprives the city of good advice. The city must give a fair and equal hearing to everyone who is willing to give his advice. In order to prevent the giving of advice under the influence of selfish motives, out of concern for the adviser's own aggrandizement or prestige, a sensible or moderate city would not honor a man more when he gives good advice, *i.e.* when his proposal is approved by the assembly, and less when he gives bad advice, *i.e.* when his proposal is rejected by the assembly; for if the suggested practice were followed, men would not speak for or against proposals merely in order to please the assembly (III 42). Diodotus seems to argue for complete equality, for the abolition even of that distinction by which democracy stands or falls, the distinction between the popular and the unpopular, between the honest men or friends of the *demos* and the corrupt men or enemies of the *demos*. If not every member of the assembly, at any rate every speaker must be treated as being equally competent and honest as every other; only in this way can ambition, striving for superiority and hence for inequality be eradicated. He simultaneously indicates the fact that citizens who are not wise cannot distinguish between good and bad advice but must identify good advice with advice convincing them or appealing to them, and leaves in the dark the fact that a speaker whose proposals are frequently approved by the assembly cannot fail to be regarded as wise and hence to gain prestige, and therefore that a man who is to the slightest degree ambitious will inevitably try to increase his prestige by making proposals which please the multitude. Differently stated, the prestige of Diodotus cannot well coexist with the prestige of Cleon: Diodotus himself is compelled to suggest, in contradiction to the principle which he advocates, that Cleon is either stupid or dishonest. Gomme underestimates the bearing of Diodotus' statement by saying that he "comes close to questioning the value of free debate." Diodotus adumbrates the problem of democracy in such a manner as to point to the regime in which only moderate and sensible men, in no way tainted by ambition, would have a say.[93] Yet surely Athens is not "a moderate city" and Diodotus is compelled to persuade the Athenians to act moderately toward the Mytileneans. He illustrates his difficulty and his manner of overcoming it by speaking of the case wherein a speaker admittedly gives sound advice yet is suspected of giving that advice for the sake of his private gain; in that case the Athenians reject the sound advice out of envy. The *demos* is then not as good-natured as Cleon had maintained (III 38.2). From not entirely pure motives, democratic assemblies are more concerned with purity of a certain kind than with wisdom. Since they will not vote for a proposal unless they have trust in the proposer, and since they trust on grounds which are so little rational, not only bad men but good men as well are compelled to deceive the assembly and to lie to it. Perhaps one cannot benefit any city without deceiving it, for no city is likely to consist chiefly of perfectly wise and virtuous people; one surely cannot benefit Athens without deceiving her, one reason being that only the speakers are held responsible for what they propose and how they propose it whereas the assembly, the sovereign, has no responsibility (III 43). With an unheard of frankness,[94] Diodotus tells the Athenians that only by using a subterfuge will he be able to plead successfully for the mild treatment of the Mytileneans.

The subterfuge which Diodotus uses seems to consist in replacing the question of justice (are the Mytileneans guilty?) by the question of expediency (does Athens derive benefit from killing them?) (III 44). Yet why is that substitution a subterfuge? In order to lay a foundation for the proposal not to kill the Mytileneans, Diodotus raises the broad question as to whether capital punishment is expedient or wise under any circumstances: in order to be wise, capital punishment must have a deterring effect which it does not have as is shown by the fact that capital crimes are frequently committed;

---

[93] Cleon may be said to state and to solve the problem as follows: you know your own limitations, you know that you lack judgment and therefore that you must trust others; but lacking judgment you cannot distinguish between those who deserve your trust and those who do not; I give you a criterion which you can understand: trust only people of your kind, people without refinement, people like me; to enable you to distinguish between me and other vulgarians, I tell you that I possess the Periclean quality of not being fickle.

[94] What Pericles says in II 62.1 approaches the trivial compared with what Diodotus says in III 43.2–3.

*nomos* is powerless against human *physis* (45). Whatever this argument may be worth in itself, its use in the circumstances seems to reveal no small lack of intelligence: by bidding the Athenians not to kill the Mytileneans on the ground that capital punishment is bad altogether, he preposterously bids them simultaneously to abolish capital punishment for murder, impiety, high treason, and other heinous crimes; he suggests that the Mytileneans are guilty of a capital crime according to the accepted standards. Yet he knows what he is doing. His statement about capital punishment implies that capital crimes are involuntary and hence, as Cleon had admitted, deserve pardon (40.1; cf. 39.2); it thus suggests that, assuming that the Mytileneans had committed a capital crime, they deserve pardon. He thus prepares his later questioning of that assumption or his proof that the majority of the Mytileneans had not committed a crime and therefore that the Athenians would commit a crime by killing them (47.3; cf. 46.5). He is then very far from simply disregarding, as he claims, the question of justice. Cleon had based his argument above all on the consideration cf justice and secondarily on the consideration of expediency; he had ruled out of court the consideration of compassion and mildness as wholly incompatible with empire (40.2–3). Replying to Cleon and knowing the nature of the city, Diodotus refuses to appeal to the Athenians' compassion or mildness (48.1) without saying however that compassion and mildness have no place whatever in an empire, and he pretends to outdo Cleon by disregarding justice altogether and by considering expediency alone while however taking up the question of justice after he has put his audience in a mood in which it is willing to listen to a plea of innocence. He prepares that mood by vaguely suggesting that the Mytileneans might deserve pardon although they were guilty of a capital crime.

Diodotus' statement about capital punishment calls for special attention. Within that statement, almost literally in the center of his whole speech, he suggests that punishments were "softer" in the past, that in the olden times even the gravest crimes were not punished capitally, that realizing the ineffectiveness of soft punishments human beings first introduced capital punishment and then progressively extended capital punishment to ever more crimes (45.3). Men do not realize that punishment does not deter men from crimes because nature compels men to commit crimes or because *nomos* is powerless against *physis*. They expect more from *nomos* now than in the olden times. In the oldest times, at the beginning, there was no *nomos* because there were no cities; there was no punishment proper; abstracting from everything else one might say that the first age was the age of Kronos. There surely has taken place a progress of the arts (and hence of power and wealth); but it would be wrong to believe that that progress is simply a progress in mildness.[95] The progress of art is accompanied by a progress of *nomos*—of law doing violence to nature, if only by concealing nature. Men are not simply milder now when Greekness is at its peak as is shown abundantly by Thucydides. The belief that man is at the peak now is therefore in need of qualification or revision. The difference between the wise and the unwise—that difference which makes it impossible for a wise man to benefit his city except by deceiving it—is not affected by the progress of the arts or of the laws. Men are not simply wiser and gentler than they were in the olden times. The belief in progress must be qualified with a view to the fact that human nature does not change.

It could seem that Thucydides himself confirms or at least illustrates Diodotus' thesis by his narrative of the Athenians' purification of Apollo's island which they undertook in compliance with an oracle (III 104). The tyrant Pisistratus had purified a part of the island; in the sixth year of the Peloponnesian war the Athenians purified the entire island. In the preceding year the plague had smitten them again and many earthquakes had occurred (87). Perhaps they felt guilty (cf. V 32). At any rate, for the sake of Delos' holiness, they forbade that anyone die or be born on the island; the dying and the women about to give birth were to be brought to another island close by which the tyrant Polycrates had dedicated to Apollo. After having purified the island, the Athenians instituted the Delian festival. In the olden times there had been a festival there which included an athletic and a music contest as well as performances of choruses sent by the cities of Ionia and the neighboring islands. This fact is proved by Homer of whom Thucydides here quotes thirteen verses whereas in the whole rest of his book he quotes only a single Homeric verse (I 9.4). The verses stand out from the rest of the work because they conjure an altogether peaceful scene. Homer exhorts the maidens who had participated in the Delian festival to remember him and to praise

---

[95] Cf. Plato, *Protagoras* 327c4–e3.

him as the sweetest and most enjoyable minstrel who frequently visited Delos. In post-Homeric times "the contests" ceased as a consequence of adversities. But now, in the sixth year of the Peloponnesian war, the Athenians restored the "contests" and added horse-races as an entirely novel feature. It is not clear whether the modern Delian festival surpasses the ancient. The horse-races surely constitute a progress;[96] but will they compensate for the absence of a Homer?[97]

## 10. *Political History and Political Philosophy*

Thucydides is not merely a political man who as such belongs to this city or that, but a historian who as such does not belong to any one city. Moreover, he is a historian who sees the singulars in the light of clearly grasped universals, the changing in the light of the permanent or sempiternal, of human nature as part of the whole which is characterized by the interplay between motion and rest; he is a philosophic historian. His thought is therefore not radically alien to that of Plato and Aristotle. It is true that he leaves matters at intimating what he regards as the originating principles whereas the philosophers make those principles their theme or, in other words, that it is evidently necessary to go beyond Thucydides toward the philosophers; but this does not mean that there is an opposition between Thucydides and the philosophers. What is true

[96] Cf. Plato, *Republic* 328a1–5.

[97] The account of the sixth year of the war or more precisely III 86–116 is characterized by the fact that "the interruption of the narrative for the sake of chronological order is carried to an extreme in the account of this campaign [in Sicily], and, since the campaign is not of the first importance and not very interesting, might, if taken by itself, justify Dionysius' and others' criticism of Thucydides' 'unfortunate chronological manner'." Gomme II 413. The fact mentioned is all the more striking since precisely in this context, in what one might call his third preface (III 90.1), Thucydides declares that as regards the things which happened in Sicily he will make mention only of the most memorable things among those which affected the Athenians. (As regards his "second preface," cf. p. 8 above.) The account given in III 86–116 consists of 15 items, 6 referring to Sicily, 3 to natural phenomena, and 1 to the purification of Delos. Demosthenes' campaign in Aetolia (including the only mention of Hesiod occurring in the book) is the central item. If one disregards the account of the purification of Delos one observes a strange regularity regarding the accounts of the Sicilian campaign on the one hand and those of natural phenomena on the other. Cf. also notes 10 and 83 above.

of philosophy in general is true of political philosophy in particular. If one does not limit oneself to contrasting easily quotable judgments of Thucydides and Plato on men like Themistocles and Pericles, if one considers that all these judgments are elliptical, and if therefore one ponders them, one realizes that the two thinkers are in fundamental agreement regarding the good and bad and the noble and base. It suffices to remind the reader of what the two thinkers indicate in regard to the order of rank of Sparta and Athens. Yet there is this difference between them: whereas Plato raises and answers the question of the best regime simply, Thucydides answers only the question as to the best regime which Athens had in his lifetime (VIII 97.2); but here again it is evidently necessary to go beyond Thucydides toward the philosophers who thematically discuss the question of the best regime simply. All of this amounts to saying that Thucydides' thought is inferior to Plato's thought. Or could Thucydides have had a positive reason for stopping on his ascent earlier than Plato?

One must compare comparable things. Thucydides did not write Socratic dialogues and Plato did not write an account of a contemporary war. But Plato in the third book of the *Laws* has sketched the development from the barbarism of the beginning up to the century in which he and Thucydides were born, and this sketch is comparable to Thucydides' archeology. In fact, apart from the *Menexenus*, which calls for comparison with the Funeral Speech, that sketch is the only part of Plato's works which lends itself to a direct and instructive confrontation with a part of Thucydides' work. As one ought to mention even in the most cursory remark, both archeologies have also in common that they equally spare Spartan feelings. We stress here only one point. Plato explains how the good Athenian regime which obtained at the time of the Persian war, the ancestral regime, was transformed into the extreme democracy of his time. He traces this change to the wilful disregard of the ancestral law regarding music and the theater: by making no longer the best and the wisest but the audience at large the judges of songs and plays, Athens decayed.[98] Shortly thereafter he contends that it was not the naval victory at Salamis but the land victories at Marathon and Plataeae which saved Greece.[99] These judgments

---

[98] *Laws* 698a9ff., 700a5–701c4.
[99] *Ibid.* 707a5–c7.

are in striking contrast to Thucydides' suggestions. On the basis of Thucydides one would rather have to say that the Athenians had no choice but to wage the battle of Salamis and, one thing leading to another, they were compelled to build the most powerful navy; for the navy they needed the poorest Athenians as oarsmen; they were therefore compelled to give the poor a much higher status in Athens than they had previously enjoyed: Athens was compelled to become a democracy; the democratization of Athens was not, as Plato wishes us to believe, an act of wilful folly or of choice but a necessity. Generally stated, it could appear that Plato in contra-distinction to Thucydides makes too little allowance for fatality as distinguished from choice. In fact however there is no fundamental difference in this respect between the two thinkers. In the very context just referred to, Plato says that it is chance rather than man or human wisdom or folly which establishes regimes or which legislates. In other words, man is a kind of plaything of the gods.[100] Plato adds indeed that within very narrow limits men have a choice between different regimes. But this is not denied by Thucydides. Hence he cannot deny that it is necessary to raise the question of the best regime. One may say that this question is explicitly answered by such Thucydidean speakers as Athenagoras and Peri-cles but it is surely not even explicitly raised by Thucydides himself. He prefers a mixture of oligarchy and democracy to either of the pure forms but it is not clear whether he would unqualifiedly prefer that mixture to an intelligent and virtuous tyranny; he seems to doubt whether a regime superior to these two—aristocracy in Plato's or Aristotle's sense—would be possible. He surely never speaks in his own name of a virtuous city whereas he speaks of virtuous individuals. There seems to be, according to him, something in the nature of the city which prevents it from rising to the height to which a man may rise.

When Thucydides speaks in the first book of the causes or justi-fications of the Peloponnesian war, he stresses three of them: the Spartans' fear of Athens' increasing power, the breach of the treaty, and the pollution contracted at the time of Cylon. He does not speak there with equal emphasis of a fourth cause or justification which would seem to be the most noble: the liberation of the Greek cities from Athens' tyranny. This cause is based on the premise that,

---

[100] *Ibid.* 709a1–3; cf. 644d7–e4 and 803c4–5.

as of right, every city is independent or is an equal member of the
whole comprising all Greek cities, regardless of whether it is large
or small, strong or weak, rich or poor. Accordingly there is a good
common to all Greek cities which should limit the ambitions of
each. The self-sufficiency of the city as Plato and Aristotle presuppose it excludes the city's dependence on such a society of cities
or its being essentially a member of it. Aristotle goes so far as to
visualize a perfectly good city which has no "foreign relations"
whatever.[101] The lesson of Thucydides' work as a whole may be
said to be that the order of cities which is presupposed in the most
noble Spartan proclamations is altogether impossible, given the
unequal power of the different cities which inevitably leads to the
consequence that the most powerful cities cannot help being hege-
monial or even imperial. But that lesson also renders questionable
a presupposition of classical political philosophy; it excludes the
kind of self-sufficiency of the city which classical political philosophy presupposes. The city is neither self-sufficient nor is it essentially a part of a good or just order comprising many or all cities.
The lack of order which necessarily characterizes the "society" of
the cities or, in other words, the omnipresence of War puts a much
lower ceiling on the highest aspiration of any city toward justice
and virtue than classical political philosophy might seem to have
admitted.

Most of the speeches and all debates occurring in Thucydides'
work deal with foreign politics, with what a given city or group of
cities ought to do in regard to another city or group of cities. But
the subject of debates is whatever is in the foreground of attention
or is primary for the citizen. For the city which is not on the verge
of civil war or in it, the most important questions concern its relations with other cities. Not without reason does Thucydides make
his Diodotus call freedom (*i.e.* freedom from foreign domination)
and empire "the greatest things" (III 45.6). Generally speaking,
even the lowliest men prefer being subjects to men of their own
people rather than to any aliens. If this is so, foreign politics is
primary "for us," although it may not be primary "in itself" or "by
nature." Thucydides does not rise to the heights of classical political
philosophy because he is more concerned than is classical political
philosophy with what is "first for us" as distinguished from what

---

[101] *Politics* 1325b23–32.

is "first by nature." Philosophy is the ascent from what is first for us to what is first by nature. This ascent requires that what is first for us be understood as adequately as possible in the manner in which it comes to sight prior to the ascent. In other words, political understanding or political science cannot start from seeing the city as the Cave but it must start from seeing the city as a world, as the highest in the world; it must start from seeing man as completely immersed in political life: "the present war is the greatest war." Classical political philosophy presupposes the articulation of this beginning of political understanding but it does not exhibit it as Thucydides does in an unsurpassable, nay, unrivalled manner. The quest for that "common sense" understanding of political things which led us first to Aristotle's *Politics*, leads us eventually to Thucydides' *War of the Peloponnesians and the Athenians*.

Yet most of the time the city is at peace. Most of the time the city is not immediately exposed to that violent teacher War, and to unsought compulsions, and hence the city's inhabitants are of kindlier thoughts than they are when at war (III 82.2). Accordingly most of the time they are given to admiration of the ancient, of the ancestral, rather than to immersion in the present (I 21.2). Not being prompted to take violent courses, they praise and even practice moderation and obedience to the divine law. Neither according to the classical philosophers[102] nor according to Thucydides is the concern with the divine simply the primary concern of the city, but the fact that it is primary "for us," from the point of view of the city, is brought out more clearly by Thucydides than by the philosophers. It suffices to remember what Thucydides tells us about oracles, earthquakes, and eclipses, Nicias' deeds and sufferings, the Spartans' compunctions, the affair of Cylon, the aftermath of the battle of Delium, and the purification of Delos—in brief, all these things for which the modern scientific historian has no use or which annoy him, and to which classical political philosophy barely alludes because for it the concern with the divine has become identical with philosophy. We would have great difficulty in doing justice to this remote or dark side of the city but for the work of men like Fustel de Coulanges above all others who have made us see the city as it primarily understood itself as distinguished from the manner in which it was exhibited by classical political philosophy.

---

[102] Cf. *Politics* 1328b11–12.

the holy city in contradistinction to the natural city. Our gratitude is hardly diminished by the fact that Fustel de Coulanges, his illustrious predecessors, Hegel above all, and his numerous successors have failed to pay proper attention to the philosophic concept of the city as exhibited by classical political philosophy. For what is "first for us" is not the philosophic understanding of the city but that understanding which is inherent in the city as such, in the pre-philosophic city, according to which the city sees itself as subject and subservient to the divine in the ordinary understanding of the divine or looks up to it. Only by beginning at this point will we be open to the full impact of the all-important question which is coeval with philosophy although the philosophers do not frequently pronounce it—the question *quid sit deus.*

# Index

243

# INDEX

# INDEX